THE EARLY BIRDS

THE
EARLY BIRDS

Jenny Minton

ALFRED A. KNOPF NEW YORK 2006

THIS IS A BORZOI BOOK
PUBLISHED BY ALFRED A. KNOPF

www.aaknopf.com

Knopf, Borzoi Books, and the colophon are registered trademarks
of Random House, Inc.

Library of Congress Cataloging-in-Publication Data
Minton, Jenny, [date].
The early birds / by Jenny Minton.
p.   cm.
ISBN 1-4000-4383-2
1. Minton, Jenny, 1971– 2. Mothers—Biography. 3. Pregnancy—Decision
making. 4. Infants (Premature) 5. Twins. I. Title.

RG525.M523 2006   618.2'5—dc22   2005044419

The Early Birds is a work of nonfiction, but the names
of certain individuals, as well as potentially identifying
descriptive details concerning them, have been changed.

Manufactured in the United States of America

First Edition

FOR
SAM, GUS, LEO, AND DAN QUIGLEY

"But if all we have to do is worry," chides the Mother, "every day for a hundred years, it'll be easy. It'll be nothing. I'll take all the worry in the world, if it wards off the thing itself."

—From "People Like That Are the Only People Here" by Lorrie Moore

"There are two ways to live your life. One is as though nothing is a miracle. The other is as though everything is a miracle."

—Albert Einstein, former preemie

THE EARLY BIRDS

Prologue

SAM IS BREATHING LIKE A FROG. I show my mother. I tell her, "I gave birth to a frog."

She says, "They are going to be beautiful boys." And she adds, "But it's good you can say how you feel."

I tell the nurse that Sam appears to be heaving more than Gus. I peek at someone else's baby in a neighboring isolette. His chest is not going from cream puff to concave each time he breathes.

"They push the preemies here to see what they can handle," she says. "He's working hard, but we'll see what the doctor decides to do during rounds. He might want to put Sam back on the respirator. They have to keep testing the babies to see if they are ready to come off."

My mother wheels me back to my room, and when she and Dan go down later to check on the twins they learn that Sam is indeed back on the respirator. One of his lungs has collapsed.

"I knew it," I say. "I knew it. How could those nurses not have seen that something was wrong with him? Why did the doctors wait so long? They were pushing him too hard."

Dan paces around my hospital room, playing with the remote. "Dr. Vanderbilt said you have to start walking," he says. I don't even try. I do not want to recover.

Later that night, I am lying in my hospital bed sipping ginger ale; Dan is flipping through TV channels, when Alex, the nurse-practitioner, knocks on our door. With his gray beard and aquamarine scrubs, he resembles an elf. He says that Sam has taken a turn for the worse and we need to sign a release for a blood transfusion. Sam is in bad shape; his system has shut down. His oxygen levels are low. Alex tells us that we probably want to come downstairs.

I have to keep reminding myself that Alex is not a doctor, although people make that mistake since he is the only male nurse-practitioner working in the neonatal intensive care unit.

Partly because I am disoriented from painkillers, I still have no idea which turns we make to get to the patients' elevator despite having made this trip several times. Dan wheels me through the glass doors.

A doctor in a white coat and several nurses hover around Sam's warming bed. They will not let us into the room.

The head night nurse-practitioner steps out of the unit and steers us toward the nursing station. She has long, dark curly hair like Debra Winger in the eighties. She sits down on a desk and says, "Sam is very sick. He is not responding to our treatments. Of the forty-eight babies in the NICU tonight, I'm afraid Sam is in the worst shape. We are going to try him on an oscillator. It may be our last resort."

Yesterday our nurse said we should be thankful that Sam was moved into Gus's room because it is overseen by nurse-practitioners, called NPs. Sam's old room was apparently run by residents, who were often making decisions based on a week's experience in neonatology. In contrast, most of the NPs have been working in the NICU for several years. But is the head night NP's knowledge of sick babies and last resorts even helpful? Is she employing a time-honored technique that gently forces parents to contemplate death as a possibility?

Sam's CO_2 level is too high, which means that although the respirator is pumping oxygen into his lungs, his body is not extracting the oxygen and releasing the carbon dioxide.

The floor is silent. No one is visiting at this hour, and aside from the huddle around Sam, there are only incubators, occasional beeps coming from behind the glass wall. It is a scene from one of the science fiction movies Dan watches, miniature babies in plastic bubbles, hooked up to computer monitors, the life's work of some mad scientist.

Dan wheels me back to the elevator, through the maze, to my room. I rest all my weight on my arms and push myself out of the chair and into my bed. I slide away the tray with its stack of unopened puddings. It is two weeks until Thanksgiving. The cribs I ordered haven't even arrived, and now I don't know if I will need two. I begin to cry uncontrollably.

Dan fits himself into the bed and puts his arms and legs over me like a blanket. He has been sleeping in his jeans on the pullout chair for the last five nights. While trying to comfort me, he accidentally sets off the nurse call button and she runs in, the first time she has ever responded so quickly.

"We're okay, we're okay," Dan assures her.

I take a Percocet. I start to feel the pill taking hold and I try to relax and give in to it. I believe Sam will die. Over and over I keep thinking terrible things happen, there is no protection from them. I am beyond anger, beyond the dread of having to go home from the hospital tomorrow leaving one of my babies here clinging to life and the other fading fast. Sam is falling away from me through a hole in the world. He should not be here yet. He has arrived and he will leave in a flash, without being hugged by his mother or father, without laughing or speaking, without our ever knowing who he really was.

I've had no more than a glimpse of Sam's fair hair and remarkably symmetrical face and already my love for him is both particular and without specifications. He is the restless troublemaker, Baby B, who kicked a hole in his sac, atypically breaking his water ahead of Baby A and hurrying his brother out. He is a heartbreaker—full of promise—who struggled mightily merely to breathe until he collapsed. Am I grasping for clues? Encoded within Sam are thousands of genes not yet expressed and I can feel the elasticity of my tenderness toward him, how easily it could expand to cover any array of strengths and weaknesses. It is conditional only in that it is nontransferable. I love Gus equally and separately.

If Sam dies I will be left reaching out for a baby I never held.

Part One

NO, I WOULD NOT GIVE YOU FALSE HOPE

Fᴿᴼᴹ ᴛʜᴇ ᴠᴇʀʏ ꜰɪʀꜱᴛ ᴛɪᴍᴇ I set foot inside an infertility clinic in New York City, I think this is what it must feel like to be a very beautiful woman. I'm thirty years old and everyone, the doctors and nurses, even the receptionist going over my insurance papers, appreciates my relatively youthful eggs. Although I'm biologically past my fertility peak, which occurs between twenty and twenty-four, I sense that I am the object of envy in the clinic's crowded waiting room.

Two minutes after I've met him, I hand to the reproductive endocrinologist the temperature charts on which I've checkmarked each time Dan and I had sex, circled when I ovulated, slashed through the days I got my period. Each chart extends onto two pages since my menstrual cycles have been averaging about fifty days.

The RE I've been referred to, across from whom I'm now sitting, is Dr. Morganstern. He has a boyish grin, a big teddy bear frame, and coarse dark hair I will later hear he dyes. I've waited two months to get an appointment. The books I read on infertility all said that women who were trying to conceive at thirty-five or older should wait no longer than six months before seeing a reproductive endocrinologist, but women under thirty-five could try for up to a year on their own. After nine months I started doing research. After ten months I called to make an appointment, and now that I've finally gotten in to see the doctor, it's been a year. He slips my charts into a folder and says in a raspy voice, "Don't worry. We'll get you pregnant." I start to cry.

Reproductive endocrinologists are gynecologists who have been trained in the field of infertility, one of the highest-paying sub-specialties in medicine. The director of the clinic I'm now at earns 2 million dollars a year. Most REs are men. All of the books I looked at warned me that the money I am about to spend will buy my RE a sports car.

An article about Morganstern that I found prior to this meeting identified him as one of four sons, all of whom credited their demanding Jewish mother for steering them toward careers in medicine.

"It sounds to me like polycystic ovarian syndrome," he says, "which affects one in ten women. Your body isn't producing enough estrogen to release an egg from your fallopian tubes each month. I see you have a history of adult-onset diabetes in your family. We think PCOS is genetic and has something to do with how the body metabolizes insulin. We'll do some diagnostic tests and then we can start with an ovulation-inducing drug like Clomid. If that doesn't work, we can add metformin to your protocol to regulate your insulin. And there's always IVF."

Dr. Morganstern leads me down the corridor to a small, windowless office. "We'll do some blood work today and see if you're ovulating at all, make sure your insulin levels aren't too high." He extends his hand, "Nice to meet you," and is gone. The nurse takes my right arm, taps it a few times at the elbow, and expertly draws blood.

I AM OBSESSED WITH oral thermometers, ovulation predictor kits, and the missionary position. I spend hours on the BabyCenter message board reading postings by women who are TTC—trying to conceive. They speak in a code of abbreviations. It takes me several tries to decipher CD (cycle day) and BD (sex). I deduce that DH is a reference to the husband, but what does it stand for? The best I can come up with is "designated hitter." If I were to have a

PET scan tomorrow, I think my limbic system might shock the doctors; the region of my brain controlling sexual reproduction would be blown up way out of proportion, like a balloon.

I'm convinced a baby will strengthen the bond between my husband, Dan, and me. I crave the intimacy I expect will come from bringing a child, who'll be a true fusion of us, into the world. I want one of those large, inviting homes where kids are always coming and going, reaching for any of the millions of windbreakers hanging on the foyer hooks.

The idea of not having children frightens me. I become claustrophobic at the thought of living for another forty years in an eternal adolescence, Dan and I responsible only to each other. Although I've volunteered in an inner-city Big Sister program since college, I wonder whether I'm selfless enough to dedicate my life to the greater good. Instead, I imagine myself as a childless middle-aged or elderly woman getting dolled up for benefits, only to arrive and have eyes dart past me, ears tune out the fascinating thoughts I've had time to develop.

On my second visit to the infertility clinic, Dr. Morganstern asks, "Did the older women give you a hard time in the waiting room? Some of my younger patients complain that they get some pretty mean looks."

I'm not aware of anyone staring me down—but then again I try not to meet anyone's eyes in the waiting room. I hate overhearing the sad stories some women blurt out to perfect strangers about their four failed attempts at IVF. I always bring several magazines and bury my head in them until my name is called, in much the same way as I won't even look at the person sitting next to me on an airplane until we have safely landed.

My blood work comes back normal. My LH/FSH (luteinizing hormone/follicle-stimulating hormone) rate is low, indicating that my eggs should be viable. High levels of FSH can reduce egg quality. As promised, Dr. Morganstern prescribes Clomid. He says,

"You'll take this on days 3 through 7 of your cycle, and once you've taken the last pill start having sex every other day for a week. We'll see you back here in a month." He shakes my hand. "Good luck."

The Clomid mixes up my hormones enough to make me upset. On the third day of swallowing the pill with my coffee I call my mother from the office on Park Avenue where I work as an editor for a book publisher. "I'm so scared I will never be able to have a baby," I say. I have closed my door and I start sobbing into the phone.

"Look out your window," she tells me. "All of those people walking down the sidewalk, hailing taxis, just remember each of them was born."

It is snowing outside, a week before Christmas, and I watch it fall two floors below onto the hoods of yellow cabs detained at a traffic light, Middle Eastern drivers appearing through the windshields each time their wipers pass. Snowflakes land on bundled men hurrying along the sidewalk with their heads down; on a scruffy twenty-something in his oversized black parka jaywalking behind a dozen dogs on leashes; on a clan of laughing tourists huddling around their street map on the corner in brightly colored hats and gloves and matter-of-fact L.L. Bean boots. My mother was trying to reassure me that wanting children isn't too much to ask for. Conception is a routine event that happened to all our mothers. But as I stare out the window the people who enter my frame form a breathtaking vision, like the clusters of lights that appear along coastlines at night, each constellation a self-contained town.

At the end of the month I return to the clinic. I don't think I've ovulated because my temperature hasn't risen. Dr. Morganstern does an ultrasound and says, "You're right. I can't see any follicles." He prescribes a double dose of Clomid and tells me to follow his instructions from the top.

"Do you think we should have sex every day this time?" I ask.

"Every other day should do it. You don't want to wear out your husband just yet."

Ten days after I've taken the last pill, my temperature spikes.

Dan and I fly to Jacksonville, Florida, to spend Christmas at my parents' home. I record my temperature each morning and am delighted to see it continue to rise, indicating increasing progesterone levels, a sure sign that ovulation occurred and, should it remain elevated more than fourteen days, a possible sign of pregnancy. On the morning after Christmas, day 15, it abruptly drops. I rinse the thermometer in hot water, raise the shades to let in the sun, then wrap myself up in the covers for twenty minutes and take it again. A few minutes later I start having terrible menstrual cramps, a side effect of the Clomid, and my period arrives.

Dan sits beside me on the bed until the six Advil kick in and relieve the cramps. In the afternoon my family rents a motorboat and we whiz up the coast, anchoring at Jacksonville Beach. We drink piña coladas at a bar on the strip decked in colored lights. Over the previous two weeks I have imagined a microscopic baby snuggling down inside me for the winter ahead. I've considered my nausea evidence of a foreign body's invasion. But it must have been a side effect of the prenatal vitamins I started taking along with the Clomid. Suddenly the baby I've conceived in my mind vanishes. I am shocked to discover she never existed.

BEFORE WE EMBARK ON A third round of Clomid, Dr. Morganstern suggests adding artificial insemination (IUI) to our strategy. Dan will have to produce a semen sample, which technicians can wash to filter out the fastest, healthiest sperm. The champions will then be inserted into my uterus through a catheter right before I ovulate.

"Aren't you rushing this?" Dan predictably asks when I inform him of the plan. "We've only been trying a year."

I force myself to stay seated at the dining table, to be patient. "We've discovered there's a problem so why wouldn't we do something about it?"

Two weeks later Dan and I are at the clinic, peering into the specimen sample room. It is the size of a closet with a single chair facing a television screen and VCR. Weathered *Hustler* magazines languish in a basket in the corner. Along the wall is a shelf with a sliding door. Taped above a sink are instructions on how to leave your sample. "Do you want me to come in with you?" I ask, not sure if we can both fit inside the room.

"I think I'll be all right," Dan says seriously. He steps inside and shuts the door. I stand out in the hallway for a while, just in case he changes his mind. Then I walk back to the waiting room. Minutes pass before I see Dan approaching, his short cropped hair a relic from his years in the marines, his expression that of a wide-eyed, innocent boy. I suddenly feel guilty for putting him through this. Why *am* I in such a hurry? I think I just want this painful period in our lives to be over as soon as possible, before it strains our relationship. So far we've avoided taking our infertility personally or blaming each other. I've heard of couples who struggled with infertility for years only to split up after they finally became parents, the years of stress having worn their marriage down. But if we get pregnant soon, no harm will be done, and we will appreciate our children. Dan sits down beside me.

When I ran into Dan at a party eight years ago, he had just come home from four years of active duty abroad. He was accustomed to rigid schedules and punctuality and all of our early fights involved my not showing up on time for dates. He loves to say that I had a crush on him at Groton, the boarding school near Boston we both attended, but daydreaming about a guy who was two classes above me and captain of the soccer team would not have occurred to me back then. Though I knew who he was, I'm not sure we ever had a conversation there. But I do remember that Dan and a friend of his played a couple of pranks on my roommate, Lindsay. And that, on a whim, one snowy night before Christmas break, I convinced her to seek revenge. Together we climbed out our bedroom window and we crouched on the roof watching the snow come down under streetlamps on the path around campus. A group of lower-school girls with wet frozen hair and hockey sticks passed below us heading back from the ice rink. Then we crawled into the boys' dorm through an open window and landed on a tile floor facing a row of urinals. We sprinted down the hall, barged through Dan's bedroom door, and threw handfuls of cooked spaghetti up at his ceiling.

At the clinic we browse through magazines in the waiting room for two more hours until my name is called. Dan and I are shown into an office where a giant Nordic doctor with deeply set eyes introduces himself as a "fellow"—an RE in training—and prepares to inseminate me. Though consciously I understand there to be no connection between an insemination and actual sex, his enormous hands alarm me.

"But where's Dr. Morganstern?" I ask. "Isn't he here? I'd prefer it if he did the procedure."

The Nordic fellow offers to look for Morganstern. I nod and he leaves the room. Finally there's a knock on the door and Dr. Morganstern enters. "I heard you were looking for me." He laughs.

"I was under the impression that you would be doing the insemination."

"Sure," he says. "I can do it. But the fellow could have done it as well. Even our nurses do inseminations." He seems amused. Surely he and the fellow shared a laugh over my naïveté that it could possibly make a difference who carries out such a menial task.

Dr. Morganstern is gripping a catheter that the fellow must have passed off to him. I'm aware that the instrument was carried down the hallway, perhaps briefly placed down on Morganstern's desk. He slips it between my legs, which have been spread in stirrups for the past half hour.

"What are our chances of it working?" Dan asks.

"About twenty percent. Good luck," he says, and shakes hands with both of us on his way out.

The next two weeks are interminable. On the fourteenth day I double over with terrible cramps again and my period arrives. Only after I've rung Dr. Morganstern's office and scheduled my next appointment do I unplug the phone and cry for five minutes, conjuring up Holly Hunter in *Broadcast News*.

Then the numerous tests begin. Dye is injected into my fallopian tubes to confirm they are open for an egg to pass through. A urologist checks Dan's DNA for gene mutations and finds all the right chromosomes. Blood work results find his testosterone level normal. Neither of us is diagnosed with a physiological problem. In fact, we find no conclusive explanations for our infertility. We proceed with another three rounds of Clomid and insemination, and when I fail to get pregnant, Dr. Morganstern says the next step is for me to sign up for IVF. He says, "We could keep going with inseminations but statistically if you were going to conceive through IUI, you would have done so in the first four attempts. I think IVF is our best option here."

By this point I've done my research. I know that IVF, in vitro fertilization, is a five-step process involving ovarian stimulation, egg retrieval, fertilization of the eggs with a semen sample, embryo transfer, and post-transfer injections of progesterone.

"First, we'll put you on medication to suppress your menstrual cycle. Then, if everything looks good, we'll prescribe you a combination of follicle-stimulating drugs. The challenge with a younger PCOS patient like you is to produce several eggs without overstimulating the ovaries, a condition that would make your uterine lining inhospitable to an embryo. But we'll use ICSI so you won't need to make all that many eggs."

"ICSI?"

"Our clinic now routinely uses intracytoplasmic sperm injection for seventy percent of our procedures. The embryologists inject a single sperm through the egg's membrane. ICSI is dramatically increasing our fertilization rates. We're averaging sixty-six percent of the eggs extracted."

The first IVF baby, Louise Brown, was born in England in 1978 after numerous failed attempts. A few years later the Browns did IVF again to expand their family. They had a second daughter, Natalie. Natalie is now grown with two children of her own, both conceived naturally, proving that infertility is not necessarily passed down to the next generation. The booklets printed by the American Association of Reproductive Medicine claim that ART (assisted reproduction technology) is no longer considered experimental, having been practiced for twenty-five years. But does that include ICSI, which has only been around for twelve?

"Do you think ICSI increases the chances of having a child who is infertile? I don't want to have to worry about my son getting dumped when his fiancée discovers he's from ICSI."

Morganstern laughs, not unkindly. "Thirty years from now IVF will be so refined it'll be like having blood drawn. But there's no reason you'd necessarily pass along infertility to your child. Even with ICSI. The children most likely to inherit reproductive problems from their parents are the cases in which the cause of infertility is a congenital disorder or gene mutation. I don't think you need to worry."

"Okay. Good. So will you actually perform my IVF or will it be whoever happens to be here, like with the inseminations?" I smile to let him know that although I now understand quite clearly how his clinic operates, I'm not convinced the setup is especially patient-friendly. By signing up for IVF I've exposed my willingness to go to extreme measures to conceive, and yet I do not want my situation to seem dire. I hope Dr. Morganstern will continue to view me as an easy and valuable pregnancy he can chalk up for his team.

Dr. Morganstern glances at his watch and picks up the pace. "We work on a rotating schedule for all procedures. You'll meet all of the doctors over the course of the month or so that you are cycling. Everyone in the practice is very good."

"It just seems so impersonal, like the patients are cattle or something."

"You can call me anytime you have a question," he says and grins. Have I flattered him too much?

He shuts my folder. I've been in his office for forty-five minutes. The waiting room must be overflowing with his patients.

Rising from my chair I ask, as if it were an afterthought, "Are there any additional risks to having a baby through IVF as opposed to naturally?"

"No," he says. "Not really. The only risks are with high-order multiples, and we'll only be putting in two embryos with you since you're young. I think you'll be fine."

Again I have to convince Dan, who does not share my sense of urgency. "Shouldn't we get a second opinion?" he asks. "Isn't IVF pretty much the end of the line?"

"Why would we go for another opinion when our clinic has the best doctors and scientists and pregnancy statistics in the country? Think of the waiting room. It's filled with women who have come from Nebraska and Italy and even Israel. Why would we go anywhere else?"

I promise him that as soon as I'm pregnant I'll be happy again.

"Besides," I add, "it might take a couple of tries."

A month before I'm set to start "cycling," the results of an Australian study on the incidence of birth defects in IVF babies are published in the *New England Journal of Medicine.* The researchers found IVF babies to be at an increased risk for birth defects. I immediately call Dr. Morganstern.

"We've obtained no such evidence here," he says defensively. Are his patients flooding the phone lines? "Our clinic has found no difference between the babies conceived through IVF and naturally born babies."

"I'll take your word for it," I say, the relief in my voice too audible; I sound desperate. I tell myself we should be fine since our clinic has produced nearly 10,000 babies via IVF and, in the world of medicine, high-volume outcomes are generally better.

Still, after I hang up, I carefully read through the list of birth defects mentioned in the study and see that most of them—cleft palate, club foot—are operable.

If my appendix bursts I will have an appendectomy. If I get cancer I'd be willing to try chemotherapy. When I broke my arm I wore a cast until the bone healed. And now I need to have surgery in order to conceive a baby. One in every eight couples of reproductive age experiences infertility. Our situation is hardly unusual. 6.1 million Americans are infertile, and of this number almost half have sought medical assistance. Each year more than 250,000 IVF procedures are performed in the United States. Over a million IVF babies have been born worldwide. Yet only fourteen states—including New York—require that insurance cover the procedure, and at $15,000 a round, the cost is prohibitive to many couples. My company's insurance plan will foot 80 percent of the bill. Most health plans don't subsidize reproductive medicine so extensively. Although we have to face infertility, we are still very fortunate to be able to afford IVF, a treatment that offers success rates of 50–60 percent per cycle.

Certain acquaintances tell me they could never do IVF. On a couple of occasions where we divulge our plans, I am asked, with just the slightest hint of condescension, why we don't consider adoption instead. I don't pretend to know, though I do say that if our attempts at IVF are unsuccessful, we won't hesitate to adopt. My desire to bear a biological child feels so primal that there's not much use speculating about it. Throughout history, haven't people gone to extremes to pass their genes to the next generation? The irony that natural selection can lead to artificial inseminations and in vitro fertilizations is not lost on me, but it only strengthens my conviction that mysterious forces are driving reproduction.

I dream that our child will be the living image of my love for Dan, that my parents' genes can be preserved in my baby. I hope our child will be able to find answers to who he is in Dan and me. Am I vain for wanting him to resemble us? Dan mostly. I hope he won't be cursed with my fine hair or short stature. Any knack for acing standardized tests will need to come from Dan, too. But even if it doesn't, evolution will surely give our child a boost, opting for a batch of chromosomes with greater potential than our own.

Dan's religion, Catholicism, is opposed to reproductive medicine, which it claims undermines God's will. The bishops state that conjugal love is the only acceptable means to human procreation. A priest in Dan's sister Cannon's church recently said that couples who pursue infertility treatments are greedy. Dan doesn't seem bothered. Why should he and I be shamed into viewing our motives for wanting children skeptically? Does thinking that the will of God could be compromised by science underestimate His power? Who can say for sure that God's giving us the genius to develop reproductive medicine is not a part of His plan to help infertile couples?

When I was a child my parents took us to the Jersey shore every July. We stayed in any one of several upside-down houses on a block that dead-ended at the beach. I loved the homes we rented— lime with evergreen trim, or pink with red shutters and doors. My younger brother, Will, and sister, Katie, and I got to sleep in downstairs bedrooms, underneath the kitchen. And most likely because the houses were already so tacky, every Fourth my mother let us decorate the front deck in red, white, and blue crepe paper. I was eight years old when Will and I were finally allowed to walk to the Woolworth's ourselves to purchase the supplies. On exiting the store, I leaned into the door and held it open for three nuns in habits to pass through. The third nun smiled at me as she entered and said, "Thank you, Jenny." I stared at her, alarmed that she knew my name. Was it possible her relationship with God gave her omniscience? My parents had raised us mostly without organized religion, and not for the first time I wondered if this was wise. Were there truths in the world I was not privy to because I hadn't had a First Communion earlier that spring like the rest of the rising first graders in our predominantly Catholic town? I dreaded when Tuesday afternoons rolled around and all but three or four of us groaned, "Oh no, it's time for CCD (the Confraternity of Christian Doctrine), the Central City Dump." I'd go home and read the Bible to my dolls, though I never made it past Genesis. Might God impart secret knowledge to the people who took religion classes and worshipped Him in pews? I let the door swing shut behind her, feeling its slow breeze.

"Did you hear that?" I asked Will out on the sidewalk. "That nun knew my name."

"Duh," he said. "Do you think it might have had something to do with the shirt you're wearing?"

I looked down and saw that I had on my blue tank top with "JENNY" plastered across the chest in bubble letters.

I was still a little unhinged that afternoon when the boy next door showed Will and me that crepe paper could serve purposes other than holiday decor. At twelve years old, he wore thick glasses and black socks with sneakers and was always reciting scientific facts he'd picked up from the NOVA series. He'd ride up on his bike and, while orbiting me, repeat, "A shark circles its victim before attacking it." Even my brother and I, no insiders ourselves, were able to identify his dorkiness. If we had nothing better to do, we might offer to help him conduct his science experiments. On that particular Independence Day he came walking across our lawn of white stones to request a roll of our crepe paper. Will and I followed him to the end of our driveway and knelt while he tore off a sheet and placed it over an anthill on the sidewalk. He withdrew a magnifying glass from his pocket, aligned it to reflect the sun onto the paper, and started a fire. Here was finally an experiment that might come in handy. I'd tried numerous times to light a flame by rubbing two sticks together and never succeeded. Now, if I were ever lost in the woods, all I'd need to get by was a magnifying glass and crepe paper. Dry leaves could even do the trick.

To this day, my religious convictions are shaky enough to occasionally overwhelm me with anxiety. And I still regard science primarily as a tool to facilitate survival. One can subsist in nature by drawing on its elements.

I START TAKING BIRTH CONTROL PILLS to regulate my hormones until the clinic is ready to begin its second IVF series of the year. Each series lasts about two and a half months; in between the lab is cleaned and the staff's work schedule reduced. The series I've signed up for runs from April into June. On the Monday the clinic reopens I stop taking the pills and Dan injects Lupron, the hormone suppressant, into my abdomen after work. The technicians don't want the blood of too many women overcrowding their laboratory so the clinic staggers its start dates; since I'm on the younger side and can afford to wait, I'm delayed for a week. Finally I receive the call to begin injections of the ovary-stimulating medications. Compared to the months we were trying on our own that I spent waiting helplessly in the dark, IVF is so proactive! I arrive at the clinic every day for ultrasounds where I can see my eggs growing. The best specialists in the country measure them, say it won't be long now, and I feel that I am in very good hands.

Each time one of the nurses opens my file I see "A+" circled across the top, which I presume categorizes me as a patient of the highest potential.

When my eggs are mature one of the doctors gives me a prescription to fill for HCG, human chorionic gonadotropin, to trigger ovulation. That night I'm to get a shot with a three-inch-long needle. I've been given this shot four times previously at the clinic before inseminations and I still have the scars. Although Dan is a perfectly capable injector, for this particular shot I want a professional. I ask my favorite nurse, a woman my age from Scotland, if she minds giving it to me. We arrange for her to stop by my apartment downtown the following night at ten. This does not fall under her job description, but is not all that unusual for the clinic, where the nurses supplement their earnings by administering shots to patients after hours.

Dan and I eat dinner at a restaurant with friends on Saturday night and excuse ourselves at 9:30. The Scottish nurse and her husband ring our buzzer precisely at ten. We give them a tour of our apartment, a two-story walk-up with a narrow steel spiral staircase. We tell them how my mother found this apartment in the *Village Voice*. The rent has not increased much over the years since our building is rent-stabilized. When I first moved to New York, I was surprised that everyone felt comfortable discussing what they paid in rent. Growing up I was taught that good manners meant never talking about money.

Dan opens a bottle of wine, and I quickly drain what I hope will be my last drink for a long time. The Scottish nurse declines a glass, and admits, guiltily, that she is eight weeks pregnant. "Congratulations," Dan says, extending his hand to her husband. I give her a hug.

"Don't mention it at the clinic yet," she says. "Some of our patients have a hard time dealing with pregnant nurses."

I nod to show sympathy, to show that of course I would not have a hard time dealing with her pregnancy, or anyone's for that matter. And so far I've been only happy when friends and relatives have announced they're expecting. But I suspect one of the reasons

I want to conceive in a hurry is so that I won't start to feel envious or resentful of other women. I try not to think about whether the Scottish nurse would have confided in me had I not offered her a glass of wine.

The nurse and I go into the other room and she draws up the needle. I pull down my pants. Dan comes in to watch. She injects it into my butt in a split second. We head back out into the living room so everyone can finish their wine. Our Village apartment may not have seen this kind of action since the drug parties of the eighties.

On the retrieval day I show up at the hospital as an outpatient. I sit in a checkered cotton gown and paper slippers with four other women while Dan is steered into another dark playroom to contribute his sperm. While he's gone I assess the women's ages, invent their stories. My favorite scenario involves a career woman who almost forgot to fall in love, but at age thirty-nine met a great guy whom she married, and they are here in the nick of time.

I'm fortunate that Dr. Morganstern performs the Monday morning retrievals. The Scottish nurse drew up the order for the morning and put me first on the list. Dan returns, flashing me a quick and subtle thumbs-up. It feels good to laugh. Soon the receptionist calls my name and I'm steered into a bright white operating room where an anesthesiologist takes my glasses before sticking a needle into my arm. The drug works immediately. I recognize the voice saying hello as Dr. Morganstern's but I can only see a fuzzy blur. I'm in a rectangular recovery room where my bed is sectioned off by curtains on both sides. Dr. Morganstern and the nurses have just rolled another woman to the spot beside me. I hear Morganstern say, "We got eleven eggs."

"That's good, right?" I smile, squinting.

"It's great. Just what we were aiming for."

"Thanks," I say, and the nurse calls Dan in.

"Can I please have my glasses back?" I ask the nurse.

"They're in your right hand."

The nurse draws two marker circles on my behind so Dan knows where he is supposed to inject the progesterone shots for the next two weeks, after which, if I'm not pregnant, he'll stop. If I am pregnant, we will keep going for three more weeks.

On Tuesday a nurse calls me at work to say that four of my eggs have been successfully fertilized by Dan's sperm in the petri dish.

"What about the other seven?"

"They didn't fertilize."

"But if they did ICSI and stuck the sperm straight into each egg why only four?" I ask.

"Think of it this way," the nurse says. "You made the right decision to do IVF. But I wouldn't worry about it. At your age four should be plenty. All you need is one."

For the next two days I'm disheartened. If only four eggs fertilized, the chance that they'll divide into high-quality embryos must be slim.

On Thursday afternoon we arrive back at the same waiting room. Although we are slated to go first again, we're the last of the five couples to show up. An unfamiliar young couple who were not a part of Monday's group are seated in the corner. Perhaps they're doing a frozen embryo transfer (FET). These are performed after thawing additional embryos from a previous IVF cycle. The blonde holds her Prada purse in her gowned lap, and I wonder why I had pegged her as thirty-nine. I slip the gown on, and an hour and a half later the receptionist calls my name.

"Remember," Dan says, "only two. Do not put back in more than two."

Dr. Morganstern has informed us about selective reduction, the process whereby one or more fetuses can be aborted in the event of a multiple pregnancy. During the procedure all of the embryos might miscarry. For both of us, but especially for Dan, who was raised Catholic, selective reduction is not an acceptable option.

I lie down on the operating table, and the doctor on rotation walks in. He's young, maybe thirty-five, with ruddy good looks. I haven't seen him before. There's no way it could have been Dr. Morganstern again since he was just at the hospital on Monday. "You have some good-looking embryos," Thursday's smiling doctor says.

A skinny middle-aged woman with spiky blond hair wearing a white coat makes her way out from behind a glass wall and warmly introduces herself as the embryologist. "Perfect embryos." She points to a video monitor in the upper right corner of the room, on which there's a black-and-white ultrasound picture of two floating jellyfish.

Is this funny, or am I just looking for an excuse to laugh? I've read on the Internet that the quality of embryos is determined by the number of cells, along with the symmetry and fragmentation of the cluster.

"How many cells?"

"We're going to put in two embryos. One eight-cell and one eleven."

"So the eleven one is really good, right?" I ask her.

"Oh, they're both beautiful."

I look at the blobs on the screen again. I think, *Beautiful.*

"What happened to the other two?"

"They also look great," the embryologist says. "We'll keep them in their petri dishes for another two days, at which point, if they make it into blastocysts, we'll freeze them."

"With two extras it's unlikely that you'll have any to freeze," the doctor says. "Only embryos of absolute top quality continue to thrive outside of the uterus more than a few days. But if we freeze them before they become blastocysts they're not likely to survive the thawing process." He pauses. "Ready? Stay still."

The embryologist says, "And they're off." This time I actually guffaw, just as the doctor slides out the catheter that contained my embryos.

"Okay," he says. "All done. Good luck. The next eleven days are going to be very long."

The embryologist hands me a printout of the jellyfish ultrasound as I'm being wheeled away. Dan is invited into the recovery room, opposite my cubicle of a few days before.

"Look at them," I say, showing him the picture. I'm relaxed and hopeful, an entirely new person from the one who left him minutes before.

I insist on lying on the bed for half an hour after the nurse clears me to leave. In that time three out of the other four women are wheeled in. I overhear the blonde with the Prada purse telling her gray-haired husband about the four embryos, each somewhere between five and eight cells, that have all been implanted in her. I realize that I'm hoping she'll get pregnant and am reassured that my infertility hasn't yet made me self-centered.

Finally I let Dan call my friend Heather, who agrees to pick us up in her car because the heavy rain means a long wait for a cab. We ride the elevator down to the lobby and I climb carefully into the back seat. Dan returns to work, but my younger sister, Katie, leaves work to play hooky and hang out with me. I've rented *Anna Karenina* for the occasion, and as always, once the TV is turned on, Katie starts snoring. Usually no one in my family will agree to watch a movie with her. On September 11, 2001, Katie met me at my office in midtown and we walked the forty blocks to my apartment, surrounded by hundreds of women in heels and men carrying briefcases. We put on the television and she fell asleep.

Today, Katie wakes up in time for the final scene.

"Do you want to order pizza?" she asks. "Or we could get Chinese."

"Which do you want?"

"Just decide," she says.

Shouldn't I be annoyed at *her* for sleeping through the movie we were supposed to watch together? "I'm too nervous to care," I say.

"It'll probably work. Don't start obsessing already."

"And don't you be condescending." At this she appears hurt; I back down. "I want it to work more than anything," I say.

"More than you wanted a permanent wave in the eighth grade?"

"Even more than a perm."

"You know I wanted to get one, too. After you left for boarding school. But Mom wouldn't let me. I would sleep with my hair in braids and wear it frizzy the next day. I never understood why she let you and not me."

"Probably because she'd seen what mine looked like."

"Maybe. But it seemed unfair that just because you freaked out about things, she thought you wanted them more." She stands up from the couch and walks to the drawer of take-out menus. "How about pepperoni?"

On Monday morning a nurse whose voice I don't recognize calls me at work and says, "Great news. Both of your extra embryos made it to blastocysts and have been frozen in our lab." Embryos reach the blastocyst stage on day 5 in the petri dish. At that point they're a heartier cluster of hundreds of cells, more likely to develop into a pregnancy. But the lab environment is harsher on the embryos than the uterus, and therefore keeping them all out to see which ones make it to blastocysts is not a risk you want to take unless there are plenty of embryos.

I stay late at the office every night that week. Before going to bed at night I recite a prayer to St. Gerard from a laminated yellow card that my mother's friend gave her to send me. On the front of the card, which is the size of a driver's license, Gerard's gazing with love at a cross in his arms, a halo above his head. On the back in cursive lettering reads the following inscription:

O good St. Gerard, powerful intercessor before God and Wonder-worker of our day, I call upon thee and seek thy aid. Thou who on earth didst always fulfill God's design help me to do the

Holy Will of God. Beseech the Master of Life, from Whom all paternity proceedeth to render me fruitful in offspring, that I may raise up children to God in this life and heirs to the Kingdom of His glory in the world to come. Amen.

Dan's mother, who never misses a mass, claims she's never heard of St. Gerard.

On sunday dan, katie, and i ride out to New Jersey so they can play golf. I drive the golf cart around, with one hand on the wheel and another on my abdomen, and each time I hit a small bump in the grass I whisper, "Sorry, guys." Every few minutes I evaluate myself to see if I've developed any symptoms of pregnancy.

We eat lunch afterward on a porch overlooking the eighteenth hole and Katie says, "I think it worked."

"Why?" I ask.

"I've never seen you order chicken fingers before."

"It's too early for cravings," I say.

"That's going to be a nightmare," Dan says. "'I want dessert. Dan, I have to have ice cream. Dan, get me ice cream. It's a *craving.*'"

"I just think you are," she says and smiles.

Monday morning I ride the subway up to the clinic for a blood test. I recognize one of the women in the waiting room from the retrieval and transfer procedures. She looks like she's in her forties, with dark hair and sorrowful eyes.

"Hi," I say.

"Hi." And then: "I'm not pregnant. I took a home test this morning. You haven't taken one yet?"

I shake my head no. I can't bear to buy another over-the-counter box. I've spent hundreds of dollars on them during the last year. They are nothing but bad luck.

"I suspected it wouldn't work anyway because I only made one embryo. My chances were slim. Dr. Morganstern said that given my age, he's not going to make me wait until the clinic starts its third series. He's going to let me do a second cycle this month."

It's the beginning of May and the second series doesn't officially end until June, so there should be enough time for her to run through a second IVF cycle.

My name is called, and a pretty Latino nurse has me extend both of my arms so she can see which one is less bruised. She pricks my skin and tells me I'll receive a call sometime in the afternoon with the results.

When I haven't heard from the clinic by 4:30, I decide I must not be pregnant. A friend in the office who got pregnant with IVF claims to have heard a rumor that they call people with positive results first, putting off the harder news until the end of the day.

I phone Dan at the consulting firm where he works and tell him it's probably bad news.

At 5:00 I walk back to my friend's office and stare at the photograph of her IVF daughter taped to the computer.

"They could at least have the decency to call me."

"Have you tried checking your messages at home?" she suggests. Later she'll admit she was just trying to give me something to do.

"Not yet. But they always call me here." I walk back to my office and dial our home phone. There's one new message.

I've spent the past eleven days imagining how I will react when Dr. Morganstern gives me the news, how I will scream with delight so that he can experience my happiness vicariously. Or I will stay upbeat, assure him I am okay, and make arrangements for the next IVF cycle before he hangs up the phone.

I hear my doctor's sweet, hoarse voice saying, "Congratulations, you're pregnant. Continue with the progesterone shots and we'll see you in a week." I replay the message three times, blushing, only partly because over the past several weeks I've developed a small crush on Dr. Morganstern. Then I sit quietly at my desk for five minutes.

I ring Dan. All I have to say is "Hello" and he knows.

On the way home from work I splurge on several pregnancy tests. I take the tests every few hours over the next couple of days for the thrill of seeing two strong pink lines immediately appear.

My life is charmed. IVF has worked the very first time.

MY FIRST ULTRASOUND is scheduled at five weeks. Dr. Morganstern says, "There's one sac." It looks like a small black cocoon. He moves his wand around my belly and calmly announces, "And there's another."

He does not mention the word "twins." But he adds, "It's a good thing we only put in two embryos. Remind me what happened to the embryos we didn't put in?" He puts down his instrument and reaches toward my manila file.

"We froze them," I say.

"It looks like you've got your whole family then."

I call Dan as soon as I return to my office. "Remember how you said the other night that it would be fun to have twins?"

A few weeks later, a couple of jumping beans appear on the ultrasound. "What you're seeing are the heartbeats," Morganstern notes.

"Do you think I should see a high-risk specialist?" I ask him. This is our last appointment before I graduate to a standard ob-gyn.

Dr. Morganstern notices the motion sickness bands around my wrists. "Morning sickness already?" He laughs. "Cici Vanderbilt sent you to me, right?" Cici Vanderbilt is a tall, pale obstetrician in her late thirties who nodded in agreement throughout my only office visit. From the certificates on her wall you could see that Vanderbilt is her married name and I'd wondered if she would have taken her husband's name if it hadn't sounded so fancy.

"You're so young," Dr. Morganstern says. "You don't need a high-risk specialist. You can go back to Cici."

Dr. Vanderbilt had seemed slightly nervous, as if she were inexperienced. But she had directed me to Morganstern, and for that I owe her. Besides, I have so much faith in Dr. Morganstern that I'm willing to do anything he tells me.

"Good luck, Jenny," he says on his way out, giving me his trademark handshake. Each time he extends his hand, I'm embarrassed by where it has been just minutes before.

While I'm dressing, I hear Dr. Morganstern congratulating someone down the hall. And I'm a little surprised that someone else is pregnant. But of course that's what the clinic is for.

I DON'T REALLY NOTICE myself expanding. I don't feel heavier. My face is a little rounder, but as early as twelve weeks, people in my office remark on my swelling stomach.

I keep saltines in my desk drawer and sometimes they help alleviate the nausea. Twice I bump into the publisher of my company as I'm squirreling back from the cafeteria at 11:00 a.m. with a hamburger and chips.

For the most part, though, I feel healthy, and fertile, and sexy. It's the start of my second trimester. I pass construction guys on the street who call out, "Doesn't matter what the sex is as long as it's healthy." They don't know about the glass vials of hormone injections, the petri dishes, and steel insertion instruments. To them I'm a woman who's had sex. And sex with Dan has become spontaneous and fun again, unbound from our arduous efforts to conceive.

At my sixteen-week checkup, Dr. Vanderbilt says, "So I'm sure you've read all that stuff about the increased risks of a twin pregnancy."

"Sure." I've already bought a book on twin pregnancy. It stresses eating a lot in the second trimester so that the babies will be big if they come early and listening to your doctor should she prescribe bed rest. I've committed to memory the signs of preterm labor listed in *What to Expect When You're Expecting*. I know to notify Vanderbilt if I feel contractions so that she can administer one of two labor-halting drugs, terbutaline or magnesium sulfate. I've read about a cervical stitch that can be sewn in surgically if my cervix appears to be weakening, and about pre-eclampsia, a maternal condition causing high blood pressure. Nearly all of these conditions are followed by assurances that "with appropriate treatment, a woman with this condition has virtually the same excellent chance of having a positive pregnancy outcome as a woman without it."

"Let's check out the heartbeats," Vanderbilt says. She rubs gel on my belly and slides a probe around until it picks up the first echoing beat. It sounds like the pitter-patter of fast little feet. She pushes the probe around some more and, above my right hip, the second heartbeat comes in.

On the way back to my office I call my mother. I tell her I think I'm the happiest I've been in my life.

"I know." She laughs. "Pregnancy is the best part."

"How can you say that?" That my mother ever had a life, much less one that had been enjoyable before she had children, is something that even at thirty rarely occurs to me.

"I'm kidding," she says. "Just kidding."

SINCE BECOMING PREGNANT I've become a harsher judge of manuscripts submitted to my publishing house. Previously I'd been agreeable to reading just about anything. Now that it's getting harder for me to climb the four flights to my apartment; I don't feel like lugging heavy manuscripts home every night. During work hours I'm increasingly preoccupied with finding a new rental in an elevator building. I click onto the Internet and look up Realtor sites, before sneaking onto the pregnancy calendars at BabyCenter.com to see that our babies already have ears and fingers and toes, that they are the size of oranges. I'm delighted by how quickly they've made the jump from olives to oranges. I've watched new mothers at my company become far more efficient at their jobs, no longer dropping by my office to chat, eliminating coffee breaks, so they can be out the door, work completed, at five. But I sense that my shift in priorities is not turning me into a more competent professional.

During week 18 one of my authors drops by. I close the door, lift up my blouse, and show her my stomach. As soon as she leaves I call my mother. "I just bared my belly to an author," I tell her.

"She probably appreciated it. Imagine how vulnerable she must feel each time she gives you a draft of her book."

I'VE SPENT A GOOD DEAL OF TIME over the past two and a half years helping to acquire the rights to and plan the paperback publication of a brilliant young writer's memoir. In addition to his extraordinary literary talents, this author has messy good looks, dark ringletty hair, and mischievous eyes. The second time we went for drinks (over which meetings in the publishing business are traditionally held), I was already engaged to Dan. The brilliant, ringletty-haired author met me at my office wearing rumpled khakis and an untucked, white button-down oxford that exaggerated the mischief in his eyes. He pushed his hands down inside his pant pockets and said, "Bet you didn't think I owned any of these." We walked to a bar around the corner in the Waldorf Hotel, and I immediately sensed his distaste for my choice as happy hour was packed with wealthy tourists and investment bankers. After we finished our business discussion, much of which had been covered earlier in the week over the phone, he casually mentioned that he'd not yet eaten dinner. But having drunk two beers I knew I had to get myself home.

I led him to the subway station, to a platform heading in the opposite direction of where we both lived, across the tracks from where I stood waiting for the train to take me home every other night. Was the beer to blame or the fact that I already regretted ignoring his remark about wanting dinner? We had to climb back up the stairs and turn ourselves around. Once we were finally on the subway heading downtown, he said my engagement ring reminded him of a ring his mother had worn. The expression in his eyes was sincere. But I couldn't adjust quickly enough. Still playing to his puckish side, I replied, "It's too big on me, but whatever, it's not like that's important. Marriage schmarriage." He looked appalled. Of course he did not know I'd spent the last year trying to persuade Dan to propose.

The doors of the subway car opened at Christopher Street; I pecked him on the cheek and hurried out. I walked the two blocks home with an extra spring in my step. I crawled into bed and wished Dan a slightly drunken and giddy goodnight.

While I'm in my second trimester we buy the paperback rights to this author's next book. He has unconventional ideas for publishing it and I become argumentative with colleagues, trying to get him the green light. I find myself increasingly regressing to the prickly personality I possessed as a child, flip-flopping between showing friendly deference to my editor in chief and publisher and quarreling juvenilely with them.

My father claims the reason I went away to Groton when I was fourteen is because he and I were at each other's throats and I was driving him nuts. Mostly I recall fighting over use of the telephone. I say to my father that he's exaggerating and he answers, "You gave me a lot of lip. I told your mom, it was either you or me." This is a story he started telling a few years ago, and it has grown particularly harsh with age, getting stronger each time it's rolled out. I moved away from home and subsequently changed. In order to fit in I became conciliatory. I stopped being so vigilant. And I found life easier to navigate once I wasn't so intense.

Occasionally my mother wondered aloud as to where I'd buried my seriously uptight nature.

Now, out of nowhere, I'm back on guard.

I mention to Dan that I might see a psychiatrist, knowing he considers both my anxiety and the entire field of psychology bullshit. But he is amused when I confess I've always wanted to visit a shrink, to lie on the couch with a cup of tea and talk about myself for forty-five minutes.

I bring a check for $200 to my appointment to cover the cost.

The psychiatrist's office has two beige Eames chairs. The psychiatrist greets me at the door, a slightly older, more professionally dressed version of Sarah Jessica Parker on *Sex and the City*. She leads me across the room, sits down, and crosses her legs. She asks, "What brings you here?"

I explain that I am fighting with my bosses, who obviously know a great deal more than I do, over every decision about a book—its cover art and layout, advertising plans. And my reversion to childish conduct is causing me stress.

"Good," she says at last. "It sounds to me like you're growing up." She motions to my burgeoning belly. "And you'll need to start taking charge since you're about to become a mother. You seem to have this naive notion that everyone is out there to protect you. It's time to get realistic about making decisions for yourself; you're on the right track. And I'm afraid we're out of time."

I walk the twenty blocks back to my office, elated. It's not that I've been seized by raging pregnancy hormones, but simply that I'm stepping up to the plate in preparation for motherhood.

The next day I'm surfing the Web for nursery furniture to calm myself down after another disagreement with my editor in chief when he enters my office, precariously navigates his way through piles of manuscripts on the floor, and rests his hand on my shoulder. He asks, "Are you feeling overworked? Do you want me to cut down your list, assign someone else to work with a few of your authors?" My editor in chief is a hippie boy-genius editor who grew up to be a revered, reluctantly tweedy editor in chief.

"No," I say, trying not to sound irritated. "I can handle it."

Months prior to a three-month maternity leave, I must be cognizant that I will soon be replaced, at least temporarily. I spent ten years photocopying manuscripts with the word "assistant" somewhere in my job title. But recently I've begun to feel as if I've finally arrived in the business. Agents send me manuscript submissions. Editors at *The New Yorker* return my calls and sometimes choose to run stories my authors have written. I show up at book parties and indicate my name, not my boss's, on the guest list.

The reluctantly tweedy, former-hippie editor in chief is looking at me with concern.

"It's okay," I manage to smile. "I promise I'm fine."

I HAVE ALL BUT CONVINCED DAN we are having girls. I have communed with my soul in dreams and awakened knowing there are girls inside me. The additional weight I'm carrying feels just like me. My in-laws have five granddaughters and no grandsons; a tendency to bear girls clearly runs in the family. At our twenty-week ultrasound, Dan hints at the gender question by asking the technician whether the babies are different sexes. She answers that they are in fact the same. I say, "See, they're girls. I knew it." As the technician finds each body part on her list, she says, "Looks good," and I exhale. Finally I say, "Okay, tell us the sex."

"Both boys. Definitely boys. And from the look of it they're well-endowed." I laugh, but Dan's in shock.

We head down York Avenue toward our offices and we don't say a word. We are rearranging everything in our heads. Just the day before, on a Labor Day visit to the Jersey shore, two of my nieces called for me to join them on their rented surrey run by foot pedals. As their father, Bruce, drove us around the streets of Cape May, his two girls, ages five and three, and I sang "The Surrey with the Fringe on Top."

"This is a pretty great surrey," I said at some point, resting my feet on the dashboard.

"It's okay," the older one answered. "But it's not like the surrey in *Oklahoma!* This surrey doesn't have any fringe on top and its wheels aren't yellow."

"And there aren't any isinglass curtains you can roll right down," the three-year-old added. I thought, *This is what it would be like having girls.*

On the walk to my office, the specifics of our future family begin to take shape in my mind. Our nuclear unit will consist of me and the guys. Dan will pass down the Quigley name to our sons, who will each grow up having a brother.

IF YOU SAY ANYTHING TO DAN about his older brother Matt, just some harmless comment like "Isn't it funny that he's a Democrat and you're such a close-minded conservative?" or "I wonder why Matt's so generous with money while you're such a tightwad," he'll jump on you. He'll say, "Leave Matt alone, he's my brother."

Lately Dan's been complaining about having once been an interesting person, about needing an adventure to avoid becoming a boring, middle-aged man. He brainstorms about trips he might take before the babies are born—dogsledding expeditions in Antarctica, rafting tours down the Amazon—and after each idea he proclaims, "I bet Matt would love to go with me. I should call Matt."

Football season is just starting and we've already spent a few weekends watching games from the couch. When the Giants played Tampa Bay, Tiki Barber went to the line to face off with his twin brother Ronde. You could only imagine how many times as kids they practiced together in the park. A boy tosses a football; it lands with a thump in his brother's arms, and back it comes. They might talk about anything then, with the ball going back and forth.

The tube-socked boys I knew in grade school whose eyes welled up in frustration after losing on the basketball court, the untucked, baseball-capped teens at Groton whose teasing cautiously hinted at affection, my male colleagues who have been arriving at the office lately wearing navy button-downs and Kenneth Cole black loafers in their first attempts to dress fashionably, all suddenly evoke in me such tenderness I wonder how I could have been numb to these feelings before.

C ANNON IS PLANNING a baby shower for me, and at the beginning of October I take the subway to Grand Central from our new apartment on East Sixty-sixth Street and catch a train out to her house in Larchmont to register at Buy Buy Baby.

First we stop at the house of Cannon's friend who has newborn twins, a girl and a boy. The mother has offered to show me some of the gear I'll need. We arrive just as she's getting ready to breast-feed. She pulls out an enormous blue Styrofoam square with a U cut out of it. "You will definitely want a double boppy." She fits the device around her waist like a life preserver, pours herself a glass of water and rests it on the coffee table, then lifts both babies out of their playpen simultaneously and floats them on either side of the boppy. "Come stand behind me on the couch so you can see," she says. She sits down, unhooks both straps of her nursing bra, and attaches each baby to a nipple. She picks up her glass of water. "Voilà, I even have my hands free. It's easy and the best thing for them."

For the first time in several months I am nauseated.

At Buy Buy Baby I register for a million essentials from a list my friend Holly forwarded to me. While Cannon is looking at crib sheet patterns, I find a spot on the floor beside the information booth and sit down.

Later that night I call and special-order the double boppy from an entrepreneurial mother of twins. It is one of the things I select that day that never makes it out of the box.

I'M TWENTY-SEVEN WEEKS PREGNANT the next time the brilliant, ringletty-haired writer comes to town and we make plans to go to dinner. Dan's plane arrives early from a business trip so he is able to join us, and the author invites along a few rising literary stars. I cannot finish my pork chops because the babies are taking over the space that had been my stomach. Dan tells a story he's just heard from a friend he met at OCS (Officers Candidate School) about a secret army force that consisted of a bunch of guys with long hair who hung around the bars in a small North Carolina town. All the longtime residents assumed they were bikers until one day a few weeks ago they disappeared. In their absence rumors flourished of a mission to hunt Osama bin Laden.

Over dessert, a beautiful black writer with an English accent outlines her exercise routine and I smile at how someday I can tell the twins about the cool people and scintillating conversations they were privy to while still inside me.

AT TWENTY-EIGHT WEEKS, I catch a virus. Early in the day my stomach is upset, and later in the afternoon I feel contractions roll across my belly. I call Dr. Vanderbilt. She isn't worried. I still have eight weeks to go before the average mother of twins delivers. But my mother is anxious and she convinces me to call the doctor again. The second time Dr. Vanderbilt says, "It doesn't sound like real preterm labor. But at your last ultrasound the technician forgot to check for any cervical change so why don't you walk down to the hospital and get an ultrasound. You worked so hard for this pregnancy."

A pretty young resident stops my contractions with terbutaline. She does an ultrasound and calls Dr. Vanderbilt, who decides over the phone that she doesn't need to come by, that it isn't serious. The terbutaline is making me feel as if I've drunk an entire pot of coffee. My heart is racing. She says, "It's just that my daughter is sick," and I answer, "Of course. Not to worry." The resident releases me and I walk back to my apartment.

Dan says, "Vanderbilt didn't put you on bed rest?"

"No."

"Well, I'm confining you to this apartment. You need to tell your office that you have to work from home until the babies are born."

I don't argue. The next day I ride the bus to the offices on Park Avenue and pack my stuff. My editor in chief understands. Computer Services delivers a laptop to our apartment.

At my weekly checkup the following Monday Dr. Vanderbilt seconds Dan's plan. "I believe in house rest. I think it's good to relax." And she offers to write a note to my boss prescribing it. She says, "Jenny, don't look so worried. We're still aiming to get you to thirty-seven weeks. Well, thirty-six at least."

Tuesday morning after working on the couch I walk ten blocks to the hospital for a routine stress test. I climb onto the metal table and am connected to two stethoscope heads with gel on them that record the babies' heartbeats. I lie there for forty minutes, trying to relax, and the nurse says the babies' heartbeats look fine.

On Friday, I arrive at my thirty-week appointment with Dr. Vanderbilt, only she's on vacation so her partner, an older Irish woman, sees me instead. "The heads are dropping," she says. "These are going to be December babies."

My due date is in the middle of January. "Do you think I should be put on bed rest?" I ask.

"We don't believe in bed rest these days."

"But my mother was on bed rest with both my brother and sister. She wanted you to know that. She's small like me."

"And did she make it to term with them?"

"Yes. With both."

"And today she probably would have done it without bed rest."

"So I can walk a little?"

"Some walking is good for you."

That night I walk the ten blocks to our first Lamaze class at the hospital. Dan meets me there, coming straight from work. We tour the labor and delivery floor, run our hands along the birthing tables. We stop to admire some sleeping babies in a window. We've been told to bring snacks, and I'm envious of the couple next to us who have a whole pizza. Afterward I'm too tired to walk home and Dan jogs down the street to hail us a taxi.

The following evening, a Saturday, something tears on my right side as I step onto the Third Avenue bus on the way to a friend's house for dinner. It's the first time I've left the apartment all day. I sit down in a front row seat reserved for disabled persons and press my fingers lightly into my side. I eye Dan warily.

"Should we turn around?" he asks.

"Maybe," I say. But just then it subsides. "I'm okay."

"Could it have been a kick?"

"More like a dagger."

While eating rack of lamb at the table, the pain on my right side returns. I wonder briefly if it could be my appendix. Then I run to the bathroom as my stomach starts to cramp. I have diarrhea, which is loud and might be embarrassing if the pain weren't so awful. We have been discussing the various discomforts of pregnancy at the dinner table. But I am certain that what I am feeling is not normal. I shout for Dan to call Vanderbilt.

She is still away, so her partner meets us at the hospital. She stops my contractions with terbutaline again and sends us home with a prescription for it.

In the middle of the night I am startled awake. I feel as if I've been stabbed in the side. I notice blood on the sheets. I call the partner at the home number she gave me. "I took another of the terbutaline pills and a Benadryl to make me drowsy, like you suggested, but my side still hurts and I'm bleeding. Do you think I may have hemorrhoids now, too?" I've been afraid of this: 85 percent of women carrying twins contract hemorrhoids.

"Do you want to go back to the hospital? Or we could talk in the morning." Her voice sounds sleepy.

"I don't think I can drag you back at this hour." The Benadryl is starting to kick in. "I'll try to sleep."

On Sunday morning Katie shows up as planned to make pancakes. I'm crying on the couch. She calls my parents on her cell phone, hands it to me.

"You should be in the hospital," my father says.

"But the doctor isn't that worried."

"I don't give a damn whether the doctor is worried. Just go to the hospital." He threatens to call an ambulance.

I ring the partner and tell her the pain is still awful. She says, "I think you should check into the hospital for twenty-four-hour monitoring."

Later, at the hospital, the partner examines me. "The heads have come down since yesterday," she says.

"It felt like they were sliding down as I walked to the hospital last night."

"It's entirely possible."

"Will she be staying here for the rest of her pregnancy?" Dan asks.

"Oh no." The partner laughs and crinkles her nose. "She'll go home tomorrow. But now it's time for bed rest." She looks at me. "For the rest of your pregnancy you'll be an incubator for the twins to grow."

We watch football and that night the stabbing sensation in my side returns. The nurse arrives with more terbutaline. When a young Italian resident checks on me, I ask him if there's anything he can do to alleviate my lower back pain. He says no. Later I will wonder if he even realized we were supposed to be preventing labor. It could have been his first day of rounds on the labor and delivery ward. An even younger nurse knocks the next morning and asks whether I want an epidural. She must be thinking I'm just a regular pregnant lady about to have a regular baby. How can it be that so many of the people taking care of me have no idea why I'm here, that the babies I'm carrying are in danger? Why don't I inform each staff member as he enters my room, "We have an emergency situation here which we need to respond to right away"? Instead I laugh with them about how I dragged the entire IV drip and stand with me into the bathroom not realizing the bag unhooked. I joke with the residents doing my ultrasounds about how the hospital needs to get HBO because I've never missed an episode of *Sex and the City*.

The Giants lose, and Katie and Dan go home. But I'm unable to sleep with the itchy monitors on my belly and the terbutaline—which is actually a form of speed, of all things—pumping through my veins, and at sometime around 1:00 a.m. I rip the nozzles and IV off me. A nurse appears immediately. I tell her I have to use the bathroom and will call her as soon as I am ready to be reattached.

I climb back into bed just as my water breaks. I feel it pouring down my legs, drenching the sheets. I page the nurse, who calls the partner, and she says to start running steroids through my IV to help mature the babies' lungs quickly.

I phone Dan to say the boys are coming. It is November 10. I'm not quite thirty-one weeks pregnant.

Over the next several hours a steady stream of doctors and nurses move in and out of my room. When Dr. Vanderbilt arrives at the hospital the next morning, she has not yet been given the news. The nurse who's washing my hair tells her that my water broke. Dr. Vanderbilt is surprised; the message her partner left her must not have been cause for alarm, but she quickly recovers and rolls with the new situation, reeling off patients who stayed three weeks in the hospital once their water broke before delivering healthy babies. "I would only let you go three weeks, though," she assures me.

"I think it will happen tonight," I say. I've lost confidence in my doctors. "The contractions get bad at night."

"That's true," she says. "Contractions are worse at night. But I bet they will be the healthiest babies in the NICU. I'm guessing they are four pounds each."

The partner pops in. She rests her hand on my sheet and says, "I wish I had put you on a stronger magnesium sulfate instead of the terbutaline."

A resident in neonatology arrives to inform me about the NICU. He says, "One in ten babies born at this hospital requires care in our NICU."

"Are you kidding?" I snap. "I've never heard of a NICU."

"Are you familiar with preemies?" he asks. "Because someone must think your babies are going to be born prematurely or they wouldn't have called me up here."

Up until now the word preemie had conjured up images in my mind of the infant Cabbage Patch Kids that were always on back order during the height of the dolls' craze.

The resident recites the various challenges preemies can be expected to face. Chronic lung disease, respiratory distress syndrome, patent ductus arteriosis—a vein to the heart that hasn't been closed off—intraventricular hemorrhages (brain bleeds), retinopathy of prematurity (which could lead to wandering eyes and blindness), necrotizing enterocolitis (a bowel disease). After pronouncing each medical term, I ask him to describe the condition, which he carefully does.

I say, "I don't think you should be scaring me." The IV in my left arm is bothering me like crazy. I ask him to leave.

Katie and Dan return from buying sandwiches in the basement

cafeteria. I'm not allowed to eat. It's Monday afternoon and I haven't eaten since Saturday. We're sitting around, shooting the breeze, when my mother pushes open the door.

"Thank God I'm here," she says. She has arrived from Florida without a coat.

Dan stands to give her his seat. He walks to the radiator where his laptop is resting and tries to get it to play a DVD. He has been tinkering with it since Saturday without any luck. Again and again the screen lights up, the opening credits to *Ben Hur* roll, and the picture freezes. I'm not terribly disappointed. I can never seem to muster up enthusiasm for *Ben Hur* even though Dan has been recommending it since our first date.

Later my mother and sister go home to sleep. But Dan stays. I listen to him snore on the pullout chair, while watching the monitor above my bed. By morning, the change of day has boosted my morale. Dan goes home to change and answer a few e-mails from work, and my mother, who slept in our bed, comes to keep me company. Throughout the day, each time I use the bedpan, the boys' heart rates drop and the alarm beeps, sending in a dozen worried residents and nurses. They pull the oxygen mask from the wall, and tell me to place it over my face, instruct me to get on all fours like a dog. We go through this routine half a dozen times before the head resident pages Dr. Vanderbilt, who runs the five blocks from her office to the hospital.

She enters the room panting. I smile at her. She finally catches her breath and says, "I've never had a patient like you." I have no idea what she means. By this point I'm wondering how many patients she has actually had.

An anesthesiologist knocks before entering, and Vanderbilt steps away from my bed while he describes the epidural procedure. The nurse who washed my hair yesterday arrives to insert a catheter so I won't have to use the bedpan anymore. Dan returns in fresh clothes.

The heartbeats dip again; everyone rushes in. I start to laugh and burst into tears, and Dr. Vanderbilt, who was just leaving to talk to a high-risk ob-gyn down the hall about my situation, says, "I think it's time to get those babies out."

The heartbeats rise and everyone's attention turns away from the monitor.

I ask Dan, "Do you agree with her?" I inquire of my mother. "What do you think we should do?"

It is 6:00 p.m. on November 12. I am exactly thirty-one weeks pregnant. My father's birthday is November 13 and I consider saying that I want to hold out another six hours so he and the boys might share an anniversary.

I no longer believe anything my doctor says. The heartbeats only drop if I shift my position. Are my movements somehow jolting the monitors? What if I stay absolutely still? But Dan and my mom are sure that now is the right time.

And so the team rolls me into the OR.

Part Two

59TH STREET
BRIDGE OVER
TROUBLED
WATER

WHILE I AM SITTING ON THE operating table the anesthesiologist calls attention to my scoliosis and I remember that my spine was slightly crooked as a child. Dr. Vanderbilt is preparing for an emergency C-section. There is no time for an epidural so she is doing a spinal instead.

Dan enters the OR in scrubs. He sits on a chair beside me and holds my hand. A sheet is draped across my stomach so he can't see much, but later he tells me that blood was squirting everywhere, that there were pools of it on the ground.

I feel Baby A being pulled from my stomach. In a twin pregnancy, the baby who is positioned lower in the uterus, nearer the birth canal, is referred to as A; the baby above him is B. The nurse holds A in front of me. Covered in blood is a small swaddled figure with dark hair. Who knows how he would have seemed to me if this had not been my first time giving birth. What I will remember afterward is how during that very first brief meeting, he looked exactly like a baby.

Dan is motioned across the room to watch while A is weighed and given an Apgar score, a tool to assess if a newborn needs resuscitation. I hear the numbers: the first one is too low, but no one says anything about it. He weighs 3 pounds, 9 ounces. The baby is crying, which must be a good sign. Out comes Baby B, looking like a replica of Baby A, like the tiniest incarnations of Dan. Someone says, 3 pounds, 7 ounces.

Just minutes before our babies were born I only loved the idea of them. They were abstract. Suddenly this changes. I am momentarily stunned by the swell of emotion I feel at witnessing the start of life. It is as if our babies have jumped out from behind a curtain. *Ta-da!* The timing is wrong. They have been thrust onstage too soon. But look how they manage to pull it off, how time accelerates during their dazzling introductions. How could they have been so unrecognizable to me until now? I want to hug them both against me, to soothe them. But they are whisked out of the room. Instantly Dan is gone.

While she is sewing me up, Dr. Vanderbilt asks, "Have you guys decided on names?"

"Sam and Gus," I say. "Or maybe Gus and Joe."

"I like Sam and Gus," Dr. Vanderbilt says. And the resident, anesthesiologist, and nurses in the room all enthusiastically agree: "Definitely Sam and Gus."

I WAKE UP IN THE RECOVERY ROOM to find my mother standing over me. The first thing I tell her is "I'm not going back to work." I know that my babies are off somewhere attached to life support. I miss them already. They should never have to fend for themselves again.

"You don't need to decide that now," my mother says.

"Why do you think they keep the recovery room so freezing?"

"It's warm in here." She smiles. "That's the anesthesia. It makes you feel cold."

Dr. Vanderbilt checks on me and says she has called Dr. Morganstern. "He said that a lot of his patients with twins have been delivering this early."

Later that night Dan arranges to have me moved to a private room, where friends find me on the phone and ask about the C-section, how I'm feeling.

I tell them I don't know. But in truth, I like being in pain because as soon as the morphine and antinausea drugs kick in, I rage at myself for not insisting on bed rest, for allowing myself to stress over a job, when I knew that stress could trigger labor. The psychiatrist had said it was time to start acting like a mother and still I hadn't left what must be the most casual ob-gyn practice on the planet for a high-risk doctor who would have demanded that I take a leave of absence from my job, and prescribed an extended course of terbutaline the very first time I showed up at the hospital and then pumped me full of magnesium the second. Dr. Morganstern had claimed I was too young to be considered high-risk, but now he's seeing twins born prematurely all the time? Could he have sent me to any other OB than the one who had recommended him in the first place? Why did I trust him instead of doing my homework to find a high-risk OB who might have bought me enough time to feel that I had done everything in my power to protect my children, enough time to have asked God for additional strength?

"I have never had a patient like you before." A patient who is such a fucking idiot.

THE NICU AND THE PICU are located on the sixth floor. The PICU, pediatric intensive care unit, is closer to the elevator. Behind its glass windows are infants of all ages, some fighting pneumonia, others unconscious from high blood sugar. To control the risk of infection, if a baby has gone home, gotten sick, and comes back to the hospital, he is admitted to the PICU rather than the NICU. The neonatal intensive care unit is past the PICU at the far end of the hall. It has five units containing a total of fifty beds. For the time being our babies have been moved to the only available stations: Baby A is in unit 5 and Baby B is in unit 4. Dan is already trying to get them moved to the same room. Each room has several rows of stations, equipped with computer monitors, oxygen tank hookups, and either a warming bed, a plastic isolette, or a crib.

Five years ago the entire NICU was rebuilt and expanded to

make room for more preemies who are surviving, largely due to the introduction twelve years ago of surfactant replacement therapy, which helps to develop premature lungs. Without it a substantial number of premature infants would not be expected to live. Some great technological advances have been made in the last few years—the oscillator, for instance: a high-frequency vibrating ventilator that gently delivers air at a very high rate, eliminating the need to inflate and deflate a baby's immature lungs. There has also been major progress in cardiac surgery for infants. The expansion of the NICU can also be attributed to improvements in fertility medicines that have vastly increased the number of twins born each year, close to 60 percent of them premature. One in eight babies born in the United States today is premature; nearly 500,000 preemies are born each year, a number that has increased by 29 percent since 1981. Prematurity is not fully understood but researchers suspect certain sociological changes in addition to reproductive medicine have contributed to its increase. Women over thirty-five are more likely to give birth prematurely, as are women who report high levels of stress. And better prenatal care may prolong some pregnancies that otherwise would have resulted in miscarriage.

Many NICUs are divided into several distinct regions: a true "intensive care" unit, an intermediate care area for babies who still require oxygen, and a quieter area for "feeders and growers," healthy preemies who need to gain some weight before they can be discharged. But at our hospital, a room is selected at random for a baby depending on where there is space for him, and he stays there until he's ready to go home.

On the consent form I signed before doing IVF, there was only one reference to the risk of premature births with multiple gestations. It was followed by a claim that the clinic limits the number of preembryos transferred according to maternal age and preembryo morphology in order to prevent pregnancies of more than one baby. I had naively inferred from the clinic's statement that they had everything under control.

In neighboring rooms, Baby A and Baby B are strapped to warming beds to restrain them from pulling off their oxygen masks. Preemies have little body fat and get cold easily so they must be kept in an incubator or a radiant warmer. Their lungs are often not fully developed so they sometimes need assistance with breathing. The oxygen masks are connected by elephant trunk tubing to ventilators, big boxes on legs next to their beds. The first time I visit, I don't understand that they will progress to the iso-lette once they are extubated from the ventilator. Nor do I compre-hend that Jack, born at twenty-seven weeks and now in the isolette next to ours, had been on a warming bed and in bad shape until quite recently. I don't see that there are several full-term babies here suffering from congenital heart defects, gastrointestinal mal-formations, or injuries from difficult births. All I see is that ours are the only babies in either room laid out naked on white sheets. Blue veins protrude through raw red skin, around their eyes, down their legs. Their flesh hangs over elbows and knees like withered fruit. Their joints and feet seem too large for their limbs. A's crying sounds like a trapped baby mouse, so soft and irate and scared, unlike anything I've heard before. His arms are twitching franti-cally, trying to break free of his armbands. The overhead lights are blinding. Everything is beeping. I tell myself that I met my babies in the OR. This visit doesn't count. Dan wheels me out one set of glass doors and in through another to Baby B. I cannot see his face well enough through all the tubes to tell him apart from his brother. Dan says, "You can touch his arm." But I'm frightened.

DAN VISITS THE BABIES SEVERAL TIMES. By Wednesday he seems to know them already. I have made fewer trips to the NICU in my wheelchair, as I'm still recovering from the surgery, drowsy from large doses of painkillers. But Dan reports that they are doing well on the respirators, that the nurses claim the first forty-eight hours are the most dangerous and we have passed them now. The doctors are talking about taking the boys off the respirators tomorrow and letting them try to breathe on their own with just a small amount of extra pressure support.

We have still not assigned the boys names although we are agreed on Sam and Gus. I tell Dan that since he has spent more time with them, he should decide who is who.

The brilliant, ringletty-haired writer has sent a huge bouquet of flowers that are perched on the windowsill. Metallic helium balloons from a friend float "It's a boy!" across the ceiling. Our Lamaze nurse (we had made it to the first class) brings us Polaroids of the boys strapped to their warming beds. Do they take Polaroids of every baby who is born? On these particular photographs, you can just see two sets of miserable squinting eyes and writhing mouths. The rest of their faces and bodies are covered with vacuum cleaner tubes that run up to a breathing mask over their noses. I do not have the idea that it would be fun to keep the snapshots for a scrapbook to show when the boys, dragging snow on their boots and hats inside after sledding, ask over hot chocolate, "Tell us again how small were we? How scared were you?" Instead, I throw the photos in the waste bin by my bed while the Lamaze nurse is still visiting.

Cannon and Bruce are due to visit on Wednesday night. I have not showered in several days, and am still wearing the checkered hospital gown. Why does no one think to bring me pajamas? Why don't I remember to ask for any? Dan leaves to meet his sister and brother-in-law in the lobby. I reach for the phone to dial my hairdresser who had said he would drop by our apartment this Wednesday night since I was unable to travel to his salon.

I've been trying to call him all day to cancel the appointment but Dan keeps repeating that it's not important right now. I imagine my hairdresser stranded in the lobby of the elevator building we just moved to on the Upper East Side, with the doorman holding out the phone like a question mark. Why should he have to make a trip uptown unnecessarily? I think I also want to hear the reaction of someone who doesn't know exactly how far along I was in my pregnancy.

"Congratulations," he says in his romantic Portuguese accent when I tell him I've just had the babies. "That's great. I am so happy for you."

My hairdresser has been cutting my hair since I moved downtown. He is one of a few acquaintances who have tracked the general developments of my life, as I have his, without needing to become actual friends. "So I guess I'll call to reschedule once I'm home," I say.

"Remember to bring pictures the next time you come in."

I am ashamed when Cannon and Bruce walk in, which I know is unnecessary—on some level I accept that what has happened is not my fault. But it is also impossible not to feel that as a child-bearing spouse I have not entirely passed muster. Dan and I went to the hospital in Westchester when each of their three girls was born. During our most recent visit, under a year ago, we ate yogurt-covered pretzels and drank champagne, and Cannon asked me to be the godmother.

But now that it is our turn to be visited, I am wary of the first impressions that the boys will make, pinned down on plastic beds, their thighs the width of my middle finger, peering out over their masks from enormously vulnerable extraterrestrial eyes.

Then when the two of us are alone Dan says that he has decided Baby A should be Gus. "He has this silent cry that's really pissed off and he keeps trying to break the tubes off his face. The nurse told me he's getting a reputation. She said once the breathing tube blocking his vocal chords is removed, we're going to be in trouble." Like Caesar Augustus then, Augustus Cannon will be our warrior. "Are you sure about Augustus Cannon Quigley?" my dad asks over the phone. "It's a hell of a name." Dan says Baby B has been mostly quiet. He will be Samuel Minton.

On Thursday Dan's younger sister, Megan, arrives to meet the boys before her first date with a young lawyer. My mother, my mother-in-law, and Megan sit in my room, deciding which of the three outfits she has brought into the city with her sends the right message. I want this conversation to go on for hours. I am hoping she will marry this young man, that he will let her talk about her new nephews tonight and manage to convince her that her outfit, a sleek black top and jeans, is marked indelibly in his mind, and that at their wedding someday Sam and Gus will carry the rings down the aisle.

But eventually it is seven and even if Megan takes a taxi she is going to be late. My mother leaves, too, and my mother-in-law helps me try out the hospital breast pump even though it is too soon to have any milk. The boys are being fed liquid nutrients through an IV. My father-in-law shows up and stands outside the door until I take off the plastic cones so he can join us.

Dr. Vanderbilt visits before going home for the night, concerned about how my cesarean is healing. With my mother-in-law and father-in-law in the room I say to her, "I wish I had stayed in bed. I would have done anything to protect those babies." I start to cry in front of my in-laws, which I hate doing, but I don't know how long it will be before I see Dr. Vanderbilt again, and without going so far as to blame her I don't want her getting out of this entirely guilt-free either. I am grateful that my own mother has gone home since her anger at Dr. Vanderbilt is palpable. My mother seethes through tight lips each time Vanderbilt enters the room. I want desperately to keep my composure, for fear that if I lose it, my rage will crush the gentleness I feel toward Sam and Gus.

Dr. Vanderbilt tells me the statistics show that bed rest doesn't work. She says, "When I opened you up there was a lot of blood. The pain that you felt might have been one of the placentas tearing off your abdominal wall. This happens to pregnant mothers who use cocaine, but we see it with twins as well. There's nothing that either you or I could have done to prevent it from happening."

I ask her, "Do you know of any long-term problems the boys might have from being preemies?" I am already focusing on long-term issues, on the hope that we can get through this and leave it behind.

Dr. Vanderbilt answers, "I would guess that there's a chance they could develop asthma. I remember that from residency, but even that they might outgrow. If they get it. Really, Jenny, at thirty-one weeks they should be fine."

My in-laws stay in the room for this conversation, looking down at the floor, out the window. Over the summer my father-in-law was diagnosed with liver cancer. He did not tell anyone for weeks. Cannon was nearing the end of her third pregnancy and he wanted the birth of her baby to be a joyous occasion.

After Vanderbilt has gone, I say, "I just hope that they're okay."

"Right now we're concerned about you" is my father-in-law's response. He lost his mother when he was eight years old and was raised by his father with the help of the nuns down the street. He must understand on a deeply subconscious level how unbearable it is for a mother to feel that she cannot keep her children out of harm. He was the child his mother could not protect.

Dan returns from a trip to our apartment where he has showered and changed clothes for the first time in days. He ushers his parents off for a last visit to the NICU before they head home to Queens. Once they've left I close my eyes. It's the first time I've been alone all day. I hope Dan brings back news that the boys are doing well.

And he does. Sam has been moved into Gus's room, to a warming bed right beside his brother. It's not till the following day, when the respirators are unhooked, that Sam comes crashing down.

It is painful to look at him. We have been told that the first seventy-two hours in a preemie's life are the most critical, but at four days old Sam has never appeared so uncomfortable. The sight of Sam's swollen stomach makes me suck in air and hold my breath. I say to Dan, "I can't believe this is our family."

Dan's brother, Matt, appears in the doorway. Matt unzips his jacket as he makes his way toward us and says softly, "Congratulations." I fight the urge to stand up from the chair Dan has pulled up for me and block Sam from Matt's sight.

"He didn't look like this yesterday," I say. "I hope they know what they're doing here."

"This is Sam," Dan says. "He's having a rough day." He motions for Matt to pass behind my chair. "And this is Gus." With his bulging eyes and gaping mouth, Gus looks like a hungry hatchling. It appears that switching from the womb where he'd been swimming to his present position—tied down on a flat bed—has given him quite a shock. But beside Sam, he is the image of health.

Matt says, "So these are the guys." Then he asks, "Don't we know anyone at this hospital? Someone we could call to make sure Sam and Gus are getting the best care?"

Dan's family has lived in New York City most of their lives. My father-in-law is a partner at a highly reputed law office. My mother-in-law's maiden name is engraved on the wall of this hospital; her father was one of its founding benefactors. After my father-in-law was diagnosed with liver cancer, the Quigleys called everyone they knew and read everything they could find before deciding who were the best oncologists in the city to treat him. In contrast, we haven't even gleaned the names of the doctors caring for Sam and Gus.

Dan and Matt decide, rightly, that our inquiries might irritate the neonatology team, who surely are indiscriminate in their efforts to save every baby that comes through the doors of their NICU. But since I phoned around for referrals before hiring a wedding caterer and moving van, it is unsettling now to know absolutely nothing about the medical team tending to my children.

At an open isolette opposite Sam, a father slips his wedding band up his baby's arm, to the shoulder, and takes a photograph. He removes a quarter from his pocket and rests it under his baby's hand. They are the same size. He snaps another picture. Did a nurse suggest that this father measure his baby's arm and hand using these objects? Do coins and rings serve as standard props for photo ops here, like the books kids are always resting their elbows on in school pictures?

I glance at Sam, who appears to be having enormous trouble breathing. His eyes are closed. Each time his stomach deflates, the catheter tube inserted in his belly button is pulled taut. Until now I have purposefully refrained from learning how to read the oxygen and heart rate monitors over the boys' warming beds, but it is increasingly difficult when the numbers on Sam's screen keep flashing and drawing the nurse back across the room.

The nurse turns up the pressure on the CPAP (continuous positive airway pressure) machine, which looks like a bubbling water bottle. A neonatologist from our hospital is credited with inventing its thin nose clamp, which is less bothersome to the preemies than in its previous incarnations.

"Isn't he supposed to be going back on the ventilator?" I ask her. "What's taking so long?"

"Several people are needed to intubate a baby," she answers. She motions to an abandoned respirator in the doorway. "The maintenance guys already brought it up so we're just waiting for the nurse-practioners to arrive. They should be here shortly."

This is the first trip I've made to the NICU on foot. Though I am in no hurry to recuperate, the wheelchair was starting to feel like a luxury I didn't deserve. I'm in a lot of pain. I decide to go back upstairs until Sam is safe on the respirator again. Dan and Matt each take an arm and help me make my way back to the labor and delivery ward. I shuffle past a room with a mother and a baby. I shuffle past another room with a mother and a baby. I shuffle past a room with a whole family and a baby. Once I'm settled in bed they head to the basement cafeteria for lunch.

I poke at the food that has arrived while I was downstairs and call the nurse to request another Percocet. I doze. At some point I open my eyes and Dan is sitting in the corner. When I look again he is gone.

At five o'clock, Dan and I arrive to find the doors to the NICU closed. A nurse at the front desk says the unit is temporarily shut to visitors. I peer through the glass wall, cupping my hands over my eyes to eliminate the glare. Every doctor and nurse in the room is crowded around Sam. Sam's nurse from this morning sees us and comes out into the hallway. She says that Sam is back on the respirator but he's still not recovering. They have maneuvered his position on the warming bed, adjusted the pressure on his vent, given him a medication to help maintain his blood pressure and heart strength. They are treating him with antibiotics, though so far the blood tests do not indicate an infection. The X-rays show a partial lung collapse. Still, this does not account for the dangerously abnormal gas levels they're seeing in his blood.

"It's good that we haven't discovered a cause," she says, addressing Dan. "When we don't find an answer medically it usually turns out to be better news."

Dan is sober and fit. I don't envy him. Bleary from painkillers and surgery, at least my senses are somewhat dulled. But the drugs don't make the possibility that Sam is dying surreal. Everything surrounding me is white and steel and sterile, and I can imagine how Sam would disappear inside these walls and it would seem ordinary.

In the middle of the night Alex, the male NP, visits Dan and me with paperwork authorizing a blood transfusion. Sam continues to nosedive. Alex's eyes shift past us when he says that Sam has been put on an oscillator, a breathing machine the NICU turns to when the conventional respirator isn't working.

———

Saturday morning—a week after arriving at the hospital in preterm labor—Sam's condition has, miraculously, stabilized. I leave Lindsay—my high school roommate—a message on her machine. She is a pediatrician and might be able to tell me something about the oscillator. Then Dan and I go downstairs. The crowd around Sam has dwindled to three. A nurse is adjusting an arterial line that Sam did not have yesterday. "We needed to put two catheters straight into his arteries since we're checking his oxygenation so often." The doctor standing over her says to us, "It is my job to consider the glass half-empty. I still don't know why his system failed so I am going to continue testing for everything I can. Infections he might have caught here. The immune system in preemies is undeveloped so they are very susceptible to infections. I've also ordered tests to check for blood disorders."

Dan explains to me that this talk of glasses half-empty is good news. "It means he is looking for stuff because that's his job. But it might not be there."

I cannot interpret what is happening from metaphors about half-filled glasses. I need the information to be straightforward.

So the young doctor who is doing a three-year fellowship to specialize in neonatology says, "Your son is very, very sick."

It's the first time someone has referred to Sam as my son. But despite the fellow's directness, I still can't understand. They have told us that babies' lungs are not brittle like those of adults; instead, they spring back like rubber. So what is the nature of Sam's sickness? Not even the doctors seem to know.

They have rendered Sam completely unconscious with Fentanyl, and laid him on an oscillator that is shaking air into his lungs. His tiny arms and legs are spread out and pinned down. His stomach is distended. He looks like a baby prisoner being electrocuted on death row. He is being drugged so that the powerful vibrations will not hurt him.

We take the elevator back up to the maternity floor and wait for a resident to discharge me. I take my first shower since arriving at the hospital. Blood spills out of me all over the tiles. I use the gel in the dispenser on the wall to wash my hair. I am hoping it is too much blood and that when I mention it to the resident she will decide to hospitalize me for another day. I don't even have a bag to pack, just a pocket-sized tape recorder that my brother bought me.

The phone rings while Dr. Vanderbilt is writing prescriptions for my discharge. I overhear Dan say, "She cannot hear anything negative right now." Then he passes me the phone.

Lindsay says, "Sam is in the right place to get the medical attention he needs. He's fortunate to be at a level 3 hospital." Before delivery I had not even known to ask whether the hospital with which my OB was affiliated was a level 3. Level 2 and 3 hospitals have neonatal intensive care units. Level 1s do not. And level 3 hospitals are prepared to care for the most endangered newborns.

"The oscillator is an amazing machine. It will do all the work of breathing for him so he can take a break." Lindsay's tone is quietly optimistic. She is choosing her words carefully. A best friend since Groton, she would never lie to me. She says, "I know someone whose daughter was on an oscillator for three weeks and when they unhooked it she was able to breathe perfectly on her own. She made a full recovery."

"They keep saying Sam's the sickest baby here. I don't understand how he is sick, medically. Why am I failing so miserably? I may never have come in first before, but I'm not usually this inept." Although it is Sam who is trailing the other babies, threatening to drop out of the race, there's no distinguishing him from me at this point. I'm still thinking of him as an extension of myself.

Lindsay says, "This is as hard as it's going to get."

On our way out we stop at the NICU again. Despite their name, the warming beds are cold and clinical. Sam and Gus went from test tubes directly into my womb, and now they have been turned into other people's experiments once again.

The doctor on call approaches us to report that the transfusion, needed to replace blood the nurses had drawn every hour to check gas levels, has improved Sam's red and white cell counts. The doctor reassures us that Sam has stabilized, but he looks worried. Later I will realize that the neonatologists aren't usually here on Saturday mornings, that the doctor had been paged on account of Sam. But at the time I miss this detail. I rest my hand on Sam's small arm as it vibrates.

I start to ask another question. Dan puts an arm around me and steers me toward the door. My discharge papers have been signed, the hospital gown returned, and now we have to go home. No longer a patient, my maternity jeans are horribly loose. We stop for pizza on the way to our apartment. It is a Saturday night and Patsy's is bustling. People smile as we pass them on the way to a table. They think I am still pregnant. I have my first beer in eight months. Dan says, "Even if Sam doesn't make it, he still lived. He will always exist. Samuel Minton Quigley was here."

I think about graffiti, about gravestones, about whether four unofficial days on a respirator more than two months before your expected arrival constitutes life. Jackie Kennedy's preemie son, Patrick, who died of respiratory distress syndrome, is buried beside his mother, father, and brother in Arlington National Cemetery. In four days I have loved this tiny baby and his brother enough for a lifetime. Dan and I do not say "I love you" very often. For whatever reason, it makes him uncomfortable, and after so many years I have stopped dangling it onto farewells and goodnights. I take another slice of pizza, let the cheese burn the roof of my mouth, and think about how my love for Dan has suddenly deepened. Without pain, you do not need this kind of love.

"You really don't think it would have made a difference if I had gone to a high-risk ob-gyn instead?" I ask him for the tenth time.

"No," he says. "A couple of days at most."

We discover the industrial-sized hospital breast pump I've

ordered has arrived at our apartment before us. It is in a big blue toolbox under the desk at the doorman's island. Dan carries it upstairs and I ask him to put it down on our coffee table. My milk has finally started to come in. He takes it out of the box. The sides and top are clear plastic, revealing a brass cylinder inside attached to two ridged metal wheels. It looks like the engine on a freight train that my breasts are going to fuel.

With the exception of the pump, I am indifferent to my belongings. I was here unpacking boxes just a week ago, and yet now I take in our brand-new apartment as if I've never seen it before. A marked-up manuscript is still spread around the floor by the couch. I will have to arrange for my assistant to have it picked up, for another editor to finish making the final cuts to the last chapter.

I sit down, attach the plastic cones from the case to my breasts, and turn on the pump. I flinch as I begin to feel the suction. I don't bother to turn on the TV. I ache for our newborn babies. And I pray for their safety. I have always been a worrier. But now that there is real danger, my fear seems to correspond perfectly to the threat and I discover that in my heart I'm not neurotic after all.

"I can't believe it's Saturday night," Dan says.

"I know," I say. Even the days of the week are gone.

SUNDAY MORNING I TELL DAN about a Catholic church I've passed several times on my way to the hospital for ultrasounds and stress tests. He wants to visit the boys early as he has work to complete in the afternoon. We plan to meet at the church at eleven.

I am not Catholic, but I am in urgent need of someone to answer my prayers. And I'd like to sit beside Dan, who is. I doubt that God minds where you choose to visit Him. I could save time by praying in the windowless interdenominational chapel right past the hospital lobby but it reminds me of the smoking rooms in airports.

I grew up begging my dad to take us to church following our breakfasts at Dunkin' Donuts Sunday morning. I was probably the first child ever to protest when my mother said I no longer had to attend Sunday school after just a month of singing "Jesus Loves Me" and walking around the neighborhood with a cardboard collection box for JESUS around my neck. Although my mother's parents were assimilated, nonpracticing Jews, she must have felt traitorous sending us off to church. But I loved the worn-out black leather Holy Bibles with red metallic trimmed pages that were relics from the days when my father's first children, from a previous marriage, had lived in our house. Their signatures were scribbled on the title pages. I lined up all three of the Bibles on the lime green bookshelf in my bedroom. My younger brother, Will, and I wore our half brothers' broken-in baseball mitts to play in the Little League—gloves endorsed by Phil Rizzuto that flipped open and shut with ease. On snow days we sat around our stereo playing the Beatles records they had left behind when they went off to college, as if these mysterious objects we'd inherited could somehow through osmosis make us cool.

During my first three years at Groton I sang off-key in the church choir. And I only resigned before my senior year because my chorale grade was pulling down my average enough to be of concern in applying to college.

Now, as a mother of two ill children, I want desperately to believe there is a God who can intervene.

At 10:45 I head out. Memorial Sloan-Kettering Cancer Center has bought the plot directly adjacent to the church in order to expand its offices. Scaffolding extends along the sidewalk the entire length of the street. There are abandoned bulldozers and two trucks, piles of sandy bricks.

I open the heavy door. The church is empty inside. A girl is straightening hymnals in the nave. She tells me that the service schedule has changed. The next mass is not until noon.

I walk, with my hands over my abdomen, to the NICU. A nurse tells me that Dan has just left. We have missed each other.

In the far corner of the NICU Sam is shaking on the oscillator. Someone has rested yellow sunglasses over his eyes and attached an overhead phototherapy light to his bed to treat his jaundice. Preemies' livers are not fully developed so they can become much more jaundiced than full-term babies. If the jaundice is too severe, it can cause brain damage. Although heavily drugged, Sam finally seems at peace.

Gus is staring out through an oval window of the incubator he moved into yesterday. I snap open the window, reach my hand through, and stroke his shin lightly. Gus flinches and kicks me away. One of the nurses said yesterday that once he grows a little bigger, his skin will be less sensitive. I wonder if my touch is actually painful to him now. I am in a hurry for my babies to grow. So far they are still not being fed any milk, only drops of vitamin-enriched water through their IVs. We have been told that the boys will lose up to 10 percent of their birth weight before they start gaining—this is apparently true of most babies, not just preemies. Do the boys look smaller today than yesterday? It's hard for me to tell.

An hour later I head back to the church. I don't expect to find Dan there and he isn't.

I sit in one of the back pews. A large man with a white ring of hair, wearing a purple robe, begins to speak and I remember to think of him as the Father. Dan's mother has corrected me when I've referred to him as the "minister" or "preacher."

I sing the hymns, recite the Nicene Creed, join in prayers for our troops in Afghanistan, for the Catholic bishops around the world, for a few members of this congregation who have passed away.

And then it is time to add our own prayers. In the past this has been a complicated moment for me. I'd apologize if it seemed I was asking for something. I would thank God that my parents are in good health, and then I would ask—for Dan to get a job offer out of business school so he'd finally marry me, and later, to please let me get pregnant.

The conversation that I have now is not like those I've had in the past. It is pursued with an unprecedented pureness of thought. As tears spill down my face, I ask unapologetically—without guilt, without bargaining—for Sam and Gus to be all right. A sort of bliss comes over me as I ask for something so simple. I stay with just that one prayer for minutes and no other thought intervenes.

Afterward I put two dollars into a tin collection box and light a couple of candles for Sam and Gus.

I arrive back at the apartment where Dan is making slides for an upcoming presentation. It turns out that all along he thought I meant a different church a block further away, where he attended the 11:00 service.

I pump, make us a couple of tuna sandwiches, and head back to the boys.

Sunday afternoon my brother, Will, shows up at the hospital to meet the boys. He arrived in town late last night from LA for a wedding that he thought was today but is actually not until next Sunday. My mother drives in to see him and the boys.

I tell Will to stand against the glass wall because his nose is stuffy, but he says all the right things anyway, that they are sweet and adorable. He does not cry or take photographs. From several feet away, he looks at Sam and Gus as if he already loves them.

The fellow walks over to us and I ask whether Sam's health is improving. The fellow appears to be in his early thirties. I've learned he is midway through an intensive apprenticeship following three years of training in general pediatrics, and he works longer hours than any other nurse or doctor on the floor. "His gas levels are back up but he isn't able to breathe on his own yet. Maybe once we reduce the sedative. For now his condition remains life-threatening."

I ask him what "life-threatening" means.

"Mrs. Quigley, are you asking me if I think your son is going to die?"

I nod. Here in the NICU I am called Mrs. Quigley. At work I use my maiden name. Nowhere else am I called Mrs. Quigley and I keep thinking the doctors and nurses are speaking to Dan's mother. I haven't yet bothered to tell the nurses to call me Jenny. Perhaps on some level I don't want to acknowledge that the updates about vacillating bilirubin levels and blood counts are being addressed to me.

"No. I don't think your son is going to die." He looks at me, and I can tell that my crying is making him uncomfortable, despite his training in handling upset parents, and he politely excuses himself and moves on.

Will hasn't eaten anything all day so we go down to the basement cafeteria and I see the carving board station where Dan has been standing in line daily to order sandwiches. As it is ten past four, the crowds have cleared. There are no windows, only artificial light and a few doctors in scrubs at a round table across the room. My brother and mother order turkey sandwiches. I rest three cups of tea on a tray and slide it down the counter, but when I try to lift it off, my hands start shaking. I take a few steps to the cashier, put the tray down, and while I am paying my brother comes and carries it to our table.

MONDAY MORNING SAM'S NURSE is a cheerful young woman who has recently graduated from nursing school. She has a high, sweet voice. Sam has his own nurse now while Gus shares a nurse with two other preemies. The oscillator requires almost constant maintenance. Because of the difficulty in drawing blood with the machine shaking Sam's body, he must be monitored by hourly X-rays. Sam's nurse tells me that he is trying to breathe on his own, and that all of the tests they ran on him for possible infections or illnesses have come back negative. Last night he had another blood transfusion. She says that if all goes well, tomorrow Sam will come off the oscillator.

Sam shares my blood type and I suddenly realize why an A+ was on the top of my medical chart when I see it on his. I am not allowed to give him my blood since I am recovering from what is called major surgery.

Dan is working from home, and he comes by at noon and stands beside Sam and me. A chair is really too low to see them, but my stomach hurts if I stand for too long. "Our boys look better today," he says.

If you had asked me before the boys were born who was the pessimist in our marriage, the answer would have been easy. Dan's outlook on life has always been more skeptical and reasoned than mine. He looks for people's motives, expecting the worst. And yet over the past week there have been times when Dan has seemed genuinely happy. Not during the forty-eight hours when we thought Sam would die. But on the days before and since, I've seen him beaming with pride at having become a father. He's already e-mailed a birth announcement to our friends, assigned the boys their names, placed a couple of stuffed monkeys in the corner of their beds, made arrangements for our baby nurse to arrive as soon as Sam and Gus come home. I've overheard him telling people that Mark Twain was also born two months prematurely and boasting to my parents that I haven't been taking my Percocets or complaining about the pain, as if even I've impressed him.

Before now I would have also said Dan was a perfectionist. I might have worried that, because he's an overachiever himself, his expectations for his sons would be too high. But it turns out he is easy to please. He is proud of his weeping wife and his fragile three-and-a-half-pound babies who can't yet breathe on their own. He stands behind me with his hands on my shoulders. The oscillator whirs like a washing machine on spin.

On tuesday, at one week old, Sam comes off the oscillator, skips over the respirator entirely, and moves straight to a thin tube giving CPAP like the one Gus has had Scotch-taped to his cheek since Friday. Both Sam and Gus are breathing, but their lungs still aren't working well enough to take in sufficient air. The narrow nasal prongs providing the CPAP makes this fact far less obvious than the ventilator and oscillator. If there were a blackout in the city, would Sam and Gus immediately die? Could their nurse administer CPR to both of them indefinitely? I ask her what would happen if the hospital lost its electricity and am reassured that the hospital has backup battery-operated generators.

Sam is moved into a clear plastic isolette just like Gus's. Each isolette resembles an early manned space capsule. The top unlatches and folds down like a glassy ironing board if the nurses need to change IVs or adjust catheters. Two small portholes on each side unlock so you can stick your hand through. The monitor wires and breathing tubes are twisted through air tunnels out the front and back. Inside are thin, sheeted mattresses, slightly angled to keep the babies' heads elevated. Foot pedals lower the isolette like a hospital bed so a baby can be removed. Neither Sam nor Gus is stable enough for the nurses to take them out or let us hold them, so their isolettes are raised up high, making it easier to reach inside. A blanket is placed over the top of the isolette to lessen the glare from the overhead fluorescent lights, which are always on.

The nurse adjusts Sam's CPAP. Then she turns off the nozzle on Gus's oxygen. For the first time in his life, Gus is breathing on his own. While I am watching him breathe, the nurse catches me wiping my nose and realizes I'm fighting off a cold. She says I have to leave the NICU. It is the boys' first really good day and I am kicked out. "The other parents wouldn't like it," she says softly, and it doesn't help that I know she's right. Because the immune systems of preemies are weak, the NICU must be kept as free of germs as possible. The rate of infection in NICUs is generally 25 percent, and some of these infections can be fatal.

I am still crying when I reach our apartment, big self-pitying sobs. Dan stands up from his computer and says that he will go sit with the boys in the morning. I call my parents, who promise to visit the boys in the evening. Then I phone the hospital's lactation consultant, and she assures me that my breast milk, which the nurses say will be running through the boys' feeding tubes any minute now, won't be contaminated from my cold.

The boys are scheduled for ultrasounds at 3:00 p.m. to determine whether they have suffered any bleeding in their brains. Since a premature baby's brain is still at an early stage of development, it is not really ready to withstand the stress of life outside the womb. Tiny blood vessels in an inner part of the brain are especially fragile. If they rupture, bleeding occurs in or near the ventricles. A technician will arrive at Gus's and Sam's incubators with a transportable ultrasound camera. He will rub gel onto the boys' heads before scanning them. Since the technician is not qualified to interpret the scans, a nurse has suggested I might avoid the procedure and wait at home until the radiologist has had time to view the images. At 5:00 p.m. Dan goes to the hospital for the results. Katie has stopped by the apartment and I ask her to wait with me until he returns. I have been warned there is a good chance that during Sam's trauma he ruptured a vessel, but whether it is damaging will depend on the level of the bleed. There are four grades, and anything beyond a level 2 is cause for concern. Major brain bleeds are linked to cerebral palsy, hydrocephalus (excess water in the brain that causes swelling), and neurologic disorders.

An hour later, Dan walks through the door whistling. He says that Gus had a sublevel 1 bleed, that it is in the germinal matrix, a jelly portion of the brain that is not even used, and that Sam had no bleeding at all.

Each morning the boys have tubes placed down their throats to drain mucus, needles stuck in their heels to draw blood, catheters inserted into their veins, and their throats and noses suctioned. They are not given any pain relievers before or after the procedures. "It doesn't hurt them," a nurse said gently the first day, after asking me to leave the room so a tube could be changed.

I finally reach Dr. Morganstern on my fifth or sixth call. He has not come by to visit the boys in his own hospital despite an earlier claim that this was his "favorite part." Over the telephone he admits that there seems to be a link between prematurity and advanced reproductive technology. While he is courteous, his chumminess is gone.

If you mix science with fate, are only you the one to take blame? Which saint is on the prayer card for all preemies? I recently read about a woman with three boys who took her chances when she and her husband decided to spin his sperm to improve the odds of having a girl. A sample of the husband's sperm was spun through a machine to separate sperm carrying the heavier X chromosome. Now, with twin baby boys, she has her own basketball team, and says she laughs at herself for messing with God. But if Gus faces a learning disability, if Sam develops a lazy eye, both problems linked to prematurity, I will not be laughing.

Katie was five years old and I was eleven when I taught her to ride a two-wheeler. On the day before she was to start kindergarten, I held on to the back of her bike and ran while she pedaled up our street, and after passing our house a few times she quickly caught on. I hopped onto my bike and we went for a short ride. Then she asked if we could go down our driveway. I said why not, and we pushed our bikes up the hill. But I had forgotten to teach her how to use the brakes. She made it all the way to the bottom, gaining momentum as she flew, and as she hit the curb she fell off her bike and hit her head. This was before kids wore helmets, and in my diary that day I described how Katie's head bled all over the pavement, how she got hysterical and my mother suspected she had a concussion. I graded the day a C−, then slashed it out and put a D, then crossed that letter out as well, wrote an F and circled it. I graded all of my days back then, in the upper right corner, I was that much of a nerd. My sister lay on the bed in the guest room off the kitchen for the rest of the day, my mother at her side, not wanting to move her. I paced back and forth in the kitchen, furious at myself. I'd enter the guest room, look at the deep scrapes all over my sister's face and body, and punch my thigh. I could not believe that no one was punishing me. The weekend before, I had dis-obeyed my father and sneaked out in a thunderstorm to stick some carrots through my neighbor's rabbit cage. Since I'd promised my neighbor I would care for her bunnies while she was on vacation, I thought my parents were wrong to ground me for keeping my word. But now, when I had acted so stupidly and caused my sister's accident, they were letting it slide.

The lesson I learned from that experience was not the obvious one, which would have been to slow down and be cautious, to remember to use the brakes. What I realized that afternoon was that if you beat yourself up for your mistakes, if you blame yourself intensely enough, no one else will.

Dan and i arrive at the NICU on Wednesday, the eighth day in the boys' lives, to discover that Sam's CPAP has been removed. He is breathing fine. Feeding tubes—inserted through the boys' noses to deliver colostrum (a mother's first milk)—have replaced the catheters in their veins. The IVs have vanished.

"They're finally getting my milk," I say, holding out the six new storage bags I've collected overnight for the nurse to refrigerate.

"Half an ounce every three hours," she says and indicates where that comes up to on one of the bags. "Because their stomachs and intestines are still immature, preemies' digestive systems can't handle much breast milk or formula. So we take it slow."

A nurse-practitioner arrives and informs us that the boys are in stable enough condition to participate in an experiment that is testing whether twins who co-bed are discharged in less time than those who don't.

Dan says, "Since the nurse-practitioners are running the experiment, my guess is that they will pay more attention to Sam and Gus if they're in it. Then again, if they're together in an isolette it might be harder to notice if anything is wrong with one of them. Could there be an oversight?"

While we are talking a young man passes us on his way into the bathroom. We hear him lock the door, turn on the shower. Some parents spend the night here; there are daybeds in the visitors' waiting room. We are fortunate to live only four blocks away.

We finally decide that since we're not here overnight, at least the boys should be with each other.

Sam is removed from his isolette, and before he is rested back beside his brother, the nurse asks if we want to hold him. I say, "Can Gus come out, too?" And the nurse says, "Why not?" She swaddles both of them and passes us each a baby as if there were nothing to it. She doesn't realize this is our first time holding them and we don't tell her.

I palm Sam's head in my left hand. His body fits snugly in the bend of my arm. His eyes open briefly. Do I sense his body relaxing or is it just mine? We stand perfectly still until the nurse returns and suggests that the boys be put back in the heated isolette as they aren't big enough to maintain their body temperature outside. I reluctantly let her take Sam from me. Dan and I stretch our arms and remark that they've gone numb.

The nurse says, "Next time why don't you pull up a couple of chairs? Some of the parents bring Boppy pillows to rest their arms on."

Dan and I look down into Gus's isolette, which now contains both boys huddled together asleep. It appears that Gus is kissing the back of Sam's head.

"Do they remember each other from the womb?"

"I think so," Dan says. "They'll be happier now."

Gus's left leg is mashed up against the side wall. Diaper cloths are stacked at the foot of the mattress to cushion the boys' feet should they slip down the incline. Enormous green and blue rubber pacifiers are at the head of the bed. Wires the color of newspaper (what's black and white and read all over?) loop around the boys' naked bodies. The new ratio of two growing babies to one isolette converts the space into a more convincing habitat for humanity than it had been with just a single baby.

Dan has to go to work but I take an empty chair from an isolette across the room and drag it over to the boys' isolette. I sit here for the rest of the day, no longer needing to slide back and forth between two stations. Then I go to pump. There is an official "pump room" at the end of the hall where the NICU mothers take turns expressing breast milk at two cordoned-off stations. The majority of preemies in the NICU are still not strong enough to latch on to the breast and suck. Milk is ingested more easily through gavage tubes or bottles that require less effort to drink from. Even the mothers who are managing to successfully breastfeed their preemies arrive in the pump room to express milk the nurses can deliver through bottles at night. I smile at another mother as we exchange places at the pump.

I return to find the boys being fed breast milk through a tube inserted down their throats. So far they have digested the milk well. I hand the nurse two twist-tied plastic bags of milk. Already over thirty bags of breast milk with the name "Quigley" are piled in the hospital freezer.

Once Gus has consumed his two teaspoons of milk, I ask the nurse to take him out so I can hold him again, but she answers that they've been out of the isolette enough for one day. She says, "If they burn too many calories trying to maintain their body temperatures outside of the isolette they won't gain weight."

At 7:00 an announcement comes over the intercom that visiting hours are ending. The NICU will reopen to parents at 8:00 p.m. I stick my hand through one of the portholes and squeeze Sam's hand then Gus's. Gus's eyes are open. He is awake more often than Sam. I hope that tonight, back in Sam's presence, Gus will sleep peacefully. I release Gus's hand and his whole arm falls across Sam's chest. Sam doesn't stir. Every time I leave I feel as though I'm orphaning them.

Dan visits the boys again on his way home from work. He steadies Sam and then Gus on the scale while the nurse records their weights. He returns to the apartment around nine and cheerfully comments that the boys have nearly reached their birth weights. For the second day in a row they have gained an ounce.

"How can that be possible when they're only fed four lousy ounces?" I ask.

"They mix the milk with a fortifier, right?"

"The fortifier is four calories!"

"How should I know?" he says. "Do you want an update or not?"

"An update. I was just there two hours ago."

"Fine, then forget it."

"No. Tell me. I'm sorry." Dan heads toward the door. "I said I'm sorry." He steps back in and comes to the foot of the bed. He has lost weight during the past eleven days. His jaw is chiseled again like it was when we started dating. He'd left active duty by then but was still putting in time as a reservist. Dan sits down on the bed and tells me how he learned to change the boys' diapers, which seem to go up to their armpits, how the nurse let him help give the boys baths. Last night the nurse announced the babies were stable enough to be bathed. But I turned down her offer to let me assist. I was afraid of hurting their chicken-bone legs in the plastic tub, of getting their bodies tangled up in wet wires, of not supporting their heads properly with my wrist. This afternoon when I hugged Sam, his hair smelled of lemony soap. He was swaddled in a towel, and I whispered to him that I was sorry he'd had such a rough start. *Yeah, yeah, yeah* is the look he gave me. *Just keep holding us like this until we can get ourselves out of here.*

"Wasn't it wonderful to finally hold them today?" I ask.

"They're pretty great," Dan says, standing up. He strolls into the living room and turns on the television. He calls, "Hey, your favorite show, *The West Wing,* is on."

"Just a sec," I say. I should go sit with him. He's offering to watch a show he doesn't even like. Instead, I slide under the covers, pull a pillow over my head, and burst into tears.

"Are you crying again?" Dan reappears in the doorway. He jumps on to the bed and hugs me. "Come watch some TV."

"Why do I have to be so small? Do you know tall women are far more likely to go to term with twins?"

Dan sees the books on my night table. "What is the point of reading this stuff now? Come on, Jenny." He picks up a stack of books on twin pregnancies and carries them into the hallway.

"What are you doing?"

"Throwing these out," he says. I hear him leave the apartment, walk down to the trash compactor. His footsteps grow louder on his way back. He shuts the door and changes the channel on the television.

A few minutes later I emerge from the bedroom. I pour a glass of water and sit down on the couch in front of the coffee table to pump. I have no idea what show we're watching but I wait until it's over and then kiss Dan good night.

———

My romance with dan began when I bumped into him at a party in New York City. The door to the party actually struck him when I pushed it open. I recognized his face from Groton, where he'd been two classes ahead of me, though I had not seen him since his graduation. I was twenty-five years old, which meant he had to be twenty-seven. Over the years I had heard he'd become a marine. He still had a crew cut.

He was wearing a gray T-shirt, jeans, and those wide-tongued leather boots people called "shit-kickers." He had a strong build and a masculine face, a Roman nose, light blue eyes.

He said hello to Lindsay as she passed him and then leaned his arm into the wall against which I was standing. "I remember you," he said. "You and your gang used to have sing-alongs out on the circle."

I laughed. I'd mostly forgotten that on a few sunny afternoons my sophomore year I'd carried my guitar outside and strummed the chords to exactly three songs I could play and which my girl-friends had cheerfully sung over and over.

As people arrived at the party, Dan steered me away from the door so we weren't in the way. Lindsay mingled with guests as they came and went.

Dan had left active duty but was still captain in a reserve unit in Garden City. He told me that when he was in Okinawa the "work-ing ladies" learned the names of all the officers and would shout at them when they walked down the street. "You're wondering how we got on this topic, aren't you?" he said.

I laughed again, because of course this is what I should have been thinking. But instead I'd been thinking about guns, which had brought to mind an odd joke. I loved telling jokes, mostly because it was so out of style.

"Want to hear a joke?" I asked.

"If it's good."

"It might be my favorite."

"Okay," he said. "Shoot."

I took my time getting started. I sipped my beer, pushed the hair out of my face, lifted my heel out of my shoe and pushed it back in. "Well," I said. "There's this guy who decides to plan a moose-hunting trip even though he's never been hunting in his life. He's paranoid because of the stories he'd heard about hunters getting shot by other hunters, even by friends. So he buys one of those neon orange vests for traffic cops and puts it on over his camouflage clothing and he even finds an orange cap and galoshes. Unfortunately, once he's out in the woods, he's way too nervous to enjoy himself. And almost immediately his worst nightmare comes true. A hunter, maybe fifty yards away, sees him and takes up his rifle. The man dressed in the orange yells to secure his safety, 'I'm not a moose!'"

I could tell Dan was not convinced my joke was heading toward humor. He appeared uncomfortable. But if I let it trail off, unfinished, I was certain any sparks between us would fizzle.

I drained my beer before continuing. "While the guy in the orange vest is sweating buckets, still shouting that he is not a moose, the hunter goes down on a knee and looks down the nose of his gun. The guy in orange jumps, waving and crying, 'I'm not the moose! I'm not the moose!' The hunter cocks his gun, and shoots. Down goes the guy in the orange vest. As the hunter approaches his prey, the guy is squirming on the ground, writhing from the pain of the bullet wound in his shoulder. His orange cap has fallen off. 'What the hell, man? What'd you shoot me for?' the orange man asks. 'Didn't you hear me shouting I'm not the moose?'

"'Oh,' said the bewildered hunter, 'I thought you were saying, "I *am* the moose."'"

"That's a really dumb joke," Dan said, irritated, and I regretted telling him.

People usually chuckled or smiled. Occasionally someone would look puzzled and I'd giddily repeat, "I am the moose."

It was all going terribly wrong and I expected Dan would soon excuse himself to get a drink. But he didn't take his eyes off of me. I thought of a line my father often used.

"My Dad will only watch a movie if someone gets shot off a horse in the first fifteen minutes."

Dan's laugh was frank and low. "That I like." He seemed relieved.

We were interrupted by the host of the party, who came over to say hello.

"Hey, listen to this. Jenny's father has a great criterion for judging movies. If a guy doesn't get shot off a horse in the first fifteen minutes it's not worth watching."

The host, who wore wire-rimmed glasses and had a framed poster of *Il Postino* on his living room wall, chortled politely. "Good one," he said.

"Tell him your joke about the moose."

I looked at Dan inquisitively, as if to say, *But you hated it.* His eyes sparkled. I turned to the host, who had lived his whole life on the isle of Manhattan, and decided Dan wasn't looking to humiliate me; he was giving me a shoe-in. Was he trying to apologize? Did I somehow relax him enough to steer his way back in to this civilian crowd?

So I told the joke again, with Dan watching me curiously. When I got to the punch line the host smiled. "I *am* the moose," he declared. "Not bad, Minton." He threw his arm around me. "Not bad at all."

Then Dan tried to talk the host into break-dancing. "No way," the host said. "There's no room on the floor."

After he left Dan said, "I just planted the seed." He shifted from his left foot to his right, uncrossed his arms and rested his hands on his waist.

Like clockwork, an hour later, the host cranked up the music, pushed back the carpet, and started to spin on the hardwood floor.

When his performance had concluded Lindsay found me and said she was ready to go home.

I told Dan I had to go and he said, "I'd like to give you a call."

"Sure." I pecked him quickly on the cheek. "I'm in the phone book."

Later he claimed he almost didn't call me. "'I'm in the phone book.' What the hell?"

But this was before everyone had cellular phones, when people were actually listed in the white pages. He called and asked me out three nights in a row, though he'll never admit it. When I tease him every now and then about cornering me at that first party he says, "What else was I supposed to do? I could see down the front of your dress."

On thanksgiving I walk over to the hospital early. Last night before I left, the nurse-practitioner suggested we try breast-feeding today. This NP is in her late twenties. She has a button nose and pale blue eyes, a fair complexion enhanced by brilliant-cut diamond stud earrings, and she is desperate for her boyfriend to propose. My first friend to visit the NICU noted that this NP is "someone we'd be friends with," by which she meant "if we'd met her on a lacrosse field, at a wedding under a tent, anywhere but here."

Yesterday at noon, two weeks from the time they were born, the boys were given their first bottles. Their suck wasn't strong enough yet and they couldn't pace themselves. They kept gulping and gagging. The WASPy NP suggested that breast-feeding might be easier since milk flows through bottles so much faster than through a breast. Since the boys are being fed nothing but breast milk it would also be the natural solution.

I have called the lactation specialist to make sure that she is available. I initially met her when I asked about renting a breast pump, which she does on the side. She is a no-frills middle-aged woman with a plethora of nursing/birthing jokes up her sleeve, leading me to wonder whether, in addition to her two day-jobs, she moonlights as a comedian at baby showers. The nurse suggests starting with Gus since he has been stable for longer. She lifts him out of the isolette he shares with Sam, untangles his monitor wires, and passes him to me. Just one feeding tube remains on his face to aggravate him. As he pulls at it, I notice that his movements are less stiff and jerky than a week ago.

I open my nursing bra, and the lactation specialist squeezes my breast along with Gus's cheeks and tries to get his mouth around my nipple. "Do you feel him sucking?"

"Not really," I say.

She takes his mouth away, sticks her finger against the roof of his mouth. "His palate hasn't come down yet," she says. "It's going to be hard for him to suck until the roof of his mouth comes down a bit. But let him practice for a while."

She shows me how to hold Gus's cheeks myself and push my own nipple into his mouth and we sit there for a few minutes until the nurse suggests I give his brother a try.

The lactation consultant squashes Sam's face against my breast, and I feel a slight pull. "He's got you. He's latched on," she says excitedly. Sam closes his eyes and holds on. I feel a tingling sensation in my breast and tell the consultant.

"It's your milk letting down. That's good." I feel another tug or two, after which I am certain Sam has fallen asleep. "Good job," the lactation consultant says. "Keep at it." Eventually she leaves but I don't move for half an hour. I let Sam sleep against my breast and pretend that he is nursing. The nurse doesn't bother us.

Dan arrives with his camera. "How'd it go?"

"Not bad," I tell him. I tuck my breast away and we snap our first pictures of the boys. I insert a tape of lullabies into a handheld player and press play before placing it in the corner of the isolette on our way out.

We retrieve our car from the garage in our building in order to drive out to New Jersey for dinner with my family. This late in the day everyone has already reached their destinations, and there is no traffic. While motoring over the George Washington Bridge I start to ache. How could we have deserted the boys in Manhattan? But once we turn off the highway into my hometown, familiar trees and streams appear, and I relax a little.

Minutes after we reach my parents' house we find a Motofoto in the phone book that is open on Thanksgiving and we jump back in the car to get our film developed. Most of the photographs are of the boys sleeping side by side in their isolette, their arms and legs reddish purple, enormous diapers extending halfway up their backs. They wear special size P diapers for babies who weigh less than five pounds. I imagine how newborn Pampers would swim on them. Their skin wrinkles in the folds where a full-term baby would have rolls of fat. In one I am holding both boys swaddled in blankets, a baby in each arm, wires draped everywhere. In another, Gus is peeking out at Dan from just one eye.

My family crowds around the kitchen table to see the pictures. They ask if they can keep some of the prints and say, "Look how cute they are."

"And today they started to breast-feed," I say. Everyone thinks this is great so I tell them about kangaroo care, holding your naked preemies against your own bare chest. Skin to skin. The pamphlet handed out by the NICU proclaims that "kangarooing" creates a profound sense of peace for mother and child, but on the day I asked for help our nurse seemed annoyed. I was self-conscious of how pathetic I appeared, wanting to sit topless in a public room with parents and nurses bustling about so that I might feel close to my babies. By this time I'd learned that certain smaller NICUs were divided into pods of two or three stations to allow the families more privacy and I wished this were the case at ours. As soon as our nurse had unswaddled Sam and draped my coat over us both, a couple of technicians arrived in the room with a portable X-ray machine to examine a baby's lungs and instructed the parents to leave. I saw that the nurses were already making their way to the door. Sam and Gus's nurse impatiently helped me slip back into my blouse and return Sam to his isolette. "Do you think it's okay for the preemies to stay in the room during the X-rays?" I asked her. "Sure," she replied. "Besides, they don't get a choice."

I explain how newborn kangaroos are all premature and continue to develop while protected in their mother's warm pouch.

After dinner Dan calls the hospital to check in. The night nurse assigned to Sam and Gus says that she just finished feeding each baby a small bottle without a problem. The boys had a couple of apnea and bradycardiac episodes while they were drinking but it's to be expected at the beginning. Apneas occur when a preemie's breathing momentarily stops and "bradys" often follow if his heart dips as a result of not taking in oxygen. The brain is not fully developed in preemies, so many of them can't suck, swallow, and breathe in a coordinated fashion without choking or forgetting to breathe. She tells Dan that we can expect the boys to have these episodes until they reach thirty-six to thirty-seven weeks from conception.

I call Lindsay for reassurance. She says, "You're not going to like the *a*s and *b*s, but it sounds like in general they are both doing great. Just remember, you're over the worst part now. Try to be thankful." Lindsay and I have been friends since we roomed together in boarding school. Even back then she lugged around dictionary-sized Advanced Placement biology textbooks, on her way to becoming a doctor. I spent study hall rearranging our beds on top of dressers to make a fortress. I threw sausages my mother sent in care packages across the room and Lindsay studied on, bent on ignoring me. I take a moment to appreciate Lindsay's industrious adolescence. I should buy those make-believe plastic doctor's kits when Sam and Gus are a few years old, start planting seeds. I wonder what techniques Morganstern's mother tried.

Downstairs I find Dan in the family room watching football with my family. I sit on his lap. I say, "Maybe Sam and Gus will want to become neonatologists."

He laughs. "Leave them alone."

I squint to see through the windows behind the couches. The entire back side of my parents' house is lined with floor-to-ceiling windows. As a child, I could tell that our babysitters felt uneasy in this room. They would ask if there weren't more outside lights, try to steer us up to my parents' room to watch television. At night I thought I heard criminals rustling through the trees, saw their shadows creeping across the backyard. Occasionally, forcing myself to be brave, I headed out into the forest with a spiral notebook and a flashlight. My red prescription glasses were held together with a safety pin, my bangs hung down straight over my forehead. That was the same year I cut the alligators off my collared shirts, started buttoning them to the top so that I wouldn't appear sexy. That was also the year I wore my corduroys a size too small, thinking loose-fitting pants might implicate me as a "loose" girl. I crouched behind trees to watch over our house as if I were Harriet the Spy.

Just a few weeks ago I was looking forward to returning for Thanksgiving, to the house where I grew up. My extended family would have a chance to see what I looked like pregnant. I could relax while my mom did all of the cooking and cleaning. I would be nearly at the thirty-three-week mark, which is what we'd heard was the gestational age needed to ensure the safety of the twins. During my final trip home before giving birth I'd happily reminisce, basking in my parents' attention while knowing that my dream of becoming a mother was very much alive in the house which had protected me and contained my past.

But without Sam and Gus I discover that my childhood home is empty. I have lost my desire to incorporate my nostalgia for a time before the boys existed into the new life I am embarking on, to hold past, present, and future together in my heart. All I want is for the boys to come home from the hospital and be all right. For the time being, there is nothing left but the dark outside.

"Let's take off early in the morning," I say to Dan. "I miss Sam and Gus."

Then I stand up and say goodnight to everyone on the couches, strewn across the floor with their heads on pillows, arms resting on full stomachs. In the dim light their voices rise and fall over the sounds from the TV. I go to my room and close the door. A moment later someone knocks. It is my brother's fiancée, Lane. "Can I watch how you pump?" she asks.

"Sure."

She sits down cross-legged on the floor while I unravel the tubes and attach the funnel cones. I turn on the machine, which picks right back up with its loud, swooshing rhythm. "Sometimes I think I hear it saying red-rum, red-rum, red-rum."

"It's cool," she says. "I can't wait to have babies."

I lean back against the bed and hold the cones to my breasts. The suction pulls on them immediately and for a second it hurts. My brother's girlfriend starts talking about their wedding plans, and I settle back, occasionally piping in, but my thoughts have already drifted to the NICU, to Sam's and Gus's small, guarded faces inches apart, Gus gazing out of their tank, on the lookout, while Sam sleeps.

BACK AT OUR APARTMENT, Dan and I settle into a routine. I fill an enormous ceramic mug to the brim with strong black instant coffee first thing in the morning before heading to the NICU. Later, in the afternoon, I take comfort in the sound of Dan's footsteps approaching our hospital crib, the swishing of his dark blue parka as he pulls his arms out of the sleeves and rests it on the windowsill.

The nights are harder. Dan suggests a movie. I insist we stay at the NICU until the movie has started and then we run ten blocks to the theater. By arriving breathlessly late, and missing the previews, I think I'll feel less guilty. A minute or two passes before the picture blurs. All I see are colors, and then my mind finds its way back to worrying about Sam and Gus. Will they someday be healthy like the boys in the front rows of the theater, slouching in their puffy parkas under enormous tubs of popcorn?

Dan usually arrives from work at the same time I get home from the NICU. We eat dinner together and then he heads to the NICU and doesn't come back until I'm going to bed. We fill each other in on any developments with the boys, and on weekends we walk down to the hospital together. Whenever Dan is home we answer the telephone, but the second he leaves the apartment I let the calls go to the answering machine.

I broil lamb chops and pork tenderloin, make Shake 'N Bake chicken, always with rice from a box and frozen vegetables. I sometimes go the whole day at the NICU without eating and arrive home ravenous. I am expressing breast milk eight times a day and starving. Once we finish eating I load the plates in the dishwasher, rinse the pots, pump without bothering to change the television channel from whatever Dan has left on, call Lindsay, and head to bed. Often I can't sleep, and against my better judgment I wind up on the computer in the living room poring through worst-case scenarios of premature babies written mostly by their angry parents.

I log off the Internet, guiltily pop an Ambien. By the time Dan comes in I am nearing sleep. I wake up a few hours later and he is snoring beside me. I usually make myself wait at least an hour before taking another pill. This is the first prescription for a sleeping aid I've had. Dr. Vanderbilt's partner gave it to me the night she stopped my contractions. After Vanderbilt promised that it would not contaminate my breast milk I took the first one; now I can't imagine how, without it, I would get through the intermittent hours of the night I am not with Sam and Gus.

A few nights after Thanksgiving, Dan accepts an invitation from our friends Heather and Nick to have dinner at the restaurant on our block. Heather was in my class at Groton and Nick was a classmate of Dan's. Unlike ours, their romance started in high school.

At the end of the summer between my sophomore and junior years, my friends and I drove from Saratoga Springs to Washington, D.C., to see the Grateful Dead. Lindsay and I followed Heather and Nick in my parents' Pontiac station wagon, and we were so happy, having just quit our summer jobs at Bruegger's Bagels. We had tickets to this show and one in the Meadowlands, and then we were heading to Nantucket for a week of sunbathing on the porch of a house that a classmate had talked his parents into renting for him.

Our friend Holly met us in the parking lot. We had tickets in the seatless section down on the field. We spread a blanket out on the ground maybe fifty feet from the stage and Heather lay down and curled into Nick. They held down the fort while the rest of us danced. At the end of my third form year a group of guys had claimed I was a wannabe Deadhead, and at that point maybe they were right. Over the next year I got hold of dozens of bootleg recordings, grainy tapes that the sound came in and out on, and that night at RFK Stadium the band played and I sang my heart out.

Lindsay was beautiful with classic blond hair, brown eyes. Heather was also beautiful with white blond hair, blue eyes, and a very subtle southern drawl. I was not blond and I was not beautiful, but I was high and dancing and every time I looked down I found Heather and Nick on our blanket, which reassured me.

At the end of the show, it took us an hour to find the Pontiac. We couldn't remember what section we all parked in. Holly drove us around the lot in her red Saab until we finally spotted it. Then we followed her on the highway to her house in Alexandria, Virginia. I kept swerving so close to the cement dividing wall that I felt as if I might brush my teeth against it. At Holly's house we ate ice cream. She steered Heather and Nick to a room off the kitchen and showed Lindsay and me to her brother's old room where we stayed up talking in the bed that was Holly's brother's before he died of malaria, and early in the morning we finally fell asleep.

Inside the restaurant, at a dimly lit corner table, Heather tells us about the woman who adopts ailing racehorses and heals their broken bodies with massage. I soon lose the thread of her conversation. When I become the focus of everyone's gaze, Dan tries to lead me in with a clue as to the question being asked. Nick is curious as to whether my OB was able to make a clean and careful cesarean incision. He's heard some women go for follow-up reconstructive surgery after cesareans. I don't have an answer. The truth is I can barely bring myself to glance down at it in the shower.

After dinner, Heather and Nick walk us back across the street to our apartment, and she slips a pair of silver coined saints into my palm.

Dan and I climb into bed. I roll over onto Dan to kiss him goodnight and stay there for a minute. The last time we had sex was several weeks before Sam and Gus's birth, and I could tell he was self-conscious making love with the boys' presence looming so large. Dr. Vanderbilt has cautioned me to refrain from sex until after my post-op visit. If we go through with it now, will it hurt? Then I remember we haven't yet called to check on the boys and I've forgotten to pump.

Dan pushes up my nightgown with his hand.

"By the way, my scar is hideous. I'm pretty sure I can feel a few stitches that haven't fallen out. I try not to look."

"Let me see it."

I pull my nightgown back down.

Dan looks at me. I'm still lying on him, chest to chest, but my mind has wandered. I reach for the phone, dial the NICU, and hand him the receiver. Then I swing my legs over the side of the bed and go into the living room to pump. I don't want to wait by the phone while the receptionist pages Gus and Sam's nurse.

THE MONDAY FOLLOWING Thanksgiving I am scheduled to meet our new attending neonatologist, who is the head of the department. The head attending, who is in his late sixties, has been employed at our hospital for forty-five years. The first neonatal unit in the United States was built at Yale-New Haven Hospital in 1965, and the head attending single-handedly opened our NICU soon after. Previously preemies had been kept in the incubators inside the well-baby nurseries. The head attending is a hands-off practitioner who doesn't believe in the increasingly popular physical and occupational "therapies" for healthier preemies who've been hospitalized primarily to feed and grow. The nurse quotes him as saying you can put preemies in a box and they will still learn to walk. I arrive in the morning and ask the nurse if the attending has been by yet.

"No," she says. "You didn't miss him."

"Oh good," I say, taking off my coat. I peek in at Sam and Gus who are both awake. "Good morning, Sam and Gus," I say. They stare up at me. I can't be sure, but I think they know my voice.

Sam and Gus will be thirty-four weeks tomorrow. They are still having several apneatic and bradycardiac episodes each day, which occur primarily after feeding. All of the babies in the NICU are fed every three hours, at 6:00, 9:00, 12:00, and 3:00. Our isolette is extremely active between 7:00 and 8:00, 1:00 and 2:00, and 4:00 and 5:00, with alarms going off and numbers flashing on the monitors as plastic doors are opened and shut and Sam and Gus are pulled out and stimulated until they start breathing again.

There is rarely a time when, somewhere in the room, one of the five different alarms isn't sounding. The most harmless is a low-pitched monotone indicating somebody's isolette door is ajar, which might allow babies to fall out. The second signal rings like a telephone if one of the electrodes taped to the preemies' chests or wrapped around their feet comes loose. An alarm, not unlike a garbage truck in reverse, sounds when a gavage feeding is done. The apnea monitor emits the fast high-pitched beep of a digital alarm clock when a baby's oxygen level is at lower than 85 percent saturation, meaning he is not breathing well. The final signal is a shrill siren that wails if a baby is having a bradycardiac episode. This is the only beep that makes the nurses run.

Lindsay had told me that the vast majority of preemies outgrow their apneatic and bradycardiac episodes by thirty-seven weeks. I tell myself we can make it.

I ask for the boys' weights. Gus is 4 pounds and Sam weighs 3 pounds, 15 ounces. As soon as they reach 5 pounds they will move out of the isolette and into an open crib. Although some babies who have no feeding or breathing problems are discharged from the hospital straight out of their isolettes, the transition to a crib still seems like progress. "Soon you'll be out in the big wide-open," I tell them.

"You have to be patient. Remember one day in the womb equals two out here," the nurse says. "Upper GI tests are scheduled for today to make sure that the boys' problem is only reflux. The gastroenterologists will squirt dye down the babies' throats into their esophagus and then track it with an X-ray to make sure they don't have a birth defect like a tunnel connecting the esophagus with the lungs. It's a rare physiological problem called a trachea-esophaegeal fistula and the chance that they would both have it is really small."

The baby in the far corner has a tracheoesophageal fistula. Born at full-term, he has had one operation already and is being discharged next week. But he'll have to come back after Christmas for a second operation as milk has continued to leak into his lungs. I feel terrible for his mother, although they will get to have Christmas as a family and we may not, and once his defect has been repaired, his parents can put the experience behind them, whereas since Sam and Gus were born prematurely, the possibility of long-term problems may linger until they are in school. And yet, could anything be worse than the dread of having to return your child to the hospital once he's grown comfortable at home? I wish I weren't weighing their situation versus ours. His mother looks up and I wave hello.

A tall, stately white-haired doctor in a hospital coat enters the room, and I hear him ask the nurse by the door for the Quigley boys.

I shake the head attending's hand and step back from their isolette so he can examine Sam and Gus. "Their scrotums have come down," he says, reattaching their diapers. "In some preemies born this early the sacs haven't come down yet." Then he smiles and I know he is thinking the boys are well hung.

He tickles Sam and Gus under their chins, then flips through their hospital records. "I know this must be hard for you to hear, but given that they are thirty-one-weekers, they're actually very lucky to have come through this without major problems."

It is mind-spinning good fortune and I have to pull up a chair and sit down, even as Gus's alarm sounds and the nurse lifts him out of his isolette. She sits him up in the palm of her hand, his head drooping, and pats him on the back, flicks the bottoms of his feet, to try to rouse him. He remains unresponsive. She pulls out the oxygen hose and waves it in front of his nose. Finally Gus breathes.

"Now we need you to cut this business out so you can go home," the head attending says to Gus once he is breathing again.

"What about the GI tests this afternoon?" I ask from my chair. "Do you think there might be a physiological defect?"

"I don't think so," he says. "It's highly doubtful. But we can't just go on our hunches. Reflux is frustrating for us because there's nothing to do but wait it out. In the meantime we want to be certain it's nothing else."

The head attending examines the boys' arms and legs. He says, "It hasn't been proven that there's any benefit to co-bedding, but these guys do look cute together." I stand up to shake his hand again.

"Thank you for visiting us," I say.

The head attending turns around to leave, the tails of his coat swinging out confidently.

"He's one of the best neonatologists in the world," the nurse says. "He sees preemies all day long and he doesn't usually call them cute."

I proceed to the elevator banks smiling. I punch in Dan's work number on my cell. I repeat every single word that the head attending said before I ask Dan if he can get out of work to accompany the boys to their GI tests. I think one of us should be there and if possible I'd prefer it to not be me. I don't want to watch the boys undergo an uncomfortable procedure or have to face the gastroenterologists and radiologists performing the test.

"Oh no," the doctors and nurses will say if you tell them it's your fault. "Every single mother we meet thinks this." But I've listened to them talking about how so many of the babies here are multiples from infertility treatments. And I heard one of the older NPs discussing a woman upstairs who made it to thirty-four weeks with twins on bed rest and delivered the day she was sent home. The NP said, "It goes to show that it works." I think about how the only names taped to the isolette say "Sam," "Gus," and "Dr. Vanderbilt." Is it a public embarrassment for Vanderbilt to have her name branded on our isolette? There is no need to identify me with a fat black marker because I am always here.

In a research paper Lindsay wrote, she concluded that although there are more neonatal intensive care resources in the United States than in similarly developed countries like Australia, Canada, and the United Kingdom, the infant mortality rates in our country are consistently higher. Presently 30,000 infants die each year in the U.S., twice as many as in Hong Kong and Japan, ranking us twenty-fifth amongst nations. While the U.S. has a disproportionately greater number of NICUs—approximately 1,200—many other countries place more emphasis on preconception and prenatal care. Lindsay suggests increasing funding for research on which prenatal interventions are most effective as a means to reduce low birth weights and improve infant mortality rates.

Might the improved outcomes of children in the United Kingdom also be related to its lower percentage of multiple births from IVF? In the United States one-third of all IVF deliveries are twins, as opposed to one-quarter in the United Kingdom. The U.K. has one-seventh as many triplets as we do. The discrepancy can be accounted for by the fact that transfers of a single embryo are attempted more regularly in Europe and laws prohibit transferring more than two.

In 2002, life expectancy reached an all-time high in our country, but infant mortality rates—which are attributed mostly to problems with prematurity—actually rose. Our government said that the climb was due to complications with older women putting off motherhood and then having multiple births via fertility drugs. But most other developed nations have socialized health care that covers both prenatal care and infertility treatments. If affordability were no longer a concern, might more American women opt for better prenatal care and more conservative usage of fertility drugs? The percentage of high-order-multiple pregnancies in the U.S. is greater in states that do not require coverage for infertility.

The clock above the door reads noon as Dan passes under it, trailed by a young technician. The nurse helps them unplug and reattach the electrodes to portable monitors under a metal cart. The technician and Dan wheel Sam and Gus in their isolette out through the glass doors. I watch them back slowly down the hallway. I stay sitting in my chair, facing the space left empty. I listen to the beeping, and look out the window at the glistening bridge in the distance, then back down at my dry, overwashed hands.

WHILE EATING DINNER at our kitchen table Dan says, "You should have seen the female GI doctors making a fuss over how cute Sam and Gus are."

"Did they seem concerned about anything they saw on the tests?"

"Not that I could tell, but we'll know for sure tomorrow." He cuts up his chicken and takes a bite. Then another. Glances at an episode of *Stargate* on the television.

"How can you be so relaxed?"

"The results are being held inside a black hole," he says. "Karma is karma."

"Are you trying to irritate me? Black holes. What the hell?" I pick up the remote from the table and turn the TV off. "Okay. Fine. Stephen Hawking is handicapped. Would you rather be Stephen Hawking or Helen Keller?" I am not sure what it is I'm really asking.

"Stephen Hawking. He gets to study the stars for a living."

"But he can't even get in or out of bed by himself. You wouldn't be able to lift that fork."

"Then Helen Keller," he says, his mouth stuffed with meat.

"You can't answer so quickly without imagining what each handicap feels like."

"Why are you doing this?" Dan asks, looking back at the television's blank screen.

"The GI doctors are checking for physiological defects that could seriously hinder the boys. And if you picture yourself as anyone with a serious handicap, you will realize that karma can be stressful."

"I disagree. Someone with a disability would need to be more at peace than anyone else."

It was in the marines that Dan learned to stay cool under pressure. Once, while Dan's troop was driving some visiting congressmen through Mogadishu, snipers opened up on their convoy. As per orders they threw the congressmen on the floor of the Humvee. The man Dan was kneeling on said, "You are going to get me out of here alive, aren't you, young man?"

Dan said, "Absolutely."

They sped through the gates of the soccer stadium and secured the congressmen behind a concrete wall. Then there was a boom and a cheer from some of the marines. "What's that?" asked Dan's congressman. Dan told him the sound was coming from the sharpshooters on the roof of the stadium firing .50-caliber rifles at the snipers.

The congressmen and marines lay in the sun for a while, hearing the occasional booms followed by shouts. When it was finally quiet, the marines bundled the congressmen into an armored vehicle and drove them to the airport, where the congressmen jumped onto a plane home with a quick good-bye.

Dan takes a sip from his water glass. He says, "Sam and Gus are not going to be handicapped."

"It happens." I start to cry. "Preemies have an increased risk of deafness, blindness, and physical disabilities like cerebral palsy, which can't be diagnosed for six to twelve months."

"You would handle it," Dan says, looking at me. "You would. But there's no sense in becoming a complete wreck when everything is indicating the boys are going to be fine."

How can he remain so rational? I stand up to clear the table.

Dan follows me into the kitchen with his empty plate. "So how did Helen Keller finally learn to make contact?"

"Her teacher ran one of Helen's hands under a running faucet and spelled water in sign language onto her other palm until she understood." I rinse my dish in the sink, extend my arm for Dan to pass me his.

"Do you think she ever married?" I ask.

"I think she did," Dan says.

I turn off the faucet and extend my arms around his waist.

People are always surprised to learn that Dan is not even six feet; they think he's bigger. He's stood next to other men to show me that his shoulders aren't particularly wide. Although he does have substantial, muscular thighs, he's not like those guys on the subway who sit with their legs spread wide apart, hogging two seats. There is already white in Dan's dark hair, although he just turned thirty-four, and deep-set crow's feet around his piercing blue eyes from years of squinting into the sun in Somalia and Okinawa.

After Dan has gone to the NICU, I interrupt my preemie surfing to do a Google search for Helen Keller's husband. It turns up a Web site of Helen Keller jokes. "How did Helen Keller meet her husband? On a blind date." Other sites reveal information about a passionate affair with her lover, on the female companions always at her side, on the numerous books she wrote and people she inspired. Although I find nothing that indicates she ever married, by the time I finally shut down the computer, fate's black holes look less bleak.

I brush my teeth and climb under the covers. I close my eyes and pull my pillow over my head to block out the noise from the cars on the street. I imagine that I am unable to get out of bed by myself. I wait for impressions to form in the muffled dark.

Finally Sam and Gus come into view, appearing like ultrasound images. They are floating on their backs, motionless, breathlessly in need of resuscitation.

THE FOLLOWING MORNING the gastroenterologists determine that the boys are suffering solely from reflux. The team prescribes several adult-strength antacid medications in minuscule doses. I stand by the boys' crib and occasionally drop into my conversations with their nurse—a floater from the well-baby nursery—how hopeful I am that the medications will work quickly. She finally calls in the order to the pharmacy and I head to the pump room, where I meet a mother whose preemie was transferred here from another hospital after developing a bacterial infection from the VP shunt in his brain. Ventriculoperitoneal shunts are tubes inserted surgically to drain excess water from the brain to the abdomen. The boy's mother says, "The worst part is that he was about to come home. If we'd only gotten him out of there a little sooner he wouldn't have caught the infection."

Initially, all of the babies in our room, attached to wires and setting off alarms, had appeared to be in the same boat. But now I perceive that breathing lapses and feeding difficulties are "normal" preemie setbacks that differ from the severe intraventricular hemorrhages and infections afflicting "sick" preemies. At a glance I can see that the new micro-preemie—a term given to preemies who are born weighing less than 1,000 grams/2.3 pounds—has abnormal muscle tone even before I overhear the nurses discussing him. Born at twenty-four weeks, he was brought down this morning and strapped to a warming bed. The nurses immediately wrapped him in cellophane to retain body heat. He is at the station closest to the door and I can't help but peek at him each time I enter the unit. His eyes are fused shut, his skin is translucent, revealing organs underneath. IVs have been surgically inserted into his arm and leg. His ears are folded over. He looks like a fetus.

On the tuesday morning the boys turn four weeks old I arrive at the NICU before 8:00 a.m. and wait next to their isolette for nearly half an hour for our nurse to take them out for me. I ask her twice from across the room, and she answers each time that she is busy. "Is there a mask I could wear?" I call back. Although my cold cleared up weeks ago I can't seem to shake a lingering cough. Yesterday I saw one of the nurses wearing a paper mask over her mouth.

"If you need a mask, you shouldn't be here," she says, peering over an isolette like a troll. A few of the mothers look up at me. There is no way I am leaving so I don't answer her. Finally the nurse trudges over and lowers the isolette with a foot pedal. I watch carefully as she opens the door, untangles Sam's and Gus's wires, swaddles Sam in a blanket, and gives him to me. An hour later she helps me put Sam back inside and return the isolette to its elevated position. Then, after making a trip to the pump room, I reach into the isolette and pull out Gus by myself.

He is tangled, and a couple of his electrodes pop off, sending the monitors into alarm mode, but I quickly stick them back on and sit down before the nurse notices. It is the smallest thing, really, to have taken him out of his crib, a feat that is not encouraged by the staff. But it means I am no longer at the mercy of whoever happens to be their nurse. And it's more than that. This minor act of independence has given me a glimpse of what life will be like once the boys are home and finally there is no intermediary between us. A little while later, holding Gus against my chest, I stand up to unlock the plastic doors. I manage to unswaddle him and lift him into the isolette when his wires get caught and he nearly rolls out. I realize I've forgotten to lower the isolette closer to the ground. Our nurse sees this happening and scolds me from across the room. I give her a big smile.

Wednesday as i exit the elevator and pass the pictures on the wall of children being treated for serious injuries by various nurses from the burn unit, I start to feel nauseated. Something will have gone wrong overnight; a new test will have been prescribed for the boys. Usually it has.

We rode these same elevators to the eighth floor for our IVF transfer last April. Descending afterward I was so hopeful, thinking that two babies were growing inside me. I didn't know as the elevator passed the sixth floor—and perhaps even picked up passengers—that this was the NICU, filled with fertility twins, which would be awaiting us at the end of our pregnancy tunnel. I wonder whether there isn't some animosity between the neonatologists and the infertility specialists. Might the neonatologists resent having to spend their weekends hanging around the hospital on call so that sick, occasionally hopeless infertility babies could be dumped on them while the reproductive endocrinologists head off in Porsches to second homes in East Hampton? When I ask the head attending he smiles and answers no.

While I am holding Sam, a pretty Filipino nurse carrying two bottles quietly pulls up a chair. "Do you want to give Sam his bottle while I feed Gus?" she asks.

I say yes. For the past two days anyone interested has been able to watch me attempt to breast-feed Sam and Gus. The parents in our room politely averted their eyes. Twice, a balding father in the neighboring unit glanced at me curiously. Familiar with the easy X holes on the bottles, the boys refused to draw hard on the breast. Sam would suck for a minute, then pull away and cry. Gus made only a feeble effort to latch on. Now I tell myself, face it, they are not going to breast-feed so I might as well practice delivering bottles.

The nurse removes Gus from the isolette. She lets him drink from the bottle for a few seconds, gently pulls the nipple out of his mouth, so he can catch his breath before he starts again. Then she sits him on her lap, holding his head up with her right hand and rubbing his back with her left. He immediately burps. The second I stick the bottle into Sam's mouth, his apnea and brady monitors sound. The nurse stands up and turns the volume on the monitor down. The nipple is too big for Sam's mouth. I try to relax and tip the bottle in through his lips, ignoring the muted beeping. I sit him up to burp him and his head flops forward. I tickle his feet to remind him to breathe again. The monitor continues to beep. I pat him hard on the back, flick his hands. Finally he resumes breathing. I place my thumb and index finger in a V around the front of his neck as support. It takes me half an hour to feed Sam the ounce and a half bottle. I finally rest him, fast asleep, back in the isolette and head to lunch feeling sweaty and euphoric.

Every year on the first Sunday in November I wake up in my apartment thankful I will never have to run the New York City marathon, that it's not some required rite of passage like the SATs. But as I head out to lunch I finally understand why millions of men and women are motivated to tape up their nipples so their T-shirts won't rub them raw on a twenty-six-mile run. Crossing the finish line, they might feel the way I do right now.

I arrive back at the NICU minutes before the 3:00 feeding. The nurse asks, "Do you want to try Gus now?"

I've timed my return poorly. I have just finished one terrifying feeding. How can it be time for another? I tell her, "I think I'll sit this one out."

A nurse-practitioner who is drawn to our isolette by Gus's ringing alarm notices that the boys still have feeding tubes in. "Why are the tubes still in?" she asks.

"We're still giving them some feedings with the tubes a few times a day so they can take in a few calories without exerting any effort," the nurse answers. "They burn so many calories just sucking. It's still hard work for them."

"The tubes are making it harder for them to swallow. You should unhook them."

The Filipino nurse doesn't look convinced. She turns her back to me, but I hear Gus cry when she removes his tube. She lets him have the bottle again and I notice from the way his cheeks are puffing out that he's sucking too hard. The apnea monitor goes off, indicating that his oxygen level is decreasing. She pulls the bottle out. Gus falls asleep without finishing the milk, and the nurse rests him back in the isolette.

I'm worried that without the half ounce of breast milk Gus will lose weight. The 6:00 feeding is even worse. Sam is exhausted. He forgets to breathe. His heart rate decelerates. The nurse lifts him up and pats his back hard to try to get him to regain consciousness. He remains limp. She flicks Sam's left foot with her index finger and still he does not breathe. She pulls the oxygen hose out from its station and holds it under his nose. Finally he inhales. She keeps aiming the hose at his face until the color returns.

Following rounds, the word is that the head attending has decided the boys should have echocardiograms, a test that uses sound waves to create a moving picture of the heart, to make sure their apnea and brady episodes don't indicate a physiological heart defect. The Filipino nurse makes the analogy that the NICU is like a roller-coaster ride, involving numerous ups and downs. The Scottish nurse at the clinic for reproductive medicine had likened infertility to a roller coaster as well.

A technician wheels in a floor-standing computer monitor with several wires attached. She hooks up the machine to Sam by patching small electrodes onto his upper body. She presses what looks to be a big electric shaver against Sam's chest. Then she unpeels the electrodes and performs the test on Gus. She says, "The cardiologist will be by later with the results."

"But do you see any problems?" I ask her frantically.

"You'll have to wait for the doctor," she says.

"Can you please tell me if their hearts appear okay." I look straight into the technician's eyes and lock her in my gaze. I will her to imagine that these are her children living in an isolette.

The technician could lose her job for giving me incorrect information.

"They look fine to me," she says softly. "The cardiologist will be by this afternoon."

———

THEY ARE NOT YET five weeks old when Gus reaches five pounds, and by the following Saturday Sam makes his weight too. To have nearly doubled their birth weight in less than five weeks is an accomplishment for a preemie. The weight gain indicates that despite their setbacks with feeding the boys seem to be thriving. I am so thrilled we are finally making progress that it doesn't even register that a baby who weighs five pounds is still considered too small. Someone who gave birth to a baby weighing five pounds might consider this a fact not worth mentioning on the birth announcement.

Monday morning two orderlies bring in a crib with metal bars and Sam and Gus are moved into it.

The boys' nurse dresses them in long-sleeved cotton wraps that say "Good things come in small packages." She swaddles them in hospital towels with a pink and blue stripe. "You can bring a couple of blankets from home too. They might like the smell."

You can see much more of the boys and of course touch them in the open crib. The nurse tapes a handwritten sign on their metallic crib. It says, "Please check freezer—my brother and I have plenty of breast milk." On the left is a name card, Quigley BB A "Gus" on the right, Quigley BB B "Sam" on the left, and they are both asleep under their cards, Gus's pacifier covering half of his chinless face. He looks like he's wearing those wax lips sold at candy stores. Sam will not take a pacifier. The boys are used to being nearly on top of each other and they inch closer together. Gus sticks his fingers into Sam's eyes. Sam kicks Gus, Gus cries and kicks him back, and the nurse decides to separate them with a towel. But when the nurse-practitioner passes by a few minutes later she says, "Aren't these boys supposed to be partaking in the co-bedding experiment? This is not co-bedding." And she removes the towel.

I head to the pump room at 11:00 a.m. to beat the rush at rounds. An Orthodox Jewish grandmother is sitting by the sink while her daughter pumps behind the far curtain. I pull aside the first curtain and set up my funnels. I've encountered several Orthodox families in the hospital. I often forget that there is one special elevator set up for them until I find myself stopping at every floor. Orthodox law prohibits operating anything requiring electricity on the Sabbath, even operating an elevator. While the boys were still in separate rooms, there was an Orthodox baby next to Gus. The father showed up every morning dressed in black and stood behind his son's isolette reading prayers in Hebrew aloud.

"Is that Jenny?" a woman asks from behind her curtain.

"Yes," her mother says.

I cannot remember the woman's name although she has told it to me several times. Her mother is always with her. "How are you?"

She opens her curtain halfway. "The nurse just told us we're going home the day after tomorrow."

"Congratulations. That's so great."

"Thank you," she says. "How are the twins?"

"They moved into a crib today, which is a step in the right direction, but they're having some feeding problems."

"Have you tried breast-feeding? Devorah does so much better if I breast-feed her. I'm only pumping now because I have to go out and buy a crib." She peeks in at the bottles attached to my machine, which are quickly filling with milk. "I don't understand how you can pump so much milk," she says. "All I ever get is an ounce or two. Maybe it's because I'm older."

Although I cannot remember this woman's name, I know that she is thirty-eight and has a malformed uterus, that she and her husband tried to get pregnant for three years before turning to IVF. Her daughter was born at thirty-one weeks and four days, and has sailed through the NICU, breathing on her own almost instantly and easily latching onto the breast. Preemie girls have an easier time than boys. The black girls do the best, then the white girls, followed by the black boys. The white boys, often referred to as "wimpy white boys" here in the NICU, bring up the rear. If only Sam and Gus were black.

"You won't need to pump if your daughter's breast-feeding," I say.

"But she wants to go back to work," the grandmother says harshly. "What will she do when she goes back to work?"

"Mama, that is months away," the woman says. "Can we not worry about it please?" She peers at my bottles again, which are nearly full, then switches off her machine. "A baby in our room died last night. A twenty-seven-weeker. Her warming bed was right next to Devorah. She was always having surgery. I guess it was finally too much for her."

I tell myself, *For God's sake, do not cry.*

A voice interrupts over the intercom. "Will the nurse please pick up for Mrs. Peterson? Line two for Baby Peterson." Whichever nurse has Baby Peterson is guaranteed to receive half a dozen calls a day. At first I wondered why the Petersons were always calling instead of visiting. Then I learned from a nurse who wasn't supposed to tell me that the Petersons have other children at home in New Jersey. Their youngest baby has been in the NICU on a respirator for almost a year.

The Orthodox woman stands up, ruffling the curtain dividing us. I hear her rinsing her funnels in the sink. The grandmother always has her hair covered under a dark blue scarf, but her daughter wears her long red hair down.

"Well, if I don't see you, good luck."

"Good luck to the twins," the grandmother says.

I am alone for ten seconds before a wave of women arrive, indicating that doctors' rounds must be starting. Visitors are cleared from the room as soon as the doctors arrive. The mothers line up outside the door, leaning against it so that it stays open. I unscrew my cones from the bottles, careful not to let any milk spill. The nurses call it "liquid gold."

On my way back to the boys' room, I pass the head attending in the hallway, surrounded by a group of nurses and residents. We were lucky to have had him for the past few weeks. But today is the end of a monthly rotation and starting tomorrow a new attending will preside over our unit of the NICU. There are five attending doctors on the rotation schedule. The first three rooms in the NICU make up one shift, the second two rooms another. The well-baby nursery is on the rotation, as are research and the follow-up clinic. The head attending's next shift is to the NICU units down the hall.

"Hello," I say into the crowd. Dan and I think we should make sure the attendings remember us, even though it's the nurses with whom we usually speak.

"Hi," he says and smiles. "Your boys are on their way."

A WEEK BEFORE CHRISTMAS I walk to Dr. Vanderbilt's office for my post-op visit. She examines my scar and says that the cesarean is healing nicely. She gives me the go-ahead to resume having sex. Then she shows me sections in her medical books highlighted with yellow marker that prove we did nothing wrong, that bed rest doesn't work, and tocolytic drugs don't halt real labor for any lengthy period of time. The medical textbooks contest all that I'd gleaned from *What to Expect When You're Expecting* about preterm labor being preventable and stoppable once started. For a minute inside her office I am soothed, but the instant I'm back on the sidewalk I start to seethe, infuriated that I was not smart and careful enough to have recognized her as an inexperienced, by-the-books apprentice. It is imperative to Vanderbilt's career that she maintain she's innocent. A patient has until her child is eighteen to file a lawsuit against the OB who delivered him.

I would not take legal action against Vanderbilt. I recognize that my anger at her is disproportional to her culpability in the boys' preterm birth, and that suing cannot reverse what happened. But I am also unwilling to accept that their prematurity was inevitable. Gus's and Sam's outcomes are too important for me to deny my role in determining them.

Back in the 1880s, when infant incubators were first invented in France, it was the obstetricians who cared for the preemies in the maternity ward right beside their mothers. If Dr. Vanderbilt's job had included treating Sam and Gus as her patients, would she have felt so comfortable leaving their outcome to chance? If Dr. Morganstern were to have remained my primary OB up through delivery might he have set a more cautious, possibly longer course to pregnancy that assured better odds for a safe birth? I long for the cheerful peace of mind that came from trusting people. I used to revere doctors. This necessary adjustment in perspective feels awful.

Should I just accept that there was nothing we could have done to prevent preterm labor? Is it only a matter of time before I stop searching for reasons and perceive Gus and Sam's prematurity instead as an arbitrary act of nature? Why do I refuse to learn the humbling lesson that we are not always in control of our fates? But the entire process that led up to and away from the sole chaotic event of our boys' birth was so efficiently micromanaged. Starting at the fertility clinic, Dr. Morganstern prescribed the precise amount of medicine to grow an optimal number of eggs. Dan and I filled the needles to the exact millimeter, eliminating even the tiniest air bubbles. The clinicians monitored my IVF cycle down to the moment I was to start fasting prior to the retrieval procedure. Then, immediately following when the boys were born, neonatologists expertly utilized technology to save their lives in a closely controlled environment where nurses record blood pressure and oxygen levels, along with the temperature in the isolettes and the amount of urine in each diaper.

We came across just one small but deep pothole on an otherwise perfectly paved, high-tech highway to bring home our children. We fell down it while under the supervision of our ob-gyn. The NICU team came to the rescue. And Dr. Vanderbilt stepped off to the side. Can you even blame her? She said, "Oh, preterm labor. Did nobody tell you? We haven't the foggiest idea about it really.

One of life's last mysteries." She threw up her hands. "Believe it or not, even if we *had* seen this coming, there was no way to have steered clear."

Starting at the end of the 1880s, doctors unveiled their incubator exhibits at various science fairs in Europe and the United States. On Coney Island preemies weighing less than three pounds shared space on the boardwalk with sword swallowers and bearded ladies. All of these live baby shows created quite a scandal. In the backlash that followed, the question was raised as to whether premature infants might be better off entrusted to their mothers at home than in the care of male doctors and their machines. It terrifies me to think that if history had run a different course, the responsibility of reviving and nursing my children back to health might have been solely mine.

THE BOYS HAVE BEEN in the hospital for five and a half weeks. Initially the nurses predicted that they would come home for Christmas, which is the day after tomorrow. Then they said without a doubt by New Year's. Now they laugh and say, Well, they surely won't be here for college. Each morning I do the laundry so Sam and Gus will have fresh preemie clothes. I throw in my sweatpants too. Initially the size P pajamas from the Baby Gap swam on them. I had to travel to three different stores to find six outfits. But it is comforting that enough preemies exist to warrant a size P.

Red and green paper stockings bearing the names of the doctors and nurses have been taped to the glass windows of the NICU during the night. I say hello to the mother of the twenty-four-weeker as I pass and try not to look down at the isolette in which her baby is recovering from heart surgery.

Yesterday the visiting parents were kicked out of our room for the morning while the cardiothoracic surgeons operated on the twenty-four-weeker. All of the babies remained in the room. At a mere month and a half, Sam and Gus have now attended two open heart surgeries, an operation to insert a tracheotomy tube, and an operation to remove part of a baby's intestine.

The twenty-four-weeker's name is Scott. The first time Alex, the male NP, explained Scott's condition to his mother I was holding Sam. Had he forgotten I was there? Or had I become familiar enough to seem harmless? Alex said that with a micro-preemie, it wasn't just that he was small. Parts of Scott, his brain, his eyes, his heart, were extremely underdeveloped. As soon as his heart was strong enough, the neurologists were planning to operate. Scott had suffered a brain bleed of the worst grade.

Hours before Scott was born his parents were asked if they wanted him to be resuscitated. After explaining to laboring mothers and their husbands the disabilities and handicaps that are likely to affect their extremely premature baby's quality of life, the hospital's policy is to then ask the prospective parents whether they want the neonatologist to attempt to resuscitate their child. Babies born between twenty-three and twenty-five weeks' gestation are considered at the threshold of viability with extremely poor prognoses for a healthy life, and a previous controversy at the hospital over whether neonatologists were playing God in the nursery has been quelled by involving parents in the decision. If the parents answer no, the baby is never attached to life support. If they say yes, the neonatologists will begin aggressive life-saving treatments immediately following the baby's birth. There are still a few hospitals that don't involve the parents in this decision. And some neonatologists limit the discussion to life or death and avoid quality of life issues altogether. After all, each baby is different, and at the time that he needs resuscitation how well he will recover is impossible to predict.

Scott's mother is always saying, "He has to live." After reading the thick guidebook on preemies that one of the nurse-practitioners had tried to offer me several times and finally sent over to my apartment with my parents, I'm aware his chances of ever being self-reliant are slim. The likelihood that an infant born at his gestational age who suffers a level 4 brain bleed will be debilitated by severe handicaps is almost guaranteed.

I head to our metal crib in the back of the room. We have the best view in the NICU, in the whole hospital. The boys' crib is next to a window that looks out on the East River. All day long barges glide down the river. The sun bursts in. At night, you can see the Fifty-ninth Street Bridge lit up in blue and white. Our chairs from last night are still nearby, and I pull one up and sit down. The boys are asleep. Soon the nurse comes over. She is the young nursing graduate whom I like. I no longer ask how they've done overnight, but they always tell me.

"They had a hard time last night," the young nurse says. "But so far today they're doing fine for me."

A few minutes later, the night nurse stops by before going home. She and the recent nursing graduate are friends. This particular night nurse does not inspire my confidence. Instead of the standard uniforms that the other nurses wear, hers must come from a nursing outlet. They are the same loose cotton pants and V-neck short-sleeve shirts with pockets, but with big flowery patterns all over them in a variety of bright colors.

The boys' reflux has gone from mild to moderate to severe pathological reflux. Their medications have been upped to the maximum dosage that is safe for babies their size. Every few days a nurse-practitioner increases the dose to correspond to their slight weight gain. Because they were born too soon, their esophageal sphincter did not have time to develop, and now that they are taking two whole ounces of milk every three hours, they spend the intermittent hours with the milk splashing back up their sphincters and spilling into their throats. They bear down and gag on it, stop breathing; their heartbeats dip, and they turn gray and then blue. The alarms sound and the nurse on duty turns on the O_2 tank at the boys' station and, whereas she used to just have to wave it past their noses, now she clamps it over their faces until they finally startle and inhale. One morning I came in and noticed that the night nurse had wound the O_2 hose around one of the bars on the crib and left it running all night. She must have gotten tired of saving them.

Lindsay keeps reminding me, "So it's pathological. It's still reflux. They will grow out of it." Still, I find myself looking up "pathology" in the dictionary: "1. *the science of the origin and course of diseases.* 2. *any deviation from a healthy, normal, or efficient condition.*"

"These boys gave me trouble last night," the night nurse says and laughs. "Yes sir. They were trouuuuuuble. This one, who is he again?"

"Gus," I tell her.

"He must have turned blue fifteen times." She laughs again.

"Fifteen times?" I panic. "Are you sure that's okay?" When I am here they hardly ever turn blue. I am always there with the O_2 gas hose by the time they turn gray.

"Sure, honey. It's just a normal preemie thing."

This is surely what she believes or she would not be laughing.

She leaves, and the doctors arrive for rounds, so I move to the hallway with the other mothers. At first I hated this part and would head straight for the pump room, but I have now been here second to longest and I know all the parents, and we spend the time catching up.

"How is Angela?"

"Her dialysis is working better today."

We are allowed back in, and the new attending, Dr. Zhukov, stops by our crib. She's a forty-something Russian woman with a severe ponytail whom I initially hated for snapping "I cannot guarantee you anyzing about preemies" when I asked her a question. But over the past week I've grown so accustomed to her accent that I hardly notice it. And I've been impressed by the thoroughness of her care. I'm starting to understand that any doctor who chooses to practice in an intensive care environment is going to be intense.

Dan has seen Dr. Zhukov working here late in the evening. Unlike veteran specialists in other fields, she will always have to take overnight call. I admire her even more since learning that the salaries of hospital staff neonatologists, $75,000–$200,000, aren't astronomical compared to those of many medical specialties in adult care that require the same or less training.

"We have decided to separate the boys and put them back on continuous oxygen," she tells me. "While we are still thinking their problem is reflux, we don't like that they are having so many episodes. Three a night would be okay, but fifteen is too much. We think this will give them a break and it will give them some more time to mature so that they can outgrow their apneas and bradycardias."

"Okay," I say.

Dr. Zhukov walks away and the nurse says, "She is a funny lady. At rounds, she said, 'Now tell me, how suicidal were these boys last night?'"

It must be that this hospital is getting to me, that all of the sadness and sickness has usurped my psyche, because I actually laugh. Then I go to lunch.

I return to find the boys' crib gone. In its place are two isolettes. Sam has gotten the window spot. It is hard to see them separated after being together for weeks, with a nasal cannula—an even thinner tube than the one used with CPAP, but still a tube nonetheless—running up each of their noses. Sam is awake. Now that he is in the warm isolette he doesn't need the preemie pajamas he wore in the open crib, and he has been stripped down to his diaper. I haven't seen him in an isolette for a couple of weeks, and it is obvious how snugly his preemie diaper fits, how much fuller his thighs are. My sons would no longer fit into one isolette as they did not so long ago. He is pale, not baby pink, but not blue or gray either. A new Crayola crayon. Preemie pale. The cannulas are a setback. We are supposed to be getting ready to go home and we are back to square one. I can't even imagine how I am going to explain it to Dan.

Two weeks of constantly delivering oxygen has started to take its toll on me. I don't know how much longer I can handle watching my babies stop breathing and turn gray. I am no longer afraid of the oxygen tank. By the time the alarm bells ring and the nurse appears, I already have the gas on and in Sam's or Gus's face. But each time it feels as if I have touched an electric fence, and after nearly fifty times, I am in a continuous low-grade shock.

At 7:00 the day nurses fill the night nurses in on their patients before they change shift.

My least favorite nurse arrives wearing black with curtain roses. She doesn't have the boys tonight—her babies are in another room—but she comes in to chat with the recent nursing graduate. "Back in the isolettes," she says, shaking her head. "A setback. Poor boys. What a shame."

I pack up my tape recorder, water bottle, empty milk-carrying case, and the dirty pajamas from this morning. I take my coat from the sill.

The alarms in our area have not gone off all afternoon.

TWENTY-FOUR HOURS LATER, Sam and Gus are returned to their crib so that the co-bedding experiment can continue. They are each connected to an oxygen tank on either side of the crib. Gus is scheduled to have his eyes re-examined to make sure he has outgrown his retinopathy of prematurity—an eye disease restricted to preemies in which new, abnormal blood vessels grow near the retina and temporarily or permanently damage it. My mother and I have been waiting for hours and the optometrist has not shown up. At noon we decide to get some lunch. I pack up the boys' dirty preemie clothes in my backpack, and as we leave the NICU a bell rings, louder and less computerized than the monitor signals, which have become like static cling. Our nurse runs up to me. "You must have accidentally taken one of their alarms," she says. I dig through my pack and in the foot of one of the preemie pajamas

I find the plastic anklet with a small square box that is always snapped around one of each boy's feet. It turns out to belong to Sam. Our nurse attaches the box to a new anklet and puts it back around his foot. I am grateful for the sweet gesture of attaching baby alarms to preemies. A preemie thief would require an accomplice parked in a car right outside the hospital entrance with an oxygen tank or a respirator. He would need to have practiced inserting feeding tubes and IVs.

My mother—who has been driving in to see the boys a couple of mornings a week—and I eat tomato and mozzarella sandwiches from the snack bar in the lobby because I am too focused on the eye exam to even bother taking the elevator at the end of the hall to the basement.

We return to the NICU to learn from our nurse that Gus's ROP has resolved. Although preemies are at risk for nearsightedness, only 1 to 2 percent of babies born at thirty-one weeks have complications from ROP so I needn't have been so worried. In the 1950s, excessive O_2 was linked to ROP in preemies, and ever since then O_2 usage in the NICU has been minimized and closely controlled. As a child I spent years fearing blindness myself, slipping out of school on the mornings the nurse called my classmates into her office one at a time for eye exams because I could not see the blackboard. On a trip to New York City my father realized I could not read the NBC sign in Rockefeller Center while standing right beneath it. He shouted at me and a week later I had glasses. But every year my prescription got stronger, surpassing legal blindness, and I feared I would someday lose my sight altogether.

I breathe a sigh of relief, and say to my mother, "Next time we have to get out of here for lunch. Why don't you make me go outside ever? I cannot eat one more tomato and mozzarella and pesto sandwich again in my life."

Two days later when she visits we walk up to a Greek diner on First Avenue. We pass two pregnant women on Sixty-ninth street, another waiting at a light on the curb outside the diner. After we've been seated, my mother and I both spot gyros on the oversized plastic menus.

"I love gyros, but only if they have the real meat," I say. "Sometimes they use that processed chicken stuff." My mother agrees.

The waitress shows up to take our order and I tell her, "We would like to get the chicken gyros but can you tell me, do they use the fake meat here?" Another pregnant woman in a heavy coat passes by the windows. Two women pushing baby carriages stop on the corner to wait for the light to change. Is it because we're on the Upper East Side or did I just never notice before that all the women in Manhattan are having kids?

"It's not fake chicken," the waitress says and scribbles on her pad.

"You're sure they use real chicken. Because if it's the fake stuff we can get something else."

"No, it's real chicken," she snaps. "Would you like a salad with that?"

We say yes and order drinks. She quickly turns away.

"I feel jealous of pregnant women on the street," I tell my mother.

"But you already have your two wonderful babies."

She is right. I have never loved anyone so overwhelmingly or instinctively as Sam and Gus. Do I want to return to a time when such strong devotion was absent from my life? Would I wish away such a mighty love? I would forsake it in a heartbeat if by doing so I could save Sam and Gus the distress of their premature birth.

"I'm going to leave as soon as we finish lunch today so I don't hit rush hour traffic this time." Over the past few years it seems my mother has begun, increasingly, to plan ahead. Or did I just never notice this about her before?

My right arm aches from supporting Sam's head. I think about how this afternoon I will give Gus a turn, though my mother held him this morning. I might even ask Dan to take Sam out of the crib when he visits after work so that the boys are each cradled exactly twice.

My mother has her black coat over her shoulders. She senses that I do not want her to cry in front of me, but she indulges my neuroses long enough to reveal her own anxiety. She has started talking mostly in the first person plural as in "This is hard on us, but we can get through it."

The waitress brings two large oval plates. I bite into my gyro and discover liverwurst-like chicken. I pry open the pita and see the pimento-stuffed processed meat. When I finally get the waitress's attention from our narrow corner in the back, I complain that this is exactly the fake chicken we did not want.

"You asked me if it was real chicken," she says, bored. "You didn't ask me if it was thin chicken. It is real chicken, just thin."

What could it possibly be to her whether we got the gyros or something else on the menu? I take a few bites and look at my mother's plate. She is pulling the chicken out of the pita with a fork, pushing it around her plate.

"Just eat it, Mom," I say. "It's not that bad." And I'm angry with her when she can't.

My mother changes the subject. "Has your coworker found out whether she's having a boy or a girl?" The colleague she is referring to recently got pregnant on her fourth in-vitro attempt.

"She decided not to ask at her ultrasound. She said the sex will be revealed through God's plan."

"So the sex of the baby can be left to God, but creating her life required the most aggressive science," my mom says.

"I guess," I say, but I understand my coworker's comment. I believe God had a hand in the science that created Gus and Sam. He was there while Sam's life was being saved, when Gus's brain bleed didn't extend to even a grade one. He is a part of every miracle. Like the Egyptian father who was interviewed in numerous papers about his previously conjoined twins, now I pray to God that our boys will be normal. There is a 65 percent chance that Sam and Gus, born at thirty-one weeks weighing over 1,500 grams, will develop normally, an additional 20 percent chance that they could be diagnosed with a mild disability like dyslexia or hyperactivity or asthma. Only 15 percent of babies born between thirty and thirty-three weeks of gestation develop severe cerebral palsy or are blind, deaf, or mentally retarded.

God has also given us a warning. He has said you may get out of this one, but watch it. He has created statistics that scare me at night.

I hug my mother good-bye outside of the diner and walk back to the hospital alone. I sit in the fading afternoon light, holding Gus in my arms, his head elevated, placing my index finger in his mouth to strengthen his suck so that he will not be out of practice when we try the bottle again in a couple of weeks. He never seems to sleep, he is always looking around, and I wonder how far he can see, what he can make out. My mother said he smiled at her this morning, but I am still convinced his slight mouth movements are gas.

A quiet beeping from our incubator indicates that Gus's gavage feeding is ending. The WASPy NP makes her way over to us and detaches an empty bottle from the feeding tube inserted through his nose.

"Hey there," she says. "Your guys are getting big." After I told her several times she needn't call me Mrs. Quigley, she has finally stopped. But I shouldn't expect her to remember my first name. She could not possibly know that she resembles so many of my girlfriends.

"They're both five and a half pounds. The continuous feeding seems to be working." Then, thinking she might appreciate a change of subject, I ask, "So what are you doing for Christmas?"

"I have to work Christmas Day," she says. "My boyfriend and I are going to celebrate Christmas Eve instead."

"Maybe he bought a ring."

"I can't imagine when. Besides, he doesn't know my ring size. My mother keeps saying I should give him an ultimatum. But it's so unromantic."

"I bet he'll come around on his own," I say.

"I sure hope so," she says and moves to a bassinet at the neighboring station, where the son of a fireman from Greenwich, Connecticut, is spending his last day before discharge. He has already been disconnected from his monitor. She lifts up the baby and sits down with him in front of a computer in between our stations. She begins to log in data with the baby on her lap.

I rest Gus back down in his crib. I decide to go home rather than wait for a machine to become free in the pump room. Dan can bring over my milk when he visits tonight.

On christmas morning the boys are six weeks old. Dan and I attend a mass at the church Dan discovered. Then we visit the boys at the hospital, where I drop off more milk. The sixth-floor freezer is overflowing with my milk. Dan loves to tell everyone how the nurses claim I have enough milk to feed the entire NICU.

We get stuck in the lobby behind a Santa who is greeting visitors. I push past the crowd to reach the elevator. Dan goes to the boys' crib and calls across the room to where I am trying to shove all my milk into the bucket labeled Quigley in the fridge. "Hey, you've gotta see this," he says.

Sam and Gus are sleeping side by side in red Santa Claus hats with white pom-poms. Their crib is filled with knitted yarn ornaments and two big teddy bears.

Our nurse approaches us. "Merry Christmas," she says. "Your parents were here already, Mr. Quigley. They brought the hats. One of the nurses made ornaments for every baby in the NICU. And Mrs. Lardner dropped by last night with her five-year-old twins like she does every year since they were born, to deliver teddy bears."

"I wish I'd brought our camera," Dan says.

"Your mother took some pictures," the nurse says.

"You have to admit they look pretty cute in their hats," Dan says.

"I know," I say, but I am already leaning in to pull them off. Gus opens an eye as I slip his off his head. He peers out at me then closes it again. I remove the hats, ornaments, and teddy bears and stuff them into my bag. I recognize that the decorations make the sterile crib more festive, that the tree and Santa in the lobby are an attempt to turn the atmosphere in the hospital less morose at Christmastime, and why shouldn't Sam and Gus get to look like they're having fun? But I proceed to ruin it because I can't shake the feeling that in their Santa hats lying on a bed full of presents, Sam and Gus resemble those sorry cats dressed in costumes on calendars.

At noon we leave for Cannon and Bruce's house in Westchester.

The house is filled with Dan's brothers and sisters, cousins, babies, children, parents, aunts, and uncles. There is Christmas music and a fire, a big tree in the corner wrapped in white lights. Everyone has brought gifts for the boys.

After I open a pile of presents, I slip into the kitchen to see if Cannon needs any help. One of Dan's cousins who is heating up some gravy says to me, "It must be hard, feeling like you have had your children, but you're not a mother yet."

I nod. She is expressing sympathy. But in truth what I feel is that absolutely the only thing I am now is a mother. Not a mother who breast-feeds her baby, like another of Dan's cousins is doing on the couch in the living room, or changes diapers and soaks her infant in the tub. But a mother who for the past six weeks has been recording herself singing lullabies on cassettes which she sets inside a pocket recorder in the corner of the crib at night before leaving the hospital, who cannot focus on the newspaper or the television or keep up her end of a conversation because she is worrying about her children.

At the dinner table we pray for everyone's health, for my father-in-law, battling cancer, and for the boys. Dan mentions that he is interviewing for a job in Farmington, Connecticut, next week, and someone asks down the table how I feel about it. I do not answer "Well, it's a little far for me to commute," or even "I'll have to see whether there's anything other than farms in Farmington." I can think only that by the time Dan has had this interview, and perhaps been offered the job, and decided to accept it, and we have driven around the town, surely by then Sam and Gus will have come home. Any home I picture has Sam and Gus in it, and therefore seems fine.

My mother-in-law serves apple pie. I excuse myself and go upstairs into the room belonging to my three-year-old niece and unpack my pump. A few minutes later Bruce's father walks in on me and I realize that he must be staying in this room. He apologizes and leaves.

We return that evening to several messages on our answering machine wishing us a merry Christmas. Messages are always waiting when I reach home from the NICU in the evening. I hit Play before I take off my coat and shoes. Friends ask how everything is going, they are thinking of us, wondering if we need any groceries. Even the message that sends me into a tailspin, from a friend who knew someone whose six-month-old preemie on oxygen had recently enjoyed her first hike into the mountains, carried on her mother's back with the gas tank strapped to the father's. Even this is meant to say, *I am thinking of you.* Familiar voices fill the room and I am momentarily nostalgic for a life that disappeared six weeks ago. But as the voices carry on, they soothe me and I think, *Oh, so-and-so must come and meet the babies once we get them home.* I never return the calls. I don't think people expect me to.

Dan asks, "Do you want to open my present?"

"Sure."

Dan's younger sister, Megan, stopped by the hospital a few days ago to drag Dan out Christmas shopping at a clothing store chain around the corner from our apartment. In the NICU, diapers are changed just before each feeding. While I was changing Gus, Megan asked, "Does his penis look swollen to you?" I didn't know. Sam and Gus owned the only baby penises either of us had ever seen. I pulled down Sam's diaper as a point of comparison and Megan thought it might be swollen too. I called over our nurse, who brought in a nurse-practitioner, who paged the doctor, who finally arrived half an hour later, took one look, and said that their penises were just fine. "See how no one will ever take responsibility here. No wonder everybody hates this place," I said to Megan so that the nurse could hear. Then I felt awful.

Dan brings out a small box. In it are two thin gold bracelets. One is decorated with tiny emeralds and diamonds, the other is braided with diamond chips and rubies. They are the most beautiful pieces of jewelry I have ever owned. There is also a note scribbled on a torn sheet of paper.

"Dear Mom. Merry Christmas. Thanks for bringing us into the world. Now please stop worrying about us so much. We are fine. Love, Sam and Gus."

A WEEK LATER, on New Year's Eve, Dan and I are sitting in our apartment when my mother phones to say that Katie doesn't have any plans tonight either. She and her boyfriend are having a quiet evening and so why don't I call her.

A few friends had invited us along to their celebrations, but we didn't feel much like partying. A casual, relaxing dinner with my sister and her boyfriend might be just what we need.

I ask Dan if he's up for it and he says yes so I call Katie. "Hey, do you guys want to meet at a restaurant?" I ask.

"Sure," she says. "Let me just check with him." She puts down the phone for several minutes. She returns and says, "He really doesn't want to take the subway uptown tonight."

"We could come down to you," I say. "We haven't been out to eat downtown in months."

"Okay," she says. "Let me think of a place and I'll call you back."

A few minutes later the phone rings. "He's not really up for going out to dinner," she says apologetically. "He might go out and buy something to cook."

"Don't worry about it," I say. "We don't mind eating in. It'll be nice and cozy."

"Let me call you back," she says.

Dan turns around from the computer. "They don't want to have dinner with us, Jenny. Just drop it."

The phone rings again and Katie says, "He doesn't feel like preparing a big meal. He was thinking of whipping up something easy for two."

"It's okay. Let's forget it," I say.

"Are you sure?"

"We'll find someplace up here. That way we can stop by the NICU. Happy New Year's," I say, trying to sound cheerful.

After I've hung up Dan says, "I guess he doesn't like us."

"Oh, I'm sure that's not it," I say, trying to shrug off the sting. "If he didn't like us why would he have come over that night a couple of weeks ago to make spaghetti with sausage?" I don't want Dan presuming the boyfriend doesn't enjoy our company. Dan would claim not to care, but I suspect he is as vulnerable as I am right now.

Dan and I head out at 8:00 to a pub on our route to the hospital. We drink big pints of beer and eat tasteless but warm potpies before heading to the NICU.

I prefer evenings in the NICU. Most of the procedures are scheduled during the day, and perhaps because there is not as much commotion at night, the alarms ring less often. There are fewer visitors. The doctors are all on call from home; only the night nurses are around, and they are a more eccentric, forgiving bunch than the social day nurses. The day nurses seem always to be yapping with each other, planning their weddings, complaining about the five pounds they can't seem to lose, showing each other apartment listings on the hospital computers. While they add some essential spirit to the place, the day nurses also insist on playing their own music on a big radio by the door. At night the nurses listen to whatever tape we want to put into our pocket tape recorder.

The second night that Sam was on the oscillator, his night nurse told me that sometimes as many as five oscillators were running on the NICU floor. It wasn't until weeks had gone by and I had yet to see the oscillator again that I realized she had lied.

Both boys are asleep when we arrive. They are still getting continuous oxygen, and now slow-flowing breast milk as well, drip by drip, right down into their stomachs. They have had only one episode or so a day for the last week. Dan and I are recording these in our blue NICU handbook along with their weights. At seven weeks, Gus weighs 6 pounds, Sam, 5 pounds, 15 ounces. As my father perfectly phrased it the last time my parents visited before heading down to Florida, "Sam is beautiful and Gus looks how a baby is supposed to look." I put on *Mozart for Mothers-to-Be,* a tape from their days in the womb, and we each take a baby in our arms and sit down. I have Gus. I am very careful to give them equal time each day.

It always surprises me that I get such a different feeling going from one baby to the other. If I'm holding Sam and he falls asleep, exhaling audibly, the kind of calm comes over me that I used to feel as a teenager sailing with a steady wind on my back. I don't seem to hear the jarring alarms or notice the intensely fluorescent lights. Whenever Sam tightens his tummy muscles and throws back his head—a reflex caused by his acid reflux—I feel like I'm gripping a main sheet that's luffing hard over choppy waters. But with Gus awake in my arms, I'm aware of his vulnerability. I worry more about Gus even though Sam had a rougher start. I whisper, "It's going to be okay, Gussy. Mommy's here. I promise everything is going to get better very soon." Dan claims that I favor Gus, which is absolutely not true.

"Sam is more like you," I tell Dan. "I never lose sleep over you. Whereas I'm beginning to feel Gus may be sensitive."

"You can't tell that yet," he says. And maybe he's right. It might be that I'm projecting. But I've felt Gus flinch from an alarm across the room, and watched his eyes pop open after a nurse absent-mindedly let the lid of the metal trash can in the corner slam shut. Perhaps having bounced back from death's door now makes Sam seem invincible.

We sit in the chairs watching our boys sleep. We don't say much for over an hour. My mother-in-law worries about me sitting here for hours at a time. She sends her daughters into the city to take me to lunch. What she doesn't understand, what no one can, is that the only time I find any peace is while keeping vigil over my children. At midnight the nurses go out to their station and exchange "Happy New Year"s. I kiss Gus. I whisper, "Happy New Year, baby."

"Happy New Year," Dan says. "Let's start getting you ready to go home."

It always takes me at least half an hour to leave. We put the boys back into their metal crib. Dan reattaches the stuffed monkeys with their Velcro hands so that they are swinging together once again, across the top of the crib. He does this every single day and I have yet to admit that I am the one who disassembles them while he's not here, afraid that one will fall onto Gus or Sam and suffocate him.

I kiss Sam, then Gus, then Sam, then Gus.

The boys were here for nearly two months before I realized I could kiss them, that I wouldn't be giving them germs. Initially the super-busy nurse troll who was always scolding me had warned me not to kiss them. But I'd had a cold at the time.

Then at the end of last week while I was holding Sam, the WASPy nurse-practitioner who had just, finally, gotten engaged stopped by to show me her diamond ring. An emerald cut. I knew it would be. The NP leaned over me and placed a kiss on his forehead.

"He's going to have a thing for you," I said. "You're the first person to kiss him."

"You haven't kissed him?"

"No. I mean, I didn't think I was allowed." I was suddenly ashamed.

"I feel so terrible," she said. "It's awful that you didn't get to kiss him first."

"Oh no, please," I said, still trying to carry the joke off, "I have a feeling he's going to be liking blondes from now on." And then I smacked a loud kiss on Sam's cheek.

Later I heard her saying to one of the other nurses that she felt bad about it.

"Come on," Dan says. "It's 12:30. Time to go."

We say goodnight to our nurse. I kiss the boys one last time and we head outside. The cold night air refreshes us as we escape from the hospital. The bars on First Avenue are still buzzing, horns are honking, people in warm coats are whooping it up on the sidewalk. We pass the empty playground. Dan is talking about whether he should accept the new job offer in Connecticut.

"You said you'd be fine with anything in the tri-state area," he reminds me.

"I know. But I was thinking someplace closer to New York." We spin through the revolving door and wave hello to the doorman. "Happy New Year," we say. This is our first doorman/elevator building in New York, a change we readily accepted when we discovered I was carrying twins. All day long old ladies cruise the block-length corridors in electric wheelchairs. Our building is referred to as God's Waiting Room. Now we may be moving out of the city altogether.

In our apartment Dan pops open a bottle of champagne from a good friend, Dorrit, whose twin boys were born last week and admitted to our NICU. There is a note thanking me for being supportive during the heart surgery one of her sons underwent yesterday. I drink only one glass so as not to contaminate my breast milk, which I then start to pump in front of the TV. There are milk stains all over the coffee table. Dan drinks a second glass, and a third; finds a movie worth watching.

I put away my milk in the refrigerator and pour the rest of the champagne down the kitchen sink so that Dan won't be hungover tomorrow.

"Did you just do what I think you did?" he calls in to me.

"Yup."

"You're unbelievable," he says. But then he laughs. "Come here. You'll have to pay for that."

I sit down on his lap. He kisses me and I smell champagne. He reaches a hand up the back of my shirt.

"It's a nursing bra. Different kind of clasp," I say and unhook it for him. My breasts feel overly sensitive. I hope that having just been pumped, they won't leak.

We undress and Dan says, "Your scar doesn't look that bad." He runs his fingers along it.

I look down at the scar, which is still bright red and puffy. "The stitches fell out at least," I say.

Dan and I make love on the couch and though I'm not fully present, it's not painful either. Briefly I'm thankful that Sam and Gus were born by c-section. Though I'm slightly self-conscious about the roll of fat that won't fall away from my middle and I don't allow myself to take undeserved pleasure in my body since

I'm angry at it for forcing the boys out early, still it's nice to feel so close to Dan again.

Afterward, clothes in arm on my way to our bedroom, the phone rings. "Happy New Year," Katie says. She sounds as if she might cry. "I'm sorry about tonight."

"It's all right, Katie. You've been with us all along. You're allowed a night off."

"Can I go with you to visit Sam and Gus tomorrow?"

"That would be great."

"So you're not mad?"

"No. I promise. Get some sleep."

She croaks, "Love you," before we hang up.

I go back into the living room and put the cordless in its cradle.

"Who was that?" Dan asks.

"Katie."

"You let her off the hook?"

I nod. "She's upset."

"It wasn't a big deal," Dan says.

"I know. And we had a nice time tonight." I lean over him, resting my hands on his shoulders. Dan puts his hands on top of mine.

I picture the pinpoint scars on the backs of Gus's and Sam's hands and the bottoms of their feet from all of the IV needles. A nurse has said they may fade with time. But as opposed to the slash across my pelvis, I tend to feel affection for the boys' tiny pinpricks, as if scars this slight were proof of wounds effortlessly healing. Perhaps in the new year the boys' entire experience in the NICU will gradually disappear, until a pale, almost imperceptible imprint is all that remains.

DURING HER LAST DAY of rounds before rotating on to a month of research, Dr. Zhukov instructs our nurse to unhook the boys' feeding tubes and call the nutritionist, who is also the "feeding specialist," for a trial run of the bottles. Both Sam and Gus gag immediately, the sirens sound, and Dr. Zhukov says, "Let's give them a second week with the continuous flow."

"They just tried it once?" Dan asks when I telephone him from the bank of phones at the elevator since it's sometimes hard to get reception on my cell phone inside the hospital. "They should give them more of a chance to get used to drinking."

"I guess their doctor thinks it's still too soon."

"So one try and now we have to wait another week."

It is worrisome to Dan and me that the boys seem to not be making progress. I am having trouble understanding how the apneas and bradycardias they now have each time they swallow anything more than a drop of milk are different from those that they should have outgrown by thirty-seven weeks from conception. A baby born at thirty-seven weeks is considered full-term. Now Sam and Gus have reached thirty-nine weeks and still their heartbeats dip, their breathing stops. The longest a baby has continued having these spells in this hospital is forty-four weeks, four weeks past his due date. In the record books it is many, many months.

When a bad situation goes on for weeks, it becomes absurd. Now that we have made it through the holidays, I seem to have lost the urgency to get the boys home by a specific date. Ever since they were put on the continuous feed a week ago, our alarms have not sounded and my visits have been less stressed. We call to check in every night and our nurse tells us, "No episodes for the evening so far." I have fallen into something resembling a life at the NICU. I hardly notice that the babies are emaciated and the nurses wear plastic gloves, which they take off to wash their hands between handling babies. Every few days a new mother in a hospital gown is wheeled up to her baby's isolette, where she starts to cry.

Dan is exasperated. He is entirely fed up at having to walk down to the hospital, sit under the bright lights, endure the beeping, talk to the boys in front of the nurses and whatever parents happen to be there. After accepting the new offer, he hoped he could spend time getting to know the boys in our apartment while he was between jobs. But his start date is in two weeks, and once he has started making the long commute to Connecticut, it's doubtful he will arrive home before late evening.

He asks me strange questions, like do I know where the word "decimate" comes from, and when I say no, tells me how, to punish cowardice or mutinies, the Romans would line up a legion and execute every tenth soldier. I ask, "Why are you thinking about being decimated?" And he answers, "I don't know."

This past weekend Dan insisted on cutting the boys' fingernails. The NICU's policy does not permit nurses to trim the babies' nails. Infants and preemies in particular have thin skin, and the NICU staff wants to avoid easily infected wounds. But Dan was concerned that the boys might scratch each other so he brought a pair of baby clippers to the hospital and proceeded to nick Gus's index finger. Blood spurted out, down Gus's hand, onto his preemie pajamas. Dan tried to apply pressure to the finger, but it wouldn't stop bleeding and eventually I had to call the nurse over. The nurse wrapped Gus's finger in gauze. It bled through. By the next morning rumors of Gus's injury were flying around the nurses' station. Now every time Dan enters the NICU a different nurse teases him about trying to cut off his son's finger.

I have become friendly with a number of the nurses. Sometimes I see them eating lunch in their common room and have to stop myself from joining them.

Early this morning, the young nursing school graduate was attending to Angela, who has developed an infection from her dialysis. Suddenly Angela's dialysis bag overflowed, spilling urine all over the floor. Angela's mother was home taking care of Angela's twin sister, and her father, usually a sweet man, lost his cool. He shouted at the young nurse, "Why is it that every time you're her nurse, Angela has problems? You should have seen her yesterday, she was doing just great. Now this!"

Urine was making its way along the floor toward our crib. I went over to the sink to grab some paper towels.

"I paged the doctor," the young nurse said, her voice even higher than usual. "He should be here in a minute." Then she saw me squatting and said, "Don't touch it! She has an infection."

Angela's father stormed out of the room.

I asked the nurse if I could bring her some lunch and she burst into tears. I said, "Everyone knows that the NPs assign you the sickest babies because you handle them so beautifully."

"But he's right," she said, looking suddenly too tired to be twenty-two years old. "I do seem to cause Angela nothing but grief."

After eating lunch at a Mexican café, I go into the pharmacy on the corner to buy the young nurse some pastel bath soaps and a box of sea salts. I make it out the door, then go back in and purchase all the fancy soaps from a big basket. I distribute them to the nurses and leave the last remaining box at the nurses' station with a note of appreciation for my least favorite night nurse.

Dr. Zhukov stops at the station to chat with me. She says she is looking forward to starting her next rotation tomorrow. "I need a break," she says. "Although after doing research for a few weeks I start to miss the babies."

I promise her that I will bring Sam and Gus over for visits once they have graduated from the NICU. I say, "We wouldn't dream of missing the annual Christmas party for graduates."

Dr. Zhukov says, "You may end up feeling differently. Most mothers get out of here and never want to come back."

I think about the Scottish nurse from the infertility clinic, and how I haven't returned any of her calls inquiring about the boys.

But I tell myself that the NICU will be different. A bulletin board in the hallway is filled with photographs of twin toddlers dressed in red and green velvet, sitting underneath Christmas trees, next to big dogs. And I think next year Sam and Gus will be beaming down at the nurses, encouraging a whole new set of mothers.

A voice comes over the intercom, "Nurse for Baby Peterson on line one."

"This is the fourth or fifth time they've called this morning," I say to Dr. Zhukov.

"Baby Peterson came off the respirator last night," she tells me quietly.

"And?"

"So far so good," she says. "But it's too early to tell."

At noon I head to the room next door to thank Dorrit for the bottle of champagne and invite her to the cafeteria. Technically parents are not allowed inside any other unit than the one where their child is stationed. Three different nurses look up when I enter. Their eyes follow me to the incubator where Dorrit is stand-ing in front of the twin who is recovering from surgery. Then the nurses return to what they were doing. A week ago a team of sur-geons made a small horizontal incision on the left side of the baby's back. They lifted up his lung to find a duct to his heart that was open. It had not had time to properly close before birth. The surgeons sealed it with a tiny permanent clip to stop blood from flowing back into the lungs.

Dorrit's other twin will be released later this week. Over tuna sandwiches we agree that it is going to be difficult for her to have one baby at home and one in the NICU. We decide she can spend mornings with the baby at home and leave him with the baby nurse to visit her son at the hospital in the afternoon. We have both booked baby nurses on the advice of mothers of twins. Baby nurses are hired for any stretch of time from a week to a year.

Dan and I have a nurse from Trinidad coming for three weeks.

Baby nurses expect to work twenty-four hours a day, and are therefore very expensive. You can use one of several agencies in New York City to employ a baby nurse—there is one that represents Filipino nurses exclusively, another organization that places nurses from the Caribbean. Baby nurses are not actually certified, though many of them have taken infant care classes in the States or received their nursing degree in their native countries. Many have experience caring for twins, as the majority of parents willing to shell out $200 a day for round-the-clock assistance have more than one newborn. Outside of the metropolitan area, most people I talk with have never heard of a baby nurse.

While we are eating, I recognize a mother in line at the soup station. Only one of her twins, born at thirty-four weeks, had needed to spend a couple of days in the NICU in an isolette by the door. We had to walk past her and her husband in order to reach our crib. My mother referred to her baby boy as "Piggy."

But the morning her son was discharged she peeked in at Sam and Gus (she wasn't there long enough to have been told that observing other people's babies was strictly taboo), and said, "They look so big compared to Owen." We exchanged weights and realized that they were all more or less five pounds.

The mother stops by our table to say hello. "You're not going to believe it," she says. "We're back here with RSV. Both boys caught it and couldn't breathe. They're over in the PICU hooked up to oxygen. We begged the doctors to give our twins Synagis shots before they came home from the hospital, but our insurance wouldn't cover it since they were thirty-four-weekers. Each injection costs over a thousand bucks. The Synagis would definitely have limited the virus. The PICU makes the NICU seem like a four-star hotel. I've been sleeping on a pullout chair here for a week because there are only a couple of nurses assigned to the whole room."

Respiratory syncytial virus is a very contagious winter virus that in most people causes a common cold. But preemies who get RSV often have trouble breathing and can develop bronchiolitis. As with most of the problems preemies are prone to, boys are more susceptible to RSV than girls.

The mother's blond curls are flat like old phone cords. We ask her to spell Synagis. Then Dorrit and I rush back to our separate NICU rooms to find out if our boys have been given the shots.

Gus is staring at one of the stuffed monkeys hanging above him. Sam is watching Gus. They are two months old and they have never been outside, felt a change of temperature, seen in the dark.

A WEEK AND A HALF before their original due date, Sam has a bad spell of bradycardias. He and Gus have been off the continuous feed for a week and slowly the doctors have been building on the amount of breast milk the boys can take in each bottle.

During this second trial run off the oxygen and continuous milk Gus's oxygen level has been desaturating into the 80th percentile. It should be 100 percent. Breathing is still hard work for him, and once he gets tired he does not pull in enough air. Every few seconds the alarm starts to blip and stops. I wonder if anyone else is aware that he is just barely slipping under the radar.

Sam is a different story. His lungs are stronger now, and as a result he is able to cry, which he does during most of his waking hours. Initially the nurses predicted that Gus would be my colicky baby, but the title is going to Sam. While asleep, he has also been having trouble, gagging on regurgitated milk, holding his breath and bearing down, and dropping his heart rate in the process. He actually goes limp and only comes to when we take him from the crib and bang him on his back. One of the nurse-practitioners agrees with me that it has something to do with how soundly he sleeps, though she mentioned this at rounds and the doctor laughed at her. For the last few days I've taken him, crying, from the crib and he has fallen asleep in minutes with his head on my shoulder, snoring softly against my breast. I can't help but let his peacefulness seep into me, even though I don't take my eyes off the monitor. The nurses tell me, "Don't look at the monitor. Look at your baby." But how can I if it's just a matter of time before his heart rate dips, swoops back up, then dips again, and sets off the alarm? A nurse runs over, grabs him out of my arms, and flicks his foot until he finally wakes up. "Oh, he's gray, definitely gray," she says and records it in his notebook. The hospital's rule is that a baby must be episode-free for forty-eight hours before he can go home. The nurses claim that Sam and Gus will be released on their due date. Are they really going to make an exception and discharge Sam, even though he has not been episode-free for forty-eight minutes?

I am tired of being incessantly asked by nurse-practitioners, "Are you saying that you feel ready to care for the boys at home?" I want to be told that the people in charge believe the boys are ready to be released. As it is now, the NPs are only willing to recommend discharge if I let them write in their notepads that it was my idea, which says to me they think Sam is still unstable. They drop hints about Gus being ready to graduate, but that after all these weeks, and with the boys' due date around the corner, having him leave Sam behind would be too sad. I'm grateful to the NPs for not suggesting to the attending that Gus be discharged, particularly since Sam and Gus could not possibly have endeared themselves to the NPs, since I suspect they have sunk the case for co-bedding.

On the setback day, a Sunday, my mother is already in the NICU when I arrive and I can tell immediately, from the look on her face, that something is wrong. "What is it?" I ask.

"Sammy just had a brady. The nurse was able to get him out of it, but she said he had several overnight."

"Yesterday he was fine. What are you, some kind of bad luck?" She starts to cry. "I'm only joking," I say, and although I actually was, I realize immediately it wasn't funny. "I don't mean it."

"Yes, you do." She is sobbing.

"Of course I don't." In the eight weeks since the boys were born, this is the rottenest thing I've said. I will repeat it a million times to different friends, all of whom will assure me that I was kidding. But even later, it will seem as if this was rock bottom.

Over the last couple of weeks I've become proprietary over Sam and Gus. Initially, once the boys were stable, I'd invited my friends to meet them, and I'd begged my mother to visit as often as possible. Now, suddenly, I prefer to be alone with the boys. I am desperate to establish intimacy with them. I become jealous when visitors stop by and I'm forced to share my babies, make conversation that draws my attention away from them. With my mother it's different. Since she's witnessed fewer bad spells, it's possible that they are even more alarming to her than to me. I want to tell her, "You have to hold yourself together. I still need you to be my mom." But I know she's trying and that exacerbates it. She's even more upset than she's letting on. She is not only my mother but a first-time grandmother as well.

I embrace my mother and plead with her to stop crying. Throughout the morning she stops and starts again.

The nurse-practitioner follows my suggestion of adding rice cereal to the boys' milk. The cereal thickens the milk's consistency so that it shouldn't splash back up into the esophagus so easily. Usually tried as a first resort and not a last, the cereal has helped several of the babies in our room. Sam drinks the new blend and has seven bradycardiac episodes in a row. Each time he falls asleep, his heart rate drops. His color changes from pink to gray to blue.

I am having trouble believing that all of these apneas and bradycardias are not going to cause permanent damage. At some point during the morning, although I surely know better than this by now, I ask Alex, the male NP.

"All the parents ask us this. We don't think so. But there is a doctor in California who posted an article on the Internet saying that prolonged periods of *a*s and *b*s can cost the babies a few IQ points. I have to mention it because you could always look on the Internet and find it yourself."

I have already found the article he is referring to, but I don't admit this to Alex. I reassure myself that if it were a matter of permanent damage the hospital would keep the babies on oxygen until they had outgrown the episodes. I'm lucky to have gotten out of another stupid question relatively unharmed, and what difference could a couple of IQ points make, anyway.

Sam's heart rate drops again and now I cannot stop crying. Dan escorts my mother and me to the hospital door and says he will stay until Sam is doing better. All of the parents in the room can hear me wail. Many of their babies are worse off than Sam is, but we have been here the longest. The other parents may be wondering if a public nervous collapse is also in their near future.

The NP stops me at the door and says, "I'm at my wit's end. I don't know what to do."

"Stop the rice cereal. No more cereal. Please, he's gagging on it."

"But we just tried it once. Didn't you agree to the cereal?"

"Please, it's not working. Please please please stop the cereal."

"We'll see," he says.

I turn to Dan, "Don't let them give him any more cereal."

"Okay," he says. "Now go home for a while."

My mother comes home from the hospital with me though her plan had been to leave early. She reads the newspaper at the kitchen table until Dan arrives at our apartment several hours later to report that he coaxed Sam into staying awake for several hours—possibly until the bout of reflux eased up, or he became more alert. In any event Sam seemed to snap out of it. The nurse did not add rice cereal to his 3:00 milk.

That evening Dan and I go back to the hospital for our infant CPR class. Sam is still breathing fine. I've taken CPR before, once to qualify as a lifeguard at summer camp, again for a scuba-diving certificate off the Australian coast. But tonight, even with the stakes so high, I cannot keep the order of things straight, when to clamp the nose, shout for help, pump the stomach, give the breaths. In an emergency I'd never get it right. While I am practicing on a plastic doll I decide that should the home alarms go off for more than an instant, I will turn on one of the emergency oxygen tanks they are sending us home with, shoot it into Sam's or Gus's face, and call 911. I announce this is my plan, and the teacher answers that turning on an oxygen tank without pumping the baby's chest will not necessarily enable an unconscious infant to breathe. But for as long as we have been in the NICU, eight weeks and counting, it has done the trick, and I tell her I'm sticking with the program.

On Monday I give breast-feeding a final try just in case it is the obvious solution to the boys' reflux. I pull the portable beige standing curtain from the corner of the room over to our crib and hike up my shirt. I smash Sam's mouth against my breast. He sucks a few times and then starts to scream. I move Sam to the other breast, then rest him back down in his crib and head to the pump room.

The staff continues to make arrangements for the boys' discharge on their due date next week. The bobbed-cut social worker pulls up a chair to inform me about Medicaid money I can file for on the condition that the boys don't yet have bank accounts. She asks, "How are you managing?" and I answer, "Fine." Does she really think I'm going to confide in her after all this time, or is she merely being courteous? A nurse I've just met—how many hundred nurses can possibly work in this NICU?—mentions that insurance companies are hesitant to continue coverage past the due date.

Dan and I request a meeting with the new attending neonatologist, who greets us in front of the boys' cribs.

"We don't want the boys to come home if there's a concern that they might not be ready," Dan says. "We're starting to feel like we're the ones in charge here. Jenny suggests adding rice to the breast milk to thicken it in the morning, and hours later it's been prescribed. Then she cancels it. We're not the doctors here."

We've been told that our new neonatologist takes a less hands-on approach than the other attendings, that since he came on two days ago he has signed discharge papers for over fifteen preemies. He is clearing the place out.

"We'll wait until they are not having episodes," he assures us.

But by the following day, it appears that Sam and Gus will be released on their due date. Since they will be coming home on reflux medication meds—which we will insert into bottles of breast milk with a dropper six times a day—a nurse-practitioner writes up three prescriptions for me to fill.

A woman from a medical equipment supplier is summoned to the hospital in the afternoon to teach me how to use the home monitors, which are the size and weight of a woman's shoe. The new attending neonatologist has recommended the boys be kept on monitors until they are six months old, by which point they should have outgrown their reflux. We tape the wires onto Gus's chest to test it, and the monitor immediately starts beeping. A couple of the nurses look up from their stations, not recognizing this particular high pitch. It rings for a few seconds and stops.

"It's because our monitors don't have the three-second delay," the representative tells me. "Ours are more sensitive than the ones here at the hospital." I can't help but notice the representative, who looks about my age, is not wearing a ring.

"No way. There is no way I'm using this," I say, looking around for my NP. "It's intense enough being a first-time mother. I'm not having this ridiculous alarm go off every five seconds." Immediately the siren sounds again and I rip it off Gus.

"Oh, so these are your first children. Now it makes sense. You wanted them to be perfect."

"Perfect?" I exclaim, incensed. I finally get a nurse to come over, and ask her to page the NP. "What I want is for my babies to stay alive. I am worried about keeping them alive." My admission softens the representative a bit, but what I am thinking is that my babies *are* perfect, a detail she is too hopeless to see.

When the NP arrives, she suggests lowering the thresholds on the home monitor to 85 percent (from 90 percent) for oxygen saturation and 80 heartbeats per minute (from 100), and this seems to do the trick.

I LEAVE THE HOSPITAL at four and head downtown, toward the Lexington Avenue subway, which I take to Vidal Sassoon. In addition to the haircut I've postponed for months, I have decided to get highlights. "One of us needs to be blond or else who will Sam resemble?" I have told Dan in advance so he won't flip when he sees the Visa statement at the end of the month.

While my hairdresser's assistant is rinsing my hair I say, "This is my favorite part," with the hope that she will continue running her hands through my scalp forever. Only now that the boys' release is imminent does it occur to me that I should have spent more time over the past two and a half months buying myself some much-needed new clothing, cashing in on a year-old gift certificate for a spa massage. My hairdresser looks at the pictures of Gus and Sam and doesn't comment that they were all taken in the hospital. Is it possible that they strike him as no different from the photographs of babies his other clients show him?

My hairdresser holds up his brush. "Your hair is falling out," he says softly. "A lot of my clients find it upsetting to lose so much hair after pregnancy." I have been noticing strands of hair on my pillow and clumps caught in the shower drain, but only when my hair-dresser points it out do I realize what's been happening.

He disappears and returns carrying a tray with chemicals and aluminum foils. "Keep them natural, okay?" I ask. The result is so subtle you can hardly tell my hair has been lightened. There are some streaks of chestnut, but my hair was brown to begin with.

I make it back to the NICU at 7:00, just as visiting hours are ending. The night nurses are getting their assignments. I slip past them to kiss Sam and Gus goodnight. "By next week at this time you'll be home," I whisper.

Part Three

THE ONLY
LIVING BOYS
IN NEW YORK

I HAVE DREAMED ABOUT THIS DAY. We will walk out of the glass NICU doors with our boys snuggled into their car seats and all the people lined up for taxis in the lobby entrance will think that they have just been born. Every time I enter the hospital there is a mother with her baby waiting for her husband to bring the car out front so that they can go home, and I think that someday this is going to be us.

On their due date, January 14, a nurse tapes probes to Sam's and Gus's feet and attaches them to portable monitors before pulling the red, black, and white leads off their tummies. Suddenly our boys are no longer hooked up to the hospital computers. They are free. I take pictures of Sam and Gus bundled up in their white snowsuits, staring out from under knit hats. Last night they weighed 6 pounds, 15 ounces, and 6 pounds, 14 ounces, respectively.

As a child I was so intensely frightened of kidnappers that I practiced making the run from my bed to my parents' room with a stopwatch. Today it feels like we are kidnapping our children. While carrying both boys in their car seats toward the door of the NICU, I drop the digital camera and break it. Dan's arms are overflowing with two emergency oxygen tanks.

The nurses have gathered in the doorway to say good-bye. Although the other parents are jealous, they know we have been here long enough to deserve to go home. We are not like the three-day visitors, who hover with their extended families over their piggy babies talking in loud voices and then disappear. The other parents wish us well. Angela's mother writes down my phone number, suggesting that once Angela goes home we take our twins for a walk in Central Park.

And then, there I am, with my boys, in the waiting area, everyone smiling at us, not even glancing at the oxygen tanks behind the couch.

"Don't you feel as if we've stolen them?" I ask Dan on the drive home.

"Shhhh," he says, concentrating on navigating the city streets as if it were his first time behind the wheel.

Dan parks the car in the driveway of our building, and we carry the boys past the doormen, who say hello as if it is not out of the ordinary for us to be lugging two infant car seats into the elevator. We step over the threshold of our apartment and set the boys down in their new home. The baby nurse, Lorna, has already arrived and changed into white scrubs. Lorna is a smart-looking woman with the firm and animated voice of a much-loved schoolteacher.

The crib that the boys will share has been made up for weeks; the diapers are on the changing table. I watch the boys in their new surroundings, wonder what they thought of the icy wind as it whipped their faces on the short walk to the car, if they have noticed yet how much quieter it is in our apartment.

I remove the boys' hats and Sam and Gus open their eyes. I lift Sam from his car seat and Dan unzips and pulls off the white down snowsuit not really necessary for the five steps to and from the car. But bundling the boys up like Eskimos had been a joyous rite of release, like throwing tasseled caps to the sky at graduation.

Holding Sam in the middle of our living room I introduce him to his new home. I stand perfectly still so as not to detach the cord connecting him to his monitor, which is resting on the floor.

Although my shoulders are relaxing, I'm still on autopilot. Dan takes Sam in his lap and a few minutes later I hand Gus to Lorna, who, strangely, suddenly appears nervous. Then I put a chicken in the oven and unpack all of our hospital supplies—the foot probes, two-ounce plastic bottles and nipples, elevated headrests. I tape the CPR instructions above the crib in the boys' bedroom. I show Lorna how to work the monitors and emergency oxygen, how to dispense the three different doses of reflux medication and at what hours.

We eat with all of the medical equipment spread out on the table. Then I clear the plates, say goodnight, kiss Sam and Gus on their foreheads, and turn in to bed. Hundreds of times previously I imagined our first night together as a family with the expectation that Dan and I would sit up all night watching the boys to make sure they were breathing. But I've grown accustomed to allowing nurses to cover the night shift. And having programmed myself to survive a seemingly endless succession of stressful weeks, I have become perhaps overly practical. Like a sensible parent I recognize the inefficiency of our staying up too late and becoming overtired. Long after I've climbed into bed I hear Dan out in the living room watching television with Lorna.

Finally I sleep, without dreaming or awakening in a sweat, until the next day at 8:00 a.m. And when I wake everybody is fine. Our two small souls are at home.

THE NURSES AT THE NICU advised us to limit the number of visitors to the apartment for the first month for fear they might carry germs, and Dan and I have decided not to have anyone come by for a while other than family.

Dan has less than a week before he starts his new job as a marketing director in Farmington, Connecticut. He will be commuting for the time being, but soon we will have to think about moving closer to his office. In the mornings we send Lorna to bed. The boys wake up at quarter to nine—even after being home for a few days their body clocks are set to the NICU timetable. We keep them on the same sides of the crib they occupied in the NICU, Gus on the left and Sammy on the right, although of course it's no longer necessary since they aren't attached to computers. Although I carried the boys' "BB A" and "BB B" name tags home from the hospital as mementos, I don't go so far as to tape them up to our crib. When they wake I transport them, one at a time, to the kitchen table where I proceed to quickly change their diapers, which are always soiled, before I am peed on. Most of the time their clothes are wet and I have to redress them entirely before adjusting the probes on their feet and taking their temperatures. I record all bowel movements in a ledger. I follow the routine exactly as I learned it in the NICU. The only step I skip is weighing the diapers as I never learned what output to expect. I rest the boys back in their crib while I measure out a few ccs of the reflux medications, pouring each into a separate bottle containing one ounce of breast milk mixed with formula. Although I am still pumping eight times a day, I'm not producing enough milk to keep up with the boys' increasing appetites. Lorna shows me how to mix formula and add it to the bottles I've pumped.

At nine o'clock I carry a bucket filled with bottles to Dan and rest another on the coffee table for myself. We are still nervous feeding Sam and Gus, although we've been practicing for weeks in the NICU. The monitors beep throughout the feedings. Each time the alarm sounds we yank the bottles from the boys' mouths and they cry for their milk. The alarms go off constantly, day and night, but the boys never appear to be in distress. We tape the speakers up to mute the sound, and still they make us jump. We seem to spend hours eliciting burps. The cricks in my shoulders and neck feel like they're permanent. We pat the boys on the back, rub up and down their spines, tickle their sides until finally the burps come and with them most of the milk. It appears that the boys are hardly keeping anything down, but Lorna pours a teaspoon of water onto the kitchen table to demonstrate how even the smallest spill can look like a lot.

We have pulled one of the cribs out into the living room, and throughout the day whenever I pump, eat, or use the bathroom I transfer whoever is sleeping on my lap into the crib under the musical mobile which plays symphonies by Beethoven, Bach, and Mozart at a slightly rundown-battery tempo. At night, Sam throws his head back and screams, his back arched. Lorna and I take turns rocking him for hours in our new glider until his discomfort passes.

Outside, the city is caught in a midwinter cold snap. Our relatives show up in parkas with scarves around their necks, over their mouths, wool hats pulled down to their eyes, mittens and boots. Once they have removed their coats and washed their hands with antibacterial soap, they are handed a baby and three small bottles of breast milk with reflux medication. Dan and I teach our mothers and sisters how to prop the boys upright between their legs to burp them rather than holding them over their shoulders, which makes the babies' heads flop forward.

Toward the end of the boys' first week in our apartment a visiting nurse stops by to check on us. Dan has gone to the Far West Side to lease a car for work. Lorna opens the door and the scowl that crosses her face suggests the visiting nurse is far too young to be of help to us. The visiting nurse is dressed in jeans and a St. John's collegiate sweatshirt. I tell Lorna she looks tired and should go rest. Then I prepare bottles and the visiting nurse and I pull dining chairs up to the living room crib. She asks who has the harder time with feedings and I indicate Sam. "Then I'll feed him," she offers, easing him out.

"So far he's had nothing but false alarms," I say, knocking on the crib. "Same with Gus."

While Sam is sucking, his alarm starts to beep and the nurse says, "This is a real brady. Not a false alarm." She pulls the bottle out of Sam's mouth, and flicks the bottom of his feet.

"We haven't had to stimulate him since he's been home," I say nervously. "He must be coming out of them on his own."

"Well his heartbeat was definitely plummeting just now. He stopped breathing. I saw it with my own two eyes."

Is she going to recommend that Sam be sent back to the NICU?

Sam quiets and does not set off the alarm again during the feeding. Afterward, the visiting nurse holds him upright between her legs and rubs his back, drawing three quick burps from him. She rests him down in the crib and stands up to leave. She asks, "Would you like for me to come back? I don't think the hospital will send me out here again, but I could stop by for a few hours on my day off."

"That would be great," I say.

"We usually charge $40 an hour for private visits," she says.

"Oh. Of course. It's your day off. Why don't I just take your number and I can call you."

The second the door to the apartment has shut, Lorna emerges from the boys' room. "We don't need her," she says.

"Do you think it's possible that all of the alarms have been real?"

"These boys are doing fine," Lorna says.

"Sam's behavior seemed to make her uneasy," I say.

"That nurse was just a kid," she says. Lorna never takes off her scrubs, which it suddenly occurs to me she doesn't need to wear since she is not, officially, a nurse.

"Well, it's not like we've been ignoring the alarms," I say, although I've already started waiting several seconds to see if the beeping will stop on its own before I approach the crib.

For the rest of the morning I run to the crib each time an alarm sounds. I scowl at Lorna if the monitor beeps while she's feeding one of the boys. Lorna delivers Sam his bottle and then goes to make herself a cup of tea. She dials various friends on her cell phone, has hushed conversations punctuated with cagey laughter.

Dan arrives home at dinnertime with a pile of car brochures and metallic swatches. The models are all sedans that look exactly the same. "But this one's got a six-cylinder engine," he notes.

A row of babies in hospital incubators appears on television. "Dan, look. It's the NICU."

The picture changes to a clip of a very tired-looking mother in her hospital bed. "I'm just so happy that I was able to carry them all," she says. The reporter explains that the woman became pregnant by insemination with quintuplets, whom she gave birth to last night. She was thirty-three weeks pregnant. The smallest of the litter is four pounds. Only one of the babies has a medical problem, a congenital heart defect doctors are working to treat.

"She made it two weeks longer than I did and she had five babies!"

"You wouldn't be happy with her outcome. It sounds like one of them is in serious trouble. They're glossing over that part on the news."

"It doesn't make me feel better that one of her children is having problems."

"Just stop comparing. Compare cars instead. I'm leaning toward the Honda Accord. Or the Toyota Camry. Which do you think?"

I go to bed late at night and wake up early. With Lorna and the babies in the next room I don't think about having sex. If sex occurs to Dan, he doesn't mention it.

Before the week is up, Dan announces his new status in our family is Number Five, following the boys, me, and Lorna in that order. It's true that I've been taking Lorna's culinary preferences—which are not necessarily Dan's—into account while cooking dinner. But fish is so good for you! It may be that I've been too busy prying the secrets of handling twins out of Lorna to pay him much attention. If I vaguely register that Dan and I are already falling into conventional parental roles, I refuse to exacerbate the situation by fussing over him like a dutiful wife. Lorna is teaching me techniques of baby massage she learned in Trinidad, for I've read that massage helps preemies thrive. Premature babies who receive massages gain more weight and are more active and alert than

those who don't. Preemies, separated from their parents and sub-
jected to trauma, lack two chemical compounds that work in an
infant's body and brain to influence behavior and stress hormone
output. Recent studies suggest that this deficiency can be reversed
through maternal touch.

Lorna shows me how to tightly swaddle Sam and Gus in light
cotton blankets. From time to time I try to get Sam and Gus to
breast-feed and both the babies and I end up crying in exaspera-
tion. All the while Dan moves restlessly around the apartment,
vying for my attention, packing his briefcase, preparing to start his
new job.

Perhaps if Sam and Gus had not been born prematurely, a
period would have followed their birth in which we longed for our
old life, the intimate evenings I spent reading while he watched old
movies next to me on the couch, the weekends we slept late, the
only invasion of our privacy being a casual brunch date. But once
the boys are home I slam the door to our past. It is as if the years
during which we would meet up after work and exchange stories
while sitting on unfinished wooden stools I'd bought at the hardware store, heat something for supper, banter jealously after I met
an ex-girlfriend, were just laying the groundwork for the moment
we'd become parents.

DAN STARTS HIS JOB the third week in January. The commute
takes him close to two hours in the car each way. He arrives home
at nine o'clock and is gone again by six.

In the morning while Lorna is sleeping I put the boys in their
bouncy seats, switch on vibrate, and read *Sam and the Firefly*. It's a
book by P. D. Eastman that a friend in our building pushed under
our door. Sam is an owl in search of some nighttime fun and Gus is
a daredevil firefly who arrives on the scene to provide it.

A few pages into the book the real Sam starts to fuss. His behavior corresponds to that of a typical preemie, difficult to soothe and more withdrawn than most infants. Sam and Gus are ten weeks old, a week past term, and I'm still waiting to see a smile. Most babies smile at six or seven weeks of age. If I calculate according to their adjusted ages Sam and Gus won't smile for another month and a half. Sensing that their infancies will be prolonged, I tell myself to be patient.

I change the leads attached to the boys' left feet, gently peeling the sticky tape off. The skin underneath is red and sore. I attach new wires to their right feet since they will have a few days to heal. Plugged back in, the monitors run through a course of several different beeps and are finally quiet.

I squirt medicine into bottles of breast milk and line them up in the fridge. The boys have not veered from the hospital's schedule of taking milk with medicine at three-hour intervals throughout the night, though within a day of her arrival Lorna said, "These are growing boys," and increased their milk intake from two ounces to three. I warm six vials that serve as bottles in two plastic hospital buckets. First we give them one ounce of milk with Prilosec, which is the hardest of the three to get them to take. I finally understand why after tasting it myself and cringing from its bitterness. Then they get another ounce with Reglan and a third with Pepcid. I turn each empty bottle upside down and stick it back in the bucket, then pull out the next one.

Holly, my old school friend, has already taken her newborn daughter to coffeehouses, to matinees at the movies, to yoga classes and clothing stores. Everywhere but to the studio at ABC, from which she is on maternity leave. This morning, on the one-week anniversary of the boys' trip home, they are going out for the first time. It takes me half an hour to dress Sam and Gus in fleece sacks, hats, and blankets. When I strap them into their car seats, their heads droop to the side. Their necks are not strong enough to support their heads. I prop them up with rolled cloth diapers and tilt the seats back as the nurse did on the day they were discharged. I hail a cab, slide their car seats into the back, and climb in between them. It is worth the time at the doctor's office unclothing and redressing them to hear him say they are gaining weight. But after we return to the apartment and Lorna greets us at the door, and helps me extract the boys from their layers, I doubt I'll take them out again for a while.

At some point I will need to schedule a meeting with my old boss to ask if I can work part-time from Connecticut if we move. I'll have to call the authors with whom I worked, see how their manuscripts are progressing, ask friends about their relationships, their jobs, their children. But right now I only want to take care of Sam and Gus. In the evening I carry one of the babies into bed with me where he takes up just a small portion of Dan's side. I fall asleep in a T-shirt with the heat pouring in through the radiators.

I feed Sam and Gus their bottles of medicine and rub their backs in circles until they burp. I change their diapers and bathe them, rub lotion on their tummies and arms and legs. Some days our extended families glide into the apartment carrying takeout lunches.

I wonder how long we'll be able to bunker down in our apartment. On vacations from boarding school and college I would retreat to my parents' home, watch movies in my pajamas, and not return phone calls or see any friends, old or new, for weeks. My current break from the outside world is going on three months, and I'm not so sure I won't want to stay here forever.

LORNA MOVES ON TO HER NEXT JOB after two weeks with us, and Dan and I spend our first weekend alone with the boys in their room on the pullout couch. Before we go to bed we decide who has whom for the night. Dan takes Gus because he is less fussy.

Dan handles the nights well. They remind him of his military training. As soon as I hear crying I nudge Dan, and he wakes up, instantly alert. He feeds Gus his bottles, then goes straight back to sleep. I drag myself back to the kitchen, prepare new bottles, and wait for the crying. I lie in bed, with adrenaline pumping through my veins, watching the clock until I finally fall asleep seemingly minutes before they next wake.

Sunday morning Dan sleeps through the cries and I don't have the heart to wake him, so I take turns feeding both boys and then make a cup of coffee. Dan gets up, on his own, at nine, and is grateful.

Sam cries for most of the morning. After Dan eats breakfast he puts Sam into a Baby Björn cloth backpack strapped across his chest and carries him around the apartment, downstairs through the lobby, up to the indoor roof garden, to try to soothe him. Typical preemies are easily overstimulated in their surroundings. In the womb a normal baby develops sensory filters to tune out certain sounds and sensations. When a baby is premature these filters have not had time to develop. Is Sam's crying prompted by our voices and the sound of cars and ambulances on the street below and the discomfort caused by his reflux? Is he oversensitive to pain because it reminds him of the NICU? A study of preemies who spent four weeks in a NICU found their pulses quickened in response to pain more than full-term newborns, indicating that the preemies were already seriously traumatized. Sam and Gus were in the NICU for more than twice that time.

Before Dan starts his second workweek we decide he should spend every other night at a hotel in Farmington across the street from his office, so that he is able to function at his new job. He was so exhausted during his first week that he couldn't remember colleagues' names, where they sat, or what he was supposed to be doing.

Dan spends the weekend taking apart the crib in the living room and reassembling it in the boys' bedroom. Sam and Gus have grown too big to sleep horizontally in the same crib. I order a second musical mobile from Buy Buy Baby.

Katie stops by Monday morning on her way to work. After she leaves, I am alone with the boys. Is every mother nervous the first time she is by herself with her child? While Sam and Gus are taking their morning nap, I boil bottles, pump milk, and mix in medicine.

At nine I lift Sam from his crib to feed him his three one-ounce bottles in succession, yanking the nipples out of his mouth every four to five sucks so that he remembers to breathe, holding him upright for twenty minutes afterward to keep him from regurgitating the milk. I move on to Gus next. And then I pump. Before long the routine becomes a kind of nonstop meditation.

I always feel a little sad when I first start to pump. I don't know if it's my body's response to the sensation of my milk letting down or because I'm pumping instead of nursing—staring out the window and not into my babies' eyes.

I call Dan on Tuesday morning, hyper from exhaustion yet elated that Sam, Gus, and I are functioning as a team. I have proven myself a self-sufficient mother, but I am deeply indebted to Sam and Gus for having alternated their waking hours.

By Tuesday afternoon I have come down with a cold.

Wednesday morning my hands start to shake, a result of all the caffeine. My breast milk production decreases. I have to pull frozen milk out of storage to mix with formula. Dan arrives home from Connecticut in the evening and encourages me to call Michelle, a nanny Lorna had referred us to should I decide to return to work.

Michelle arrives at our apartment for an interview on Thursday morning. She is a voluminous Trinidadian woman in her early thirties with a big beautiful smile, a loud, warm voice. While she is cradling Sam to her enormous bosom he doesn't fuss. He pulls at her hennaed cornrows and I think I detect a smile. She feeds him his bottle without the alarm sounding. I ask her two questions: Are you willing to live in for the first month? And how soon are you available to start? My throat is killing me.

"You're sure you don't need me to meet her first?" Dan asks over the phone on Thursday night.

"No, trust me, she's great. Besides, it's not like I won't be here with her. At least for the beginning," I say, trying to change the subject. I've already given Michelle the job.

Dan bites. "Are you thinking you might go back to work?"

"I don't know. I'm not ready to decide."

"You should call your boss."

"Mmm hmm."

"Why don't you see if you can go back part-time. You loved your job. Remember?"

"Kind of," I say. I hear Sam's and Gus's rhythmic snores coming from the crib. Following their 9:00 p.m. bottles I should force myself to transfer the boys to their bedroom. Lorna claimed the change of scene would help them learn to differentiate day from night. But lately I haven't had the energy to shuffle them back and forth between rooms. Gus has spent the last two nights in the living room crib and I have lain awake on the couch with Sam resting on my chest. Lorna also warned me that every time I let Sam fall asleep on me I made it harder for him to learn how to doze off on his own. But in the middle of the night I will do anything to stop his crying.

"Well, I remember," Dan says. "You were fanatical about working on books."

"Don't we have to move to Connecticut?"

"We could live somewhere on the commuter train line. You should think about it," he says.

"Okay."

"I'm serious."

"Okay. I'll see you tomorrow night," I say and rest the phone down beside me on the couch. I fall asleep with my forehead pressing into the receiver.

———

THE SECOND TIME I TAKE the boys to see their pediatrician we are late. The pediatrician detects a heart murmur in Sam. He asks me whether anyone caught it in the NICU. I say no, starting to panic. The pediatrician guesses that all of the noise must have made it hard to hear. The pediatrician reassures me it is an innocent murmur, one out of three babies has one, and Sam's already had an echocardiogram, which was fine. But I remember the cardiologist on the day of the echos saying something about a zipper being slightly open at the top of a duct. No blood was leaking through, and so the cardiologist did not find it a cause for concern. Now I wonder—might it have unzipped? Could a murmur have something to do with his collapsed lung? I took biology. For two weeks I dissected fetal pigs that smelled of formaldhyde, but I cannot remember how the lungs and heart are connected.

The Friday night before, I heard a soft gushing sound coming from our kitchen. I ran in to discover water leaking from a pipe under the sink and pooling on the tile floor. I left Dan and our superintendent urgent messages. As the water slowly spread across the room and lapped up against a cable stapled along the bottom of the wall I wondered if a wet wire might cause an electric shock. I hurried to our fuse box and, not knowing which lever controlled the kitchen, flipped them all off. I was making my way to the hall closet to search for flashlights when I noticed Sam and Gus crying. They could tell I was upset and it was rubbing off on them, or maybe they were scared of the dark.

Dan finally arrived home. He switched the electricity back on before tightening a valve under the sink with a wrench. Then he mopped the kitchen floor.

This is what I am like at the pediatrician's office. If even one small part comes loose, I am flooded back into the NICU.

I RECENTLY READ AN ARTICLE in the *New England Journal of Medicine* that summarized the results from a study group of preemies who'd had similar NICU experiences. At the end of a year the infants whose mothers had worried least showed fewer signs of developmental delays. I must try not to let my paranoia infringe on our family's reality.

I've also read about a psychiatrist in Boston who is curing patients of their fears by flooding them with its source. A person who is claustrophobic is locked in the trunk of his car every day. Is someone assigned the task of getting him out? The psychiatrist treats a woman who is afraid of cancer by prescribing the movie *Terms of Endearment* several times a week. It seems to be about raising the level of adrenaline until it combusts and loses its power.

I consider how I might put his method into practice. But I visited the NICU every day for nine weeks, and my fear of it did not dissolve. Would it have required just a few more weeks until the translucent micro-preemies failed to disturb me? Before my breathing remained steady during the boys' medical exams? Until I stopped denying that Sam nearly died?

I START BY UNPLUGGING the monitor while I'm feeding Gus. He is thirteen weeks old. We've been home for a month. I watch his face closely for signs of distress as the NICU nurses and, later, Lorna instructed. He starts to look tired so I gently pull out the bottle for a break. His breathing slows down and I give him back the bottle. A week passes before I get up the courage to try feeding Sam without his monitor turned on. At a certain point his head droops toward his chest and I know the alarm would be sounding, but when I remove the bottle from his mouth Sam opens his eyes and straightens his neck so I continue with the feeding. Soon I don't bother to reattach the boys to the monitors immediately after feeding them. I place Sam and Gus on the floor under the Gymini mobiles and watch them carefully from the couch.

The first night I leave the monitors off I can't sleep. But the following nights I do. Friday evening Dan arrives at home and says,

"I'm fine with you turning them off during the day, but I'm not so sure about at night."

Sam and Gus have their baths and I dress their right feet with new probes. I set up the monitors on the folding tables at the head of Gus's crib and the foot of Sam's. But I never plug the foot probes into the monitors. The boys sleep with wires dangling out of their cribs. In the morning the skin on their right feet is raw where gravity from the hanging cords has pulled on it. Dan must have noticed when he fed Gus during the night that his machine was not connected, but he doesn't say anything, so I don't either. The next evening I resume my practice of not putting probes on the boys' feet. But I leave the monitors perched on the card tables like bookends for the adjacent cribs, backs plugged into the wall, their blank screens guardedly facing forward.

At the end of February I proudly push the boys' stroller through the slush to their follow-up at the preemie clinic. The clinic is located across the street from the hospital, in the same building as the center for infertility. I've pulled the headrest out of Gus's car seat and placed it behind him in the stroller to hold his head straight. I have not been back to the hospital since the boys came home six weeks ago. In fact, except for the NICU's routine, which I continue to follow, I've refused to reflect on our time there.

My father-in-law has told me that the dreams people tend to remember are the ones they have after they've already started to stir. The nightmares I keep awakening from, in which I am running from a man with a gun and getting shot repeatedly, may be partly a delayed reaction to the NICU, but could just as conceivably be inspired by the boys' violent cries upon waking next door. It's possible that in the still of the night, when all four of us are deep in sleep, my dreams are serene. I'm grateful that, at least thus far, Sam and Gus and Dan have not come under fire.

Before entering the hospital, I check on the boys behind their plastic wind cover. Sam looks up at me inquisitively. Gus's eyes are half-closed.

I pull the stroller out of the elevator and see Dorrit in the waiting room. Her twin boys are asleep in their stroller. Their faces have filled out since I saw them a month ago. She says, "Why, hello. It's Sam and Gus. One of the nurses just came out and mistook us for you guys."

"Who was it?"

"I'm not sure, but it might have been the troll. She wasn't assigned to our room very often."

"She kept her butt planted in ours." We laugh about the NICU as if we were gathered at a tenth year college reunion.

"Have you been to many follow-up appointments?" she asks. "We've seen doctors all over town."

"Sam and Gus had all of their follow-ups in the NICU. I guess there are benefits to sticking around for nine weeks."

A young boy with blond curls, about three, is limping around the lobby. His father follows him back and forth down the corridor, blocking off office doors. Two African American twin girls in wheelchairs stare at Sam and Gus.

Two hours pass. Finally, when the waiting room has almost emptied, our name is called. Dr. Zhukov, the neonatology fellow, a nurse, and another woman I don't recognize are milling around the doorway of an office. I push the boys' stroller into the examining room and while I am taking Gus out I mention that I unhooked the boys' monitors a week ago. Dr. Zhukov gasps, flips her tightly pulled hair, and leaves the room. A few minutes later she is back. "Ze head of our department sez you are a smaert mozzer."

"So you'll give me a prescription to send the monitors back to the company?" I ask Dr. Zhukov. "They refuse to pick them up without a prescription."

"Daring mother," she says. "We were just whispering about you in the hallway. But the head says you're smart."

Yes, it has been daring to let the boys continue to sleep on their tummies without the monitors, though I am well aware that preemies are at an increased risk of SIDS (sudden infant death syndrome), and that back-sleeping is safer. But after they have been falling asleep on their stomachs for two months in the NICU it seems cruel to force them to turn over, and we have already been though so much, too much really, so I pretend SIDS is not our concern.

But as for shelving the monitors, there is no doubt that the bleeping has decreased over the past four weeks. Not once did we have to stimulate either Sam or Gus. Our pediatrician counseled me to keep the monitors on until we visited the follow-up clinic. He said, "Since the neonatologists prescribed them in the first place, they'll most likely want to decide when to turn them off." The pediatrician is affiliated with the same hospital where our neonatologists work. Perhaps he didn't want to step on anyone's toes. I unplugged the monitors anyway.

The realization that I know my boys better than any professional does is thrilling. Having made my first important decision as a mother, I feel a sudden surge in confidence. At last I am ready to take charge. Without the urgent care of well-meaning and knowledgeable physicians Sam and Gus would not have survived. We will forever be indebted to the NICU medical team for saving the boys' lives. But even good doctors must consider hospital politics, potential lawsuits, and the expansion of their research database while evaluating their patients. Now that Sam and Gus are out of the woods it is conceivable that I'm their best advocate.

Dr. Zhukov says we have to continue with all three of the reflux meds until our next visit in a month. In addition, she prescribes an antibiotic to be applied to the boys' tongues three times daily to combat thrush. Then the physical therapist does an exam and concludes that among other things, the boys' big toes hyperextend, which she says could, if it doesn't right itself, make walking awkward. She tells me to bend their toes forward whenever they are flexed. She says, "Their muscles are tight. The reflux must be making them arch their backs and straighten their legs. People may comment that your babies appear to be strong, but what they are noticing is actually stiffness." She coos at Gus, trying to get him to smile, but she startles him, and he wails instead. She recommends that they do physical therapy with her.

I ask what the physical therapy would be for and the fellow answers, "They don't have cerebral palsy. But there could be something wrong with an ankle. If they had been born at thirty-two weeks we'd be more optimistic than we are at thirty-one." It is so strange to see this fellow again. Before leaving the NICU I learned he was a year older than I, he and his wife had a newborn daughter, and he had a year of training remaining before he could become a full-fledged attending.

Of more than 3,000 board-certified neonatologists in the United States, 80 percent are younger than fifty. What does it say that the number of young doctors specializing in neonatology and reproductive endocrinology is on the rise while the percentage specializing in obstetrics and gynecology is declining? The fellow says, "I would definitely advise you to take advantage of physical therapy. I've been trying to convince my insurance company to pay for our daughter to attend."

"Why do you want your daughter in physical therapy?" I ask.

"Just in case our expert trainers detect a problem I'm unaware of," he says. "They're great that way."

"The head does not believe in physical therapy except in cases where we detect particularly poor muscle development," Dr. Zhukov says. "But we do not see it this way. In any event, it doesn't hurt. Think of it like a gym class. We could all stand to go to the gym."

We emerge from the examining offices to find the waiting room empty. Dorrit and her boys have gone. I think about dropping by the NICU to say hello, but the boys are fussing and I'm tired too, so I decide to head straight home.

That evening the representative from the medical equipment supplier rings our buzzer. Before I answer the door I hide one manual air pump and an oxygen mask in the back of the hall closet. The lonesome-looking representative takes a step into the foyer. I motion her inside. "How are you?" I ask. "Do you often work this late?"

"Not always. I'm just running behind today," she says, brushing away hair that had fallen in her face. I hand over the O$_2$ tanks and the retired monitors. The representative takes inventory of the equipment she's collecting and doesn't even notice that two pieces are missing. I walk her to the door.

Perhaps she'd been right to suggest that wanting perfect children pegged me as a first-time mother. Perfection as a starting point may turn out to be something that we as a family were spared. There aren't many better places you can get to from there.

Beaming, I say, "Thank you so much for your help." She exits and I leap across the room. Sam and Gus have finally graduated from endangered species to newborn babies.

PHYSICAL THERAPY IS WITH Aida on the eighteenth floor of the hospital. Aida is a pretty Asian woman in her thirties who speaks in hushed tones. She tries to get Gus to follow a toy with his eyes, to lift his head up off the mat. Aida says, "His neck is weaker on the right side. He keeps turning toward the left."

"I think the light through the window has caught his attention."

Sam will have nothing to do with physical therapy. He screams if Aida even gets near him. Therefore he is left alone to fall asleep and Gus has to work through both of their appointments. Aida pulls him into baby sit-ups, crosses and uncrosses his legs, tries to get him to hold his head up while resting against an exercise ball. I try to think of Aida as a personal trainer at a gym for babies, but it is hard not to feel that she is criticizing Gus. She can tell I am doubtful about whether this session is benefiting the boys, and at the end of the class she asks for the date of our next preemie clinic appointment, when I assume she is planning on getting rid of us by pushing us onto the early intervention people. Early Intervention Services is a government-funded program designed to assist children with developmental delays from birth to age three.

My mother-in-law frequently tells me she thinks that I should take advantage of such government services, but all I want is to leave the preemie world behind and give Sam and Gus a fresh start. I panic when an obviously bored Aida smiles sympathetically while handing over paperwork on early intervention and infant exercises, along with catalogs of toys and products for children with gross and fine motor delays. Am I in denial? I don't care. I want to get away from this crowd. I have no interest in joining the local mothers-of-multiples chapter or an online organization for parents of preemies. It is reassuring to know such support systems are in place. But what I want most is to to navigate our own course as a family.

Following physical therapy Gus is so overtired that he cries all afternoon. My mother doesn't want us to ever go back to Aida. She thinks that Gus can tell what is going on, and that it's bad for him to feel he is letting people down.

THE FIRST SUNDAY IN MARCH is unseasonably mild. Cannon and Bruce and Dan's brother, Matt, bring their children into the city to the Central Park Zoo. The second we put Sam and Gus in their double stroller Sam starts to wail. So they are right back out and into the Baby Björns against our chests.

The sun warms our faces. We walk to the park and through the swarms of families strolling along its paths. People smile as they pass us and say, "Twins?" One woman who stops to admire Sam and Gus and to see if they are identical then asks, "Fertility?"

Will Sam and Gus be asked this question as we are almost daily, almost casually? I can envision them playing kick ball at lunch when some little pest asks, "Hey, are you guys IVF?" Or will it be the sort of information that everyone seems to already have, that the Thompson twins covering two of the bases are identical, the Franco girls waiting against the fence for their turn to kick are from donor eggs? Will it be a classification that splits them from their peers? Will the fact that Sam and Gus are IVF children have any effect on potential girlfriends, or will their dates have younger brothers selected through sperm-sorting procedures like PGD (preimplantation genetic diagnosis)? Whatever the future holds, Dan and I can tell Sam and Gus an origin story full of enough struggle and bravery to make them proud.

We rest on a bench with Sam and Gus, Cannon and her baby, while Bruce and Matt take the older girls to look at the polar bears. Sam and Gus alternate between sleeping and peering out from faces smushed against us. I imagine the Björns feeling like the womb with a view. We sit peacefully for a few minutes, and then Cannon's baby throws up all over the ground at our feet. Cannon looks surprised. The baby vomits again.

"Don't worry," I say as passersby heading toward the trash can beside our bench back away. "We see the stuff every day."

"But she never throws up. This is the first time ever. She must be really sick."

"Oh," I say. Dan and I scoot down the bench away from them. A few minutes later we look at our watches and say we'd better get going. It's almost time for Sam and Gus to have their bottles. We walk to the playground, keeping a healthy distance from Cannon's baby, wave good-bye to Matt and Bruce and the kids who are going down the slide, and head home, our backs aching but our bodies still warm.

With the last of the 6:00 bottles drained, Dan puts on his bathing suit and climbs into the tub. Usually I bathe them in the kitchen sink. "Okay," he says. "I'm ready for whoever's coming in first."

"You know there's no one else here watching." He amusedly claims that he is wearing his suit to bathe with the boys so as to avoid potential future charges of sexual abuse. I've gleaned that Dan's propensity for such laughably gloomy responses grew out of his experiences in the military, though he rarely discusses this period of his life. Only occasionally, when his buddy from Okinawa visits, most recently bearing camouflaged onesies and bibs, does he get pulled into stories that shed light on his state of mind during his years as a marine, the hours in Okinawa whiled away reading paperback novels, being passed on the ascent of a mountain by old Japanese ladies in sandals with groceries on their heads, the open dinner invitations to apartments of married officers, guys who had gotten hitched at twenty, nineteen. The wife was always sitting outside on her two-by-one-foot balcony, drinking and smoking. The husband would whisper that the previous evening the stars had miraculously lined up to bring the usually fuzzy Playboy channel in over perfectly clear TV airwaves.

Gus splashes in the tub and Dan says, "Do you see what he's doing? Gus is going to be a great swimmer." I have Sam in my arms. In a few months we will have to bathe Sam and Gus together as neither will be willing to wait for his turn. But at this point they are still too young to be fully aware of what is going on.

Gus is singing a vowel song. Although he seems to be enjoying the warm water, at fourteen and a half weeks he's not yet smiling, so I can't be certain. In this regard both he and Sam act more like five-week-olds, their age if I correct for prematurity. But their eyes follow objects that are at a further distance than infants can supposedly see at five weeks. Is it possible that the boys' eyesight is developing more rapidly than their social skills? Can Gus recognize me standing in the doorway? Preemie babies are at risk of myopia. Dr. Zhukov claimed, "If you see a baby wearing glasses, you can bet she was a preemie." Even if I were able to pinpoint Gus's developmental stage, his awareness of his surroundings would remain a mystery. What I'm sure Gus is conscious of is this: in his father's strong arms he is secure.

Later that night Dan and I make love. It is our initial attempt at intimacy with the boys at home. Prior to now I worried that we might make noise and wake them next door. Tonight I forget that concern, though not about our sons altogether. Attracting me to Dan is the stirring thought that he is Gus and Sam's father. Having not felt his body pressing down on mine for a couple of months, I register his weight as both fresh and familiar, similar to stepping outside earlier this morning and rediscovering the spring.

D AN HAS TO TRAVEL TO A conference in Asia in the middle of March. The war in Iraq is starting. Rumsfeld has announced Operation Shock and Awe. Bush has put the country back on to code orange alert, and after speaking on the phone to a buddy from the military who is now in the CIA, Dan decides that I should get out of the city with the boys while he's gone. Sam and Gus are four months old. They have finally broken out of their hospital routine only to adopt schedules that are completely independent of each other. There is rarely a time, day or night, when both of them are sleeping.

"Why don't you take the boys to your parents' house in New Jersey?" Dan suggests.

My mother loves visiting us in the city. Last time she stayed in a hotel right across the street from us, and flashed her lights when she went back to her room at night so I could find her from my apartment window.

"But what about SARS? Isn't that dangerous? Maybe you shouldn't go to China."

"I have to," he says. "There is no reason you have to stay in this apartment."

Dan directs my attention to the Iraqi war coverage on TV. "Do you know what they call those aircraft? Puff the Magic Dragon." He notices I am staring into space instead of the television. "Look," he says, "there are things we have to decide. You need to resolve whether you're going back to work so we can decide where we should live." He walks to the bookshelf, pulls out a road atlas, and circles towns in Connecticut between New York City and Farmington. He is frustrated by my ambivalence toward everything but Sam and Gus.

Gus burps several times and I put him into his crib, turn on his musical mobile. I return to the couch. A minute passes and Dan asks, "What are you doing right now? You're not doing anything. Why don't you get out of the apartment? Take a walk. How about going through our insurance papers?"

"I have to pump," I tell him and pull myself up from the couch to get the funnel cones.

On Sunday night my mom drives into the city and Dan leaves in a cab for the airport. Gus falls asleep on the couch around 10:00 and my mother says, "I don't think we should wake him up. Let's see how long he sleeps. I'll stay out here with him." She sits at the foot of the couch and turns on CNN with the volume all the way down. A war correspondent is reporting from somewhere outside of Baghdad. He is crouching behind a wall while soldiers run around him, aiming guns and hurling things.

"He looks like Kermit the Frog reporting live from Humpty Dumpty's fall," I say.

My mom puts her hand on top of Gus's feet. She tells me, "Get some rest. We'll be fine."

Sam wakes up at 1:00 but not Gus. At 3:30 a.m. I emerge from my room for more bottles and say, "Why don't we wake Gus for a bottle and put him down in his crib so you can lie down."

"Let's let him sleep," she says.

"But what about his medicine?"

"He can miss one dose," she says.

"Aren't you tired? There's room in my bed."

"I slept for a while. I'm fine here. It's sort of peaceful." Bombs continue to blow up Baghdad on TV. Gus's face is turned toward the back of the couch; his lids are perfect half moons. His arms are spread out in a perfect T, his legs form a diamond. I have been told that full-term babies sleep hugging their arms and legs close in to their bodies, but that preemies lacking in muscle control have a tendency to sprawl out.

In the morning Michelle arrives from Brooklyn. We pack my mother's car with the boys' gear; their bottle sterilizer, two Pack 'N Plays, their gym mat and mobile, cans of formula and bottles, my breast pump, a suitcase of clothing. By the time we are done you cannot see out the rear window.

Michelle figures out how to latch in the car seats. Finally we are ready to put the boys in the car. Each time my mother stops for a light, Sam wails. "Just a little bit longer and we'll be out of the city," we tell him.

We take turns carrying Sam around the house all day while Gus lies on the floor and bats at the tiny cushion animals hanging from the mobile on his gym mat. About a week after Sam, Gus threw his arm across his side, planted his face into the floor, and finally flopped from his back onto his belly. Now he rolls onto his stomach, lifts his bald head a few inches off the mat, and spreads his arms like an airplane. I overhear my mother whisper to him, "We appreciate your cooperation."

Gus and Sam are smiling, at last. Generally, I make the first move with a practice grin; they beam back, and my smile becomes real. Soon exchanging smiles feels natural to me. Sam and Gus are four months old when they first smile. Full-term infants usually smile in half that time—perhaps in a rush to be understood. Sam and Gus have taken their time, but we are finally making a connection.

I haven't told Michelle that we did IVF, but my mother keeps saying things assuming she knows, and eventually I tell her. Having worked as a nanny in New York for eight years she is familiar with the procedure. She says, "All the moms at the park want to talk about is each other and IVF."

I say, "It's weird. Several of my friends have had to do it."

My mom asks Michelle, "Do they have IVF in Trinidad?"

"No, Moms," she says. "Not really. Not as far as I know. That is to say, I don't know anybody personally who has needed it."

Of course there are people in Trinidad who would benefit from IVF. It's a procedure that is performed around the world. But Michelle, who is exactly my age, had her children almost ten years ago. Most of her friends from Trinidad have children, but no husbands to help support them. She came to New York ten years ago so she could make enough money to send her kids to the private school she attended back home.

She has never lived with her children for any extended period of time. They are cared for by their grandmother in Trinidad. Michelle seems to adore Gus and Sam already, and I find myself wondering about how painful it must be for her to be helping with my children instead of raising her own. How could she have left her family behind and continued to exist? Yes, it was an economically driven decision, but most of the time she seems okay without them. Could she be putting on an act, or is it truly possible to adjust to your kids growing up far away?

Until this moment I've understood my reluctance to return to work as an emotional response to being separated from the boys after their birth. But suddenly I wonder whether my sentimentality isn't something I've created so that I don't have to deliberate over an option that is impractical at best. If I want my children to see their father, and I want to spend time with my husband, and have him support us financially, I'm going to have to move out of Manhattan where my low-rent job is located, and not just to commuterville Connecticut, but far upstate. I can inquire about a part-time position, as Dan keeps encouraging me to do, because I did love my job, *I do remember*, but if it doesn't work out, there's no reason to agonize or feel sorry for myself. Leaving my profession will require a much smaller sacrifice than Michelle has had to make.

AT THE END OF APRIL I visit my company's new offices on the West Side. I am supposed to discuss my return date with my editor in chief, catch up on a few outstanding projects that can't be kept on hold any longer. In the lobby are glass bookcases showcasing brightly lit books, some facing out, others lined up along their perfectly crisp spines. I walk along the corridor, peering into symmetrical offices each equipped with brand-new computers, one bookshelf, and swivel chairs.

I am swarmed by my colleagues who want to see the most recent pictures of Sam and Gus, now five months old. They fill me in on gossip. There is a fiftieth anniversary party for the advertising director, who is in her eighties, and I stand at the back of a conference room while the publisher makes a toast, and the publicity director gives her a year's subscription to the flower of the month club. Everyone says hello, they are happy I've come, and it feels wonderful to be out of my apartment, to see all of these familiar faces.

After the party I hang around the office that has my name on the door. I play with the phone, with the fancy new computer, wonder what Sam and Gus are doing at home. Friends have warned me that I will feel lost on this first trip back to the office, that my brain will be fossilized from lack of use. They have promised that it gets easier. But I am not lost, or overwhelmed or homesick; I am simply visiting a place that was a part of my life a long time ago. I am thinking of this period fondly, like you might remember listening to Squeeze on bunk beds at summer camp or giggling during secret late-night visits from your boyfriend at boarding school. I once belonged with these people, but life has swept me away.

I have not read an entire book—other than the preemie bible—since the boys were born. This is a rather big deal. As a teenager on vacations I read two novels a day, was annoyed if my father suggested a drive through the rain forest, or if Katie begged me to take her sailing. For ten years in publishing I read, on average, four novels a week. Now the thought of reading fiction no longer appeals to me. It's more than that I'm too tired or that there is a war unfolding in Iraq. What keeps me from opening any of the new novels that friends from work send over is a feeling that fiction is hubris. With all of the real pain going on in the world, it strikes me as gratuitous, objectionable even, that writers feel a need to create tragedies. So many already exist.

By 5:30 I am missing Sam and Gus. I poke my head into the reluctantly tweedy, former hippie editor in chief's office to say goodnight and he inquires, as if casually, about my start-back date.

"How about next Thursday?" I suggest, leaving my options open, as Dan has made me promise to do.

He agrees. He asks me if I'm still planning to go to California to attend the brilliant ringletty writer's wedding to a beautiful ringletty writer with whom I've also worked.

"Definitely," I say. "I wouldn't miss it for the world."

I hand back my visitor's pass on the way out and nearly start to run up the block. I make it back to the apartment in ten minutes less than it took to walk over.

Over the weekend I spend hours with the phone attached to my ear. I talk to my mother and the airlines fifty times, making reservations to fly to California to the wedding, and canceling them. Fatigue is making me indecisive and I am driving Dan crazy. He says, "We can go or not go, just decide." My mother has offered to babysit, Michelle is available to help out. There will be wine and dancing, some of my favorite writers, and the Golden Gate Bridge, which I have never seen.

But I can't go.

On the drive to Queens, to the church in Forest Hills where my mother-in-law has arranged to have the boys baptized, I sit in the back between their car seats. Gus turns his face toward the window. He laughs at the white-and-blue checkered pattern of the material against which his head is resting and emits some vowel sounds. What about the pattern strikes him as humorous? A couple of weeks ago the boys laughed for the first time when Dan tickled them—creaky, high-pitched giggles. Now all sorts of things make them laugh: venetian blinds, lamp shades, red airplanes on their crib bumpers. I love that they are so easily amused by their surroundings for what it highlights about human nature—that we are programmed to find the world funny, that laughter is as instinctive as crying. My brother, Will, who has come from California, is riding shotgun. We are caravanning with three cars of friends and family, my sister riding behind us.

Several friends from high school along with Dan's family are gathered in the church when we arrive. The boys are dressed in old white baptismal gowns that have been in Dan's family for generations. The older kids gather around the fountain and Sam cries as the priest pours water on his head. Then he smiles while everyone snaps photographs, which catch Gus startled and wide-eyed.

I stand back, pleased at the sight of Sam and Gus up at the altar in the arms of my brother and sister. Back in the NICU I had dreamed about the boys' baptism at the Quigley family's church. What had seemed most extraordinary was to picture Sam and Gus outside of the NICU, unhooked from oxygen tanks, and living in the everyday world. I had not pondered the significance of the gates to God's kingdom opening today for the boys to pass through. In my mind Sam and Gus entered His world on the day they shed the ventilators and breathed freely on their own. But it is wonderful to see them looking like healthy babies blending into a lovely church scene.

Afterward everyone is invited to the Quigleys' backyard for lunch. It is a gorgeous afternoon in early May. There are babies on blankets in the grass, children holding on to a hula hoop and running circles around it, friends drinking soda from clear plastic cups. Heather and a friend, both very pregnant, are laughing together. Another friend who recently gave birth to her daughter prematurely has left her apnea monitor back at their apartment for the first time. Lindsay is wiping cake off her two-year-old's mouth, Sam is uncharacteristically calm on his grandfather's lap at a round folding table. Despite having had two-thirds of his liver removed by a surgeon, my father-in-law still looks remarkably healthy, and I can almost convince myself he will be in our lives for years to come. Gus is in Cannon's arms over by the drinks, where she is talking with Megan and her new boyfriend, the lawyer she met right after Sam and Gus were born.

I walk over to greet Holly, now a producer for ABC News. Her six-month-old daughter, born a week before Sam and Gus, is sitting up and playing; Sam and Gus don't yet have the muscle control to hold up their heads for more than a second. They are still wobbly like newborns.

Holly says, "Aren't you finding this exhausting? I can't imagine how you do it with two. I was at my rope's end before I went back to work. Changing diapers, breast-feeding, I was so bored I thought I might go crazy."

We marvel at our differing experiences in becoming mothers. She thinks she was wasting away uselessly at home whereas my invisibility feels as if I've disappeared behind my babies. I don't know basic facts about myself anymore. How much do I weigh? Am I still a book editor?

Guilt is surely playing a part in my willingness to erase myself if it will help Sam and Gus to thrive. But, oddly, I have very little remorse.

Holly is looking at me with concern. How can I explain to her that there is a spiritual element to my exhaustion from a day of changing twenty diapers, drawing two baths neither of which is for me, feeding them a dozen bottles, rocking Sam on the glider while Gus sings himself to sleep underneath his musical mobile in the crib right beside me. The feeling I have is not unlike the tired peace I used to find on weekend camping trips in college when after hiking up and down mountains for twelve hours, we finally stopped to eat macaroni and cheese that had been heated on a Bunsen burner and then curled into down sleeping bags under the stars.

"I found the first months so hard. Are you really doing okay?" she inquires, her face close to mine.

I cannot have this conversation right now so I smile and step away.

Holly, Lindsay, Heather and Nick, so many of our friends congregating in twos and threes on the lawn, went to high school with us. Franklin Roosevelt, who also attended the school, wrote that the friendships he cultivated there were like bonds made in the trenches of warfare. Comparing a school of mostly privileged WASPs to warfare may be absurd, yet there was something about the intensity of Groton—of the school's outdated mission to shape America's next generation of leaders, of the six-day class week, mandatory exercise and chapel—at such a vulnerable age and in the absence of our parents and siblings that cemented us together.

At Groton you did not dare campaign to be head prefect. The school's motto, *Cui Servire Est Regnare,* "He who serves leads," stipulated that you were to answer the call to public duty if it was made by your peers but you should not be so vain as to seek it. Is it a coincidence that none of our Groton friends who now work in the city were class officers? I have run into former head prefects on occasion over the years, and many of them seem to be drifting, still waiting wistfully to receive their next calling. Should Sam and Gus want to go to Groton, as Dan is convinced they will, I'll have to warn them not to take the school motto too seriously.

It's dizzying trying to envision the infants and toddlers on the lawn as high school students. Though I can't quite transform them into adolescents, it's not hard to imagine their parents looking basically the way we do now, but with deeper facial lines. So far our appearances haven't changed drastically since high school. My girl-friends' faces have lost some of their roundness and our salon-shaped eyebrows are much improved.

Will Sam and Gus be accepted to Groton if they apply? Although the school regards legacies favorably, its application pool is rather competitive. There's no real reason why our boys should not be even better students than Dan and I. But I can't shake my knowledge that half of all neurological disabilities in children are related to premature birth and that by age eight, one in five prema-ture kids has repeated at least one grade in school. I wish I could promise our boys this afternoon that if they want to attend Gro-ton, they can; that the strong friendships and rigorous education, the cold crystallized air, and our mostly happy memories of four carefree years living on campus, can someday be theirs. It's not that I'm eager to relive my life through my children or provide them with formal leadership training. But I would love to be able to guar-antee Sam and Gus, at the very least, the opportunities I've had.

Dan and I could move up to Boston to be near them.

There is a cake, and Gus takes his first nap in a Pack 'N Play out-side as the party is winding down. People pull on sweaters, wrap their babies in blankets, touch our arms as they say good-bye.

By the time we head back into the city it is dark. Katie's ride left hours ago so she sits on my brother's lap in the passenger seat with her head mashed against the roof. I hold two bottles, one in each hand, up to Sam's and Gus's mouths, and they both fall asleep sucking. The *Sesame Street* platinum album is playing softly the difficulties of being green. As a child, on the occasions I did not feel carsick, I loved pretending to fall asleep while we were driving at night. Will and I would convince Katie that the prime sleeping spot was up on the back ledge along the rear window. I would curl up, listening to the Mets game on the FAN, while the lights from passing cars streamed in, and I knew I was temporarily safe. Kidnappers could not steal me from a moving car.

Since I have had children the intensity of my childhood fears has come back to me. During youth I was irrationally afraid of shadows, and as I became older and less vulnerable I found myself trying to recall why I had been so terrified of who was coming around the corner. But now there is a reality series on television about children vanishing without a trace, and what fascinates me is how in my young adult years, I managed to cast off such a rational fear of danger. Lindsay tells me that, in addition to the universally vulnerable position mothers are in, aware they could not survive the loss of their child, what I have is clinically called "sick-child syndrome." Having seen my children in critical condition, I now fear for their futures. Syndromes aside, I believe I now see more clearly.

Early this morning I studied Sam, whose favorite thing to watch on TV these days is coverage of the Iraqi war that is supposed to have just ended. He cried when I tried to change the channel to Big Bird. So I went back to the grave talking heads on CNN, to the overplayed clips of American troops toppling Saddam's statue. Now that night has fallen I wonder whether as a young man Sam will want to follow his father into the marines. I'm terrified by the possibility of a military career for either of the boys, but also slightly reassured that it will signify they have grown up ableminded and strong.

Do we find clarity after we have children and can see life sharply, not in the daze that we ourselves lived it, but with a keen awareness of all that is beyond our control? In the car beside me,

Sam and Gus look like angels in their filmy white gowns. We are all warm, if uncomfortable. Dan is proud and competent behind the wheel. The headlights illuminate the road right before us and the red reflectors of the car ahead.

On the second saturday in May I pump using my traveling breast pump in the car on our way to look at houses in Milford on the Connecticut shoreline, a few towns before New Haven. Dan is convinced that everyone on the highway can see my breasts. The train ride from Milford to New York City takes an hour and twenty minutes. I have told Dan that I cannot imagine making this commute several times a week. But he doesn't want me to quit my job. He has always envied how much I loved book publishing. And Milford is the halfway point between New York City and Farmington.

We meet a middle-aged real estate agent in the parking lot of her office. She drives us through the rain to several houses. She keeps referring to me as a "working mother," shows us houses that are within walking distance of the train station, a grocery store that stays open late at night.

I find something wrong with every house. The living room is too dark, the bathrooms are old, the low ceilings make me claustrophobic. The agent drives us to half a dozen listings before deciding to skip our remaining appointments. She shows us the town of Milford instead. The center is lovely with an old-fashioned square, the village green flanked by a couple of churches, and an old bridge that crosses a stream in the center of town. But subsequently, to get back to the highway we have to pass through the gloomy industrial section where cars are stacked up on top of one another and old smokestacks pepper our view of the sea.

On the way home Dan says, "I thought I'd be the picky one."

"I hate that town," I answer. "It's depressing and it's not convenient for either of us. I don't want to live there."

"Well, I can't live in that motel much longer. My company only gave me so much money for relocating. I have a right to see my children too."

"Well, you should have thought of that before you took the new job."

"That's not fair. You told me I should. You agreed to move to Connecticut."

"All my friends think it's lousy you're making us leave the city and my job after we've already been through so much this year."

"Don't blame me if you don't want to go back to work. I'm willing to compromise. I'm fine with Milford. What do you want us to do, live on your salary while I look for a new job? There are no operations jobs in New York City. You can't say I haven't been telling you this for some time." He's angry now.

We need Dan's salary. I am relieved he is enjoying his new job, the business trips that take him abroad to China, Korea, and India. But I am also aware that if we move I will often be left alone with the boys in the middle of nowhere.

"Let's go look at towns around Hartford next weekend," I say. There's a part of me that has known I would come around to this idea. And another part that has resisted. Hartford is the place where 84 merges into 91 and you always get caught in traffic. It's the city John Gunther Jr. poked fun at while dying of a brain tumor at age seventeen in *Death Be Not Proud*.

"You just want to drag this out as long as possible."

"No, I'm serious. If I go back to work at all it's going to be part-time, in which case Hartford makes more sense." I hate the terms "working mother" and "stay-at-home mom." These are my two choices and neither feels right.

"It's okay with me, as long as you've really thought it through," Dan says finally. "Which I'm not sure you have. But you cannot come to me later and say it's my fault you gave up your career. For the record, you have to acknowledge this."

"Fine," I agree. But over the next months, whenever I am lonely or bored, I will casually mention that he's to blame.

"We could drive up to Hartford now," he says. He is so impatient. "We could call your mom and see if she can spend the night."

"No, I have to bring back all this milk," I answer. "Besides, we have to find someone to show us houses."

I change the radio station and sit back. I've bought myself another week in Manhattan.

"I CAN COMMUTE TWO DAYS a week to the office, and work one morning from home, but it's going to be hard to manage so I can't take a pay cut." I am sitting on the couch inside the reluctantly tweedy, former hippie editor in chief's office on my alleged return date wearing my portable backpack pump over my windbreaker.

"I need you in the office at least four days a week."

"There's no way. I can't do it."

He appears sad even though he is smiling. "Am I making the choice easier for you?"

"Even if I weren't going to be coming in from Connecticut, I couldn't leave the boys four days a week."

"You're already forgetting what it's like here, how you worked night and day. Your position requires someone full-time. But the publisher said he would arrange something else for you if you wanted to do some part-time work. He suggested putting together a contract for you to continue developing your hardcover authors."

"That sounds great."

"Figure out how much you want to do and talk to him about it." The editor in chief has been making eye contact but now he really looks at me. He asks, "How do you feel?"

"Okay," I say. "I'm not sure when it'll hit me that I'm really giving up my position."

"You're making the right decision for those boys. Gus Cannon and Sam Minton are great names. They sound like a couple of ballplayers."

We are quiet for a minute, listening to the cars honking on

Broadway, to the managing editor out in the hallway screaming about a missed deadline. I've been the addressee of the managing editor's fury enough times to appreciate that right now he looks just like the guy Edvard Munch painted in *The Scream*. I say softly, "For a while it was horrible. I mean really truly bad."

The reluctantly tweedy, former hippie editor in chief rests his hand on my right shoulder, on top of the vinyl backpack strap. "I know," he says. "We're going to miss you. We already miss you."

Seven months have passed since I last came to work here every day. I pull some photographs of Sam and Gus out of my pocketbook to show my former editor in chief, and then I hug him good-bye.

Monday morning I call the publisher. I had worked as his assistant for a couple of years before becoming an editor. He takes my call and says he is happy for me to continue editing my hardcover authors. This is a real coup to have found him so amenable. The publisher, the son of an Indian diplomat, is famously inscrutable and inaccessible. He learned long ago that silence coupled with a dark, penetrating stare is an advantage in any negotiation. We schedule a lunch for the following week.

While the boys are sleeping, I ring everyone on my Rolodex. I tell them that I will not be continuing as a paperback editor, so that I can concentrate fully on hardcovers. Since hardcovers are considered more glamorous than paperbacks, everyone thinks it's a promotion.

"How often will you be in the office?" the agents and authors ask.

"We haven't figured out all the details. I think I'll balance it so that I do some work from home and some in the office. I just thought you'd want to know I'll be back."

"Great," they all say and start shooting questions about their books. I promise I'll get back to them with answers and quickly end the calls.

A week later I leave the boys with Michelle to meet the publisher for lunch at an airy midtown restaurant around the corner from the new offices. The smoking ban has gone into effect in New York City. Still, without prompting, the young waiter charmingly rests an ashtray on our table in front of the publisher. This is the kind of loyalty the inscrutable Indian publisher, who presides over a large company while remaining defiantly mistrustful of authority, inspires.

The publisher lights an American Spirit and asks, "So, Jenny, tell me. What have you been up to?" While I was his assistant he occasionally sent me downstairs to the newsstand in our lobby to buy his cigarettes. He also introduced me to opera, taught me to edit, and gave me his first edition of *Vanity Fair* illustrated by Thackeray himself.

He has a gentle, regal voice. He often pauses to inhale and does not resume talking. Following these uncomfortable breaks in conversation, I've heard numerous people blurt out the most embarrassing confessions as an automatic response to the silence.

"I haven't been up to much of anything. Taking care of babies mostly. I did go out to Long Island City to see the new Museum of Modern Art."

"How was it?"

"They had a great Matisse and Picasso exhibit. The setup is pretty cool too. You should go while it's still out there. The 7 train stops a block away."

The publisher scoffs and I laugh knowingly. He would never ride the subway. But I am fairly sure he would like it.

"I think you should decide soon if you want to come back now," he says, and drags on his cigarette. "Otherwise we'll need to redistribute your authors. The ones with books coming out may be getting anxious."

"Would I be working from home?" I look at him searchingly. Has he figured out a way for me to represent my authors without actually coming in to the office?

"If that's what you want."

"I doubt my authors would appreciate their editor going AWOL. How would I fight for their rights?"

He smiles. "Some might not like it but others wouldn't mind."

"It's not like there's a spare office you could keep empty for my occasional trip to town. I'd have to set up shop in the hallway. How would I acquire new authors? Agents aren't going to send me submissions up in Connecticut when there are a million editors right here in New York. I'd have a handful of writers following me out to pasture. It sounds like the kind of thing you do when you're moving toward retirement. I don't really feel old enough to retire." The waiter arrives with our plates. I hate prattling on and getting flustered in front of the publisher.

"How old are you again?" he asks, stubbing out his cigarette. The waiter swoops in to remove the dirty ashtray and replace it with a new one.

"Thirty-one."

"You have a few years yet," he says gently. "But we should get your authors reassigned if you're going to bug off for a while."

"I've stranded fifteen authors." I think this number will impress him.

"Twelve," he says, quickly adding, "We can find a desk for you somewhere. You'll let me know what you decide."

At that he changes the subject, asking what movies I've seen lately (none), which books I've liked (still none), whether I've been watching the Iraqi war news coverage on the BBC? Graciously he steers the conversation to subjects on which I can converse, and if he notices that this morning's headlines are the only ones with which I am familiar, he lets it slide.

After we've finished our lunch, I awkwardly hug him good-bye outside the company's new high-rise and promise to get back to him in a few weeks with my answer. He passes through the revolving doors. I stand under the scaffolding for five minutes because it has started to rain, and then I request a new visitor's pass, and am asked to show my ID a second time to the same guard who examined it earlier in the afternoon. I run back up to the publisher's office. He is reading his e-mails on his laptop and looks neither surprised nor overjoyed to see me again so soon.

"I can't think about this for another minute. I'm not coming back. I need some time to pull my act together, to get set up somewhere in Connecticut." Somehow I can't bring myself to say "relocate to Connecticut" though this is how I worded it to myself in the elevator. "For now it's probably better for me to be with my boys."

"Okay," he says.

"Can I call you in six months if I really miss my job?"

The inscrutable Indian publisher smiles. "You won't miss your job," he says. How long has he known I would arrive at this decision?

A minute later I'm out on the sidewalk again, walking home for good, and I take my time even though it's raining. I pay attention to the cool, hard water falling on my face, weighing down my hair, soaking through my jacket sleeves. The reliable umbrella salesmen appear out of nowhere on every corner, ready to serve those of us who are caught forever unprepared, but right now I choose to expose myself—whatever cannot be stripped away—to the impartial, open sky.

At home I flip through my Rolodex again, possibly the last nonelectronic Rolodex in Manhattan, and make another round of calls. "I know I said I was coming back to work, but it turns out that I'm not."

Everyone is gracious. No one is devastated. They all say they understand. They have already moved on.

———

IT DOES NOT CONCERN ME that at six and a half months the boys cannot sit even with support or bear some weight on their legs, as they should be able to do according to *What to Expect the First Year*. I met the parents of a baby with Down syndrome who claimed they threw this book across the room after it failed to predict a single aspect of their baby's first year correctly. Why do I continue to refer to it even though I know that Sam's and Gus's maturation will lag behind the developmental milestones by at least two months? But usually, if I use the boys' due date rather than their actual birth date to calculate their age, the book confirms that they are developing appropriately. It does bother me a little that Gus still cannot, on his stomach, raise his head off the ground at a 90-degree angle, something that, according to the book, he should have mastered at four months.

At a get-together with Holly I notice that her six-month-old is self-feeding from her bottle. I comment on it and Holly tries to instruct Sam and Gus how to drink by themselves. But their muscles are still too weak to hold the bottles properly.

Was I wrong to defect from physical therapy? This is what I worry about in the middle of the night, while trying to block out Sam's and Gus's cries. Dr. Zhukov has finally discontinued the boys' reflux medication. We dropped the medications one by one and held our breath waiting to see if they had outgrown their reflux. Although they continue to projectile-vomit now and again, their stomachs seem fine. And since Sam and Gus no longer need to be fed medicine, we are trying to wean them off night feedings. If it were solely Dan's responsibility he might succeed, as he has learned to sleep through their crying. But, to me, every whine is torturous.

One night I throw my pillow at Dan. "How can you possibly sleep?"

"I'm not anymore."

"I can't stand this."

"What do you want to do?" he asks. "Give them a bottle?"

"I don't know. Why am I always the one who has to decide? I don't know any better than you do."

Dan is falling back to sleep.

I kick the sheets off the bed. "Fine. I guess we should feed them."

I make my way, through the dark, into the bathroom. I sit down on the toilet and fall through the hole. My bottom is soaked. "Ugh!" I yell. "Dan, can't you *please* just put the toilet seat back down?"

I hear him chuckling in the bedroom. "It's not funny," I say, feeling along the wall for a towel.

"Actually, it is."

I trudge into the kitchen and fill two bottles. I poke my head back into our room. Next door, the boys' cries are growing louder. "Come on. The sooner we get it over with, the sooner we can sleep."

"I was sleeping."

He follows me into the boys' room and sits down with Gus on the couch while I rock Sam across the room. Occasionally a car passes below on the street, shining its lights through the window. Once I'm in the glider I relax. At this hour, even in Manhattan, the night is mostly shadows. I can feel Sam's heart pounding.

D AN'S PARENTS RENT A HOUSE in Jamaica for a week in June so all of their children and grandchildren, nieces and grand-nephews can celebrate my father-in-law's seventieth birthday.

Gus is miserable in Jamaica. He gets a rash from the heat, his eyelids are puffy and swollen, he catches a cold and throws up. He flinches in the sun, cries when I put him down on the sand.

Sam, on the other hand, has found his element in the hot, salty tropical air. He loves watching the overhead fans, laughs as the Jamaican cook lifts him up, passes him off to the housekeeper. The staff is crazy about him. His cousins compete to spoon-feed him bananas. For the first time in his short life Sam seems happy. His grandparents ask, "Is Sam really the difficult one?" Dan and I laugh at how Sam has discovered how to turn on the charm.

At night it cools down a bit, and we are able to relax and enjoy dinner. Dan's siblings tell their childhood stories, which by now I know by heart. I chime in with details from their family trips through Jordan, arms getting broken, appendixes being removed.

One evening toward the end of the week, we drink too much wine and Matt overhears me earnestly telling his wife that I think I peaked intellectually in the seventh grade. Matt reports back to Dan and Cannon, who decide that the only way to disrupt such an uninteresting conversation is to jump in the pool, which they proceed to do immediately, fully dressed.

Bruce dives in next, then Megan. I turn to Matt's wife, Elizabeth. "We have to go in."

"In our clothes?"

"Right now."

I do a cannonball. Dan's cousins jump in, along with my mother-in-law, who is wearing a long skirt, the only adult still sober. The older children who haven't yet been put to bed come outside bug-eyed from watching TV in the dark, and are thrilled to have finally found some excitement. Of course they are conveniently wearing their bathing suits underneath their shorts; two of them have goggles around their necks. In they come. Soon we are all floating in the pool, under the stars, in our summer clothing.

There is still uncertainty about my father-in-law's cancer.

There is still the trip home to look forward to: the van to the airport, customs, piling onto the plane, which is then delayed. Two nights from now I will slam Dan on the back as hard as I can when we finally land at Kennedy after midnight and he cancels the van I ordered because they refuse to pull up to the Arrivals curb. I'll hit the redial button and beg the dispatcher to send another car to Departures, Arrivals, anywhere because we have twin infants and too much luggage to fit into a taxi, and there aren't any around anyway. Sam will be screaming in the background.

"I'll do it only because it's late and you have two babies," she'll say. "But I do not appreciate your husband acting so rude."

I'll hang up and punch Dan again even harder, after which he won't talk to me for a couple of days.

But on this clear night in Jamaica we dive underwater weighed down by our blouses and skirts. We rise up through the surface, laugh when we meet each other's eyes, at the dangling earrings, the bubbling T-shirts, at peaking intellectually in the seventh grade. We put on dry underwear and climb, wet-haired, into bed under our mosquito nets. And when I wake in the early hours of the morning before Sam and Gus, I feel like I have a secret, that even when Sam rolls over in his crib and smiles up at me mischievously, he does not understand.

THE TOWN OF WEST HARTFORD looks like it still belongs in the fifties. Tudor-roofed shops line the streets downtown. Rows of saltbox houses are set further back from the curbs than in the suburbs of New York. What we like immediately are the sidewalks, which we imagine ourselves pushing Sam and Gus down in their double stroller. We are the underbidders for the first house we bid on. Then we get the second one, a square brick colonial that is losing its coat of white paint. The backyard abuts a golf course, and I am happy that although we will have neighbors on both sides, we will be able to see through to wide-open space. I imagine taking Sam and Gus sledding on the rolling hills during winter if the course is open to the public.

I moved to New York when I was twenty-two. Ten years later I'm leaving. Although the city will always be there for visits, I will no longer have a subway route home, a corner bodega to run out to at 11 p.m. for milk or more ice.

Unable to catch a cab, jostled by the crowds, out-of-towners tell me, "I could never live here." I nod sympathetically and offer them a drink of cold water. On humid summer days I run into acquaintances waiting for the subway and can think of nothing else to talk about but the smog. I have, on occasion, briefly longed to live in a place where the birds weren't all flying rats, the riverfront wasn't jammed with honking cars, and the people weren't so aggressive. But grass and clean air aside, New York City encompasses nearly everything I love.

IN MID JULY, DAN AND I INVITE Angela's parents and her twin sister along for our last walk in Central Park. I don't mention to Angela's parents that we're moving because I don't want to have to discuss it. Angela is still in the NICU. After her kidney infection, she developed NEC (necrotizing enterocolitis). It is caused by a disruption of the blood flow to a section of the intestines, causing it to deteriorate. Surgery is required to remove that part of the intestines, which can in turn lead to severe, chronic malabsorption, which creates nutritional problems that retard growth and often cause life-threatening infections.

Earlier this week a woman stopped on the sidewalk to admire Sam and Gus. She told me her five-year-old twins, a girl and a boy, were born prematurely and except for the shunt in the boy's head to prevent hydrocephalus—too much brain fluid caused by a serious peripartum brain bleed—both of them were doing great. At summer's end they would be starting kindergarten. Since more than 50 percent of twins are born prematurely I should not be so surprised that mothers tell me such stories.

I prop bottles on top of burp cloths, but most of the milk spills out onto the boys' T-shirts and soon they are fussing. Dan pushes our stroller toward the big lake as the rest of us fall behind. We cross a bridge and look out at the skyscrapers sparkling along Central Park West. The view of the Dakota is timeless. It is my favorite spot in the park. There are tourists in rowboats bending over the water to escape the humidity in the air.

"We don't know that Angela will ever make it out. She's still on a respirator," Angela's mother tells me. The father looks me in the eye for an answer, possibly, instinctively, because I have both of my boys. I wonder if this is one of the first outings Angela's parents and sister have been on as a family. And if her parents have started to scale back their visits to the NICU.

"I'm sorry Angela's had to stay in the hospital all this time. But she's hung on for so long I bet she'll be okay."

The mother says, "Thank you." The father turns his gaze onto his daughter, who is asleep.

I wonder if I have just said the entirely wrong thing to Angela's mother. Did I sound vacantly upbeat? I hope I have not made her feel worse.

I tread so cautiously around sorrow. My tendency is to be relentlessly optimistic. I adopt a tone I've overheard my mother use with my sister and brother on the phone. Faced with a problem, my mother will map out the next several steps her son or daughter should take to get back on track again. A person is permitted a certain amount of remorse and then it is time to make a plan. But can I actually believe you must wait to share your story until you are able to illuminate the bright side? Is it only fair to burden an audience with your pain if you can provide a silver lining?

I hear Sam and Gus crying in their stroller ahead of me. I try to ignore them. A passerby stops Dan and we catch up with him just as she is saying, "Twins? I don't know how you do it." I smile uncomfortably.

"Okay, enough," I say to Dan. "Let's take them out."

"Aren't babies supposed to fall asleep in strollers? Look at their baby," Dan says logically.

"Let's just carry them for a while."

Angela's parents smile patiently while I pull Sam out and hand him off to Dan. I take out Gus and hoist him over my shoulder, leaving Dan to carry Sam in one arm and push the empty stroller with the other.

We walk over to the fountain. Both boys are crying. "Maybe they're hot," I say. "Let's let them dip their feet in the fountain. They love swimming."

I pull off their socks. At eight months, they have no reason to wear shoes. Then we dangle their legs in the fountain. Pigeon feathers and cigarette butts drift past their feet; green poop is stuck to the sides of the stone bowl.

Angela's sister wakes up, and her father carries her to a nearby ice-cream stand. He returns holding a Popsicle for her to suck. A smart solution to the heat.

By the time we reach the park exit at Sixty-eighth Street, Dan's and my T-shirts are drenched with sweat, our arms are killing us.

I hug Angela's mother good-bye. Dan shakes her father's hand.

"We should do this again," Angela's mother says.

Dan starts to answer, but I shoot him a look: *Don't.* "Sounds great. I'll call you," I say.

Then Angela's parents head up Museum Mile and we cross at the light.

"Why didn't you tell them that we're moving?"

"Our friendship is too new to endure a move to Connecticut. They have enough on their plate as it is."

"I think you're in denial."

At home I leave each boy in the tub with Dan for half an hour. He washes their bodies and then I kneel down with a washcloth and scrub their arms and legs again. The next day, on the Toys R Us Web site, I find a red plastic car with a blue handle and yellow hood that looks like an old VW bug. I order two and have them shipped directly to our new house in Connecticut.

I t's the end of july and we are officially leaving. We have a moving date and a truck. But before we go, it is essential that we get our eight-month-olds sleeping through the night. Although according to *The Essential Guide for Parents of Premature Babies*, by the time premature infants are six months from their actual due date, which is their age if corrected for prematurity, they may start to settle into longer periods of sleep, on most nights our boys still wake up every few hours and I can't take it anymore. So while Dan spends four nights a week at a hotel in Connecticut waiting for the closing on our house, I hire Lorna, the baby nurse, to come back for two weeks to get my boys on a schedule. I tell Dan that I am willing to sacrifice all of our savings toward the goal of having our boys learn to sleep.

Within a day I have agreed—no, insisted—that Lorna's twelve-year-old daughter, Venicia, should take the subway down from the Bronx and stay with us. Michelle is also spending the nights in order to learn the schedule. So there are six of us, three black women from Trinidad, the boys, and me, living in a two-bedroom apartment.

Lorna's method is similar to a baby-scheduling book that arrives in the mail addressed from Holly at ABC. The book instructs us to make the boys' room as dark as possible. I walk to the hardware store to purchase room-darkening shades. Lorna copies the routine from the book onto a piece of notebook paper and sticks it on the refrigerator. She says that the timetable is simply a stricter version of her own system. Does she presume I'm a person who likes to do things by the book? We put the boys down for an hour nap in the morning and two hours in the afternoon, but when they doze off at any other time we jostle them awake. She increases their bottles to seven ounces hoping they will consume enough during the day to carry them through the night, and the bigger bottles do seem to better satisfy them whenever they don't vomit all the milk up. Although their reflux had been under control when they were drinking less, it flares up again now. Each time the boys stir during the night Lorna pats them to sleep without giving them a bottle. She tells me to quit rushing in to change the boys' diapers every time they cry, since the feel of cold air on their bottoms wakes them more fully. Lorna, Michelle, Venicia, and I take turns sitting silently in pitch darkness to deliver bottles.

Then after Sam and Gus have fallen asleep, Lorna cooks dinner, "something with protein"—she loves the word "protein"—and the four of us watch scary movies. Venicia is timid and skinny and wants to be a forensic pathologist when she grows up. Each night she and I head to Blockbuster and return with a more terrifying tape. She has, of course, already seen *The Bone Collector*. But we rent it again anyway, along with *The Fly, Final Destination, Final Destination 2, Panic Room, Hannibal*. I am surprised to find they are still making the Halloween movies. I haven't watched films like these since I was a kid; I bury my face in a pillow and giggle at the bloody suspense. When the movies are over, Venicia and I go to sleep in my bed while Lorna and Michelle take to the pullout couch in the living room. Lorna doesn't sleep much anyway. At the smallest sound, she wakes and goes in to hush the boys without allowing them any milk. Sam accepts the change readily and on the third night sleeps through, but Gus has trouble falling back to sleep without a nipple in his mouth, so we flood his crib with pacifiers that he can find in the dark.

On the weekends, Michelle heads to Brooklyn and Dan comes home, and we are still six. Venicia moves onto the couch with her mother. Sunday afternoon, Lorna asks us if it is okay for her to invite her older daughter and son up from Brooklyn for supper. Of course we say yes. I go out and buy pork chops.

I return to find Dan sitting amidst Lorna's entire family. They are laughing and teasing one another and he has joined right in. Venicia and her sister are holding the boys on their laps.

Now that his work has taken him out of they city, Dan has relinquished our spot in our building's garage. After dinner he goes to move his car to the alternate side of the street, where parking is legal on Saturdays, and on his way back runs into a friend who offers to buy us a beer.

"Are you guys okay here?" I ask.

"Oh sure," Lorna tells me. "Go and have your fun."

They are all gathered around the TV, still laughing, as they send us off.

"This is insane," Dan says while we wait for the elevator. "Our apartment has been taken over by a family from Trinidad. And we're going broke paying for it. I've been demoted to number seven. First Sam and Gus, then Michelle, then Venicia and Lorna, then you, and I'm last, working my butt off to pay for everyone."

I laugh at how ridiculous it is. Our boys sleeping in their bedroom while our apartment and bank account has been handed over to an entirely new family. I have tears in my eyes; it is that kind of laughter.

We sit with Dan's friend on leather bar stools and they fall into old stories, which I am easily amused by tonight. We arrive home past midnight and I am still giggling, even after we are in bed and Dan is fast asleep.

By the end of the week, I have taken the boys and Venicia swimming in the basement pool of a neighboring apartment building; I have bought her the new Harry Potter book, and she has finished it; I have taught her to hit a tennis ball on a public court between First and Second avenues. We have stood outside our building trying to find the window from which, early that morning, an octogenarian had jumped. The driveway and main entrance are cordoned off in orange tape. We see the police enter the building and a few minutes later poke their heads out a window three stories from the top. Each time we return to the apartment, the boys appear to be happy under their mat with its fabric mobiles. When I tickle them, they giggle and squirm. Gus can finally raise his head to a 90-degree angle. Sometimes we come home to find the boys in their bouncy seats being fed baby food with a single spoon. They look at me with recognition and occasionally smile and then they go back to watching *Baby Mozart* on the television.

On their last night, a Thursday, before Dan arrives for the weekend, Venicia and I decide we are finished with scary movies, we have seen at least a dozen, and so we rent *Harry Potter and the Sorcerer's Stone* instead.

On the walk home from Blockbuster, Venicia asks me if I've had fun.

"Sure," I say. "Why?"

"My mom said you needed to have some fun in your life again."

Part Four

LAUGHING ON THE BUS, PLAYING GAMES WITH THE FACES

THE FIRST WEEK IN AUGUST I quit pumping. I drop one session at a time starting with the 11:00 p.m. I am surprised by how much it hurts to stop. It takes me ten days to wean myself off the pump. Sam and Gus are now nine months old. The pump rental lady who doubles as a lactation consultant stops by to pick up the machine and once it's out the door I feel liberated in a way I had not anticipated. All of a sudden I cannot imagine how I spent nearly three hours a day with my breasts attached to an engine. Early on Holly had sent me a package postmarked from ABC News. Inside was a strapless pumping bra with two holes to insert the cups. "It'll free up your hands so you can talk on the phone or work at your computer or even knit," she'd scribbled in the note. But I'd never gotten the plastic cups to fit onto the bra correctly.

We are scheduled to move to Connecticut two days before Dan and I fly to my brother's wedding in California. The boys will stay with Dan's parents in Queens while we're gone. My mother-in-law drives to our apartment, having just learned that her husband will soon need to schedule a third procedure to remove recurrent cancer cells from his liver. It is a hot, hazy summer day and the windows in the apartment are shut, the air conditioners on high. Sam and Gus are both crying, frightened by the movers banging shut wood crates. My mother-in-law and Michelle leave with the boys, and I follow the movers up to West Hartford. I immediately find the box I marked "sheets" and make our bed for the night. The movers ask me where to put the cribs, and although I decided I would give Sam and Gus their own bedrooms, I answer, "You can put them both in the blue room."

Dan meets me at the house at the end of his workday. We have dinner at an Italian restaurant in town. I am happy to be out at a restaurant for the first time in months, but Dan eats quickly, more interested in getting back to unpacking.

The next day Dan and I drive down to Queens to spend a few hours with the boys before we fly out to the wedding. Sam and Gus are intrigued by their grandparents' German shepherd, and I wonder if I will eventually have to get them a dog. Sam has just started to sit unsupported. Gus still flops forward awkwardly even when propped up with a Boppy pillow. He shifts himself into the yoga position called downward-facing dog and tries to push off. Why can't he just sit up? Even if I adjust for his corrected age, which is seven months, according to the books he should be able to sit without support by now. Will excitement at Sam's achievements always be undermined by our wanting his brother to catch up and vice versa? We play a game my brother invented on his last visit in which we press our noses against theirs and say "near," pull our faces away and say "far" in silly nasal voices that make Sam and Gus laugh and laugh.

Out in California, Will and Lane are married outdoors by a gray-bearded Unitarian minister in a white robe, which Lane has requested rather than risk the hippie poncho and patchwork pants he wore to their first meeting. Under a perfect blue California sky, Lane looks stunning in a strapless mermaid gown. Katie and I are the only two bridesmaids who chose not to have our hair pinned up by a stylist. We are also the only two women in the wedding party who primped by applying mascara and lipstick and eating sandwiches on Lane's bed. Beside Lane and her girlfriends' red-carpet elegance, Katie and I look like sorority dropouts. The difference in our styles can be attributed to our East Coast background: the other women all hail from out west. But for a moment, while we are all squeezing in close to Lane, I wish we had gone along and had our hair done up too.

If I am with Sam and Gus, making eye contact or laughing with them, I can note their intelligence. But across the continent, worry clouds my recollection of them and questions resurge. Why is Gus so much easier to engage in toys and books than 'Sam, who can seem remote? Recent studies suggest that premature babies may differ biologically from full-term babies, that the stresses of preterm birth might derail the normal development of brain cells. Is this why preemies are disproportionately prone to psychiatric illnesses like anxiety and attention-deficit hyperactivity disorder? When will I start to define motherhood according to my experience of having boys rather than girls, twins rather than children of different ages or an only child, as a parent of a lanky brown-haired boy and a smaller blond boy, instead of primarily as a mother of preemies?

A study of preemies who struggled with behavioral and learning problems during childhood and adolescence concluded that they led well-adjusted, normal lives once they reached adulthood. *The Essential Guide for Parents of Premature Babies* says that most do reach average weight and height, though often not until late adolescence. If I can just make it through eighteen more years will the shock finally subside?

My brother and his bride exchange vows and I start to cry. Not because they look so happy together, which they do, but because there will be difficult times ahead, because minutes after the service has ended Will has already requested a strong scotch from the bartender, and the day is achingly beautiful, because we are unable to see splendor without contrast, because there will always be near and far.

MICHELLE HAS AGREED TO TRAVEL to Connecticut to continue working for us. She takes the train up on Monday morning and stays until Thursday afternoon. Her children are visiting from

Trinidad for the summer, and I feel guilty that she has to leave them in her apartment in Brooklyn while she helps me take care of Sam and Gus.

I have spent more time with Michelle lately than with anyone other than my boys.

I'll lift up Sam if he's cranky and say, "Come on, Michelle." Then she'll pick up Gus and we'll dance around humming Beethoven's Fifth. I'll lean in close to her so that Sam's and Gus's noses are practically touching.

What I often forget, while we're watching *Access Hollywood* and *Extra,* baking fish in Italian dressing on the nights Dan works late, is that Michelle is my employee. And perhaps the reason she laughs at my jokes and seems to concur with everything I suggest is that I am the boss. She maintains a professional boundary while, in the absence of my girlfriends from the city, I treat her like my new best pal. I tell her she should bring her kids up to Connecticut with her, that they would love the playground and pool. They visited our apartment in Manhattan once and sat quietly in front of the television while Michelle fed Sam his bottle. "I can do it," I told her. "Why don't you show your kids the roof garden?"

"Because I'm working," she answered matter-of-factly.

I believe that she loves Sam and Gus. Today she shouts, "Jenny! Come here. You've got to see this!" I reach the top of the basement stairs down which Gus and Sam are inching their way backward.

"I taught them to turn around. And they're both getting the hang of it."

Not five minutes after they've learned to crawl, Sam and Gus head for the stairs. The doctor had said Gus would sit up before he crawled, but yesterday he stuck his butt in the air and crab-walked across the room, and he is still not sitting. Sam slides along the floor on his stomach.

Later in the afternoon, Michelle and I have our first quarrel.

Exhausted from unpacking boxes and a red eye fight home from the wedding, I tell her I am going upstairs to rest. She doesn't answer so I snap, "Don't be mad because I'm not going to help you for a few hours. You're only here four days. I never get a break."

"I didn't say nothin'," she replies.

"Exactly." I march upstairs wondering how I have gotten to the point where my babysitter expects me to assist her all the time. I sulk for half an hour and then apologize.

The next day I suggest that we take the boys for an introductory class at the town pool. Michelle agrees and we set off. She wears spandex shorts and a T-shirt because she doesn't have a bathing suit. She removes Gus's pink pacifier from the clip-on string and attaches a blue one. "Is that because he can't be seen with pink in public?" I ask.

"Of course." Once we're in the car Michelle mentions she can't swim.

She slips on the top step of the pool as she is holding Sam, but manages to protect him in her arms when she falls. Everyone turns to ask her if she's all right. She is the only black person in the pool. We line up along the wall and recite Humpty Dumpty. Sam and Gus are the first babies whose lips turn blue. They have no body fat to insulate them. The only father points to Gus and says, "Aren't all babies supposed to be fat like me?" Feeling cold doesn't seem to upset the boys. We lower them back into the pool and Gus dips his head into the water, trying to drink, while Sam splashes around smiling. He reaches for Michelle's sunglasses, pulls them off her head. The boys are covered in goose bumps when we climb out of the water half an hour later.

We all shiver in the women's locker room, where it takes us forever to strip off the wet swimming diapers and dress ourselves without putting the boys down on the dirty floor. On the way out I switch our session to Saturday mornings and tell Michelle that I wouldn't want Dan to have to miss out.

"I can't put you through this again, Michelle," I say.

She laughs and pulls her stash of cashews from the diaper bag. We gossip about one mother who kept trying to boss everyone about another who pulled her daughter away from Gus after he coughed up some water.

I stop at the Walgreen's on the way home. "I'll just be a sec. I want to get Sam some sunglasses of his own so he doesn't keep trying to break yours."

In aisle three I find a rack of sunglasses for children three years and older. I quickly grab a pair of silver plastic rims with a small Spiderman on the bottom left corner of the lens and a pair with blue-webbed rims and red frames. Tobey Maguire's *Spiderman* has been playing in theaters all summer. I open the back door of the car, and slide the silver ones onto Sam's face, the blue ones onto Gus's. They both immediately pull them off. Sam bites on the earpiece just like my father does when he's reading. Gus tries to put his on again and cries in frustration so I fit the glasses back over his ears. He yanks them off. His hands are freezing. He must have terrible circulation. I put his glasses on for him a few more times before folding them onto his lap and climbing into the driver's seat, ignoring his cries.

Michelle reaches back to unfold the frames and adjusts Gus's glasses onto his nose. She turns to face forward and says, "Those silver glasses really suit Sammy. He looks like a little white roughneck. You know what I'm sayin'. Not in a bad way."

"It's okay," I laugh.

"He reminds me of those blond surfers I've seen around."

"In Brooklyn?"

"Those blond surfer types. To me they're always wearing silver shades. I think Sammy will be a Miami bad boy with the girls all after him. "

"What about Gus's? You think the blue is right for him?"

"Gus is Joe Cool. Gussy is going to be a romantic," she says.

"He'll take wining and dining very seriously. At least that's how I see it."

"That's how I see it too," I say.

We stop for a red light. Gus is absolutely still with his glasses on as if he's afraid they might fall off. "What do you think we should give them for supper?" I ask her.

"How about meatloaf?"

"I think so. They haven't had meatloaf in a few days."

"You think Sammy will eat it?" she asks.

"We can make some fish sticks just in case."

The boys are boycotting baby food. They clamp their mouths shut when they see a spoon coming and push it away. If I shove a bite into their mouths, they scream and immediately cough it out. So we cut frozen entrées into tiny pieces on their trays, and they occasionally stick a morsel into their mouths. Sam is far pickier than Gus. Most foods, including all fruits and vegetables, he immediately spits out. Could this be, as I have read, because certain preemies associate the pain or discomfort of being intubated with any object inserted into their mouths?

I turn on the radio and we sing along with Beyoncé. Michelle has a lovely voice. She sings in her church. I check the rearview mirror. Sam and Gus are facing backward, but I can see they still have on the glasses. I imagine they are staring out the window, wiped out from swimming.

"Another day," Michelle says as we pull in to the garage.

"Another day."

Tomorrow Michelle will take the train to Brooklyn. She tells me that on Sundays she always cooks something after church. A few years ago she literally shopped for churches and ended up a Baptist. Maybe this weekend she and her mother will bake a macaroni pie. Will they laugh about the Stouffer's meatloaf and Gordon's fish sticks that I microwave for the boys because I am a terrible cook? About my spending money on sunglasses and swimming lessons for nine-month-olds? I can't say for sure, but somehow I don't think so.

BEFORE DAN AND I WERE MARRIED I agreed to raise our children Catholic. If I shop around enough, will I be able to find a Catholic church that condones scientific advances like reproductive medicine? Mary didn't need to have sex in order to conceive the son of God. Why can't Sam and Gus be His children too?

You can now buy books that explain reproductive technology to children between ages three and five. There are several different versions to choose from—the traditional IVF adventure, ICSI (injecting a single sperm straight into an oocyte), donor eggs. Still, I imagine Dan and I will want to devise our own version of the boys' conception and preterm birth. We will need to fortify them with an interpretation so that they never worry that their origin is "undignified," as the American Society of Catholic Bishops claim. I hope to teach Sam and Gus that everyone's origins are scientific, not just their own. To me, the sciences—including mathematics and psychology—make the world seem more miraculous, not less.

I anticipate the day Sam and Gus come to me with a theological question, and only partly because it will mean they have learned to talk. On the one hand I will be sad to see the end of the present stage, in which their curiosity about how things work has not yet led them to fret over where they came from. But I am eager to instill in our boys my belief that they were conceived through hope, that God and science are behind the unknowns of the universe.

ALL THROUGH AUGUST, Gus has a terrible wheezing cough. I am certain it is asthma, for which preemies are at risk. At the boys' nine-month checkup I inform the pediatrician, who says we should keep a close eye on him, but that asthma is difficult to diagnose in children under two.

"Any other concerns?" The pediatrician my mother used to take us to once told her he clocked numerous hours of boredom at his office interrupted by moments of sheer terror. I should not have accepted the appointment slot right before lunch.

"The asthma is really my primary concern at the moment. Gus coughs an awful lot at night in his crib and during the day if he's active. But I worry about all sorts of silly things." I have not called our pediatrician once in the past three months. Instead I have been compiling a list of questions I planned to ask at this appointment. That I did not have to bother him with phone calls to return at the end of his day struck me as seriously unneurotic. Now I smile to downplay what I'm about to say in person. "Gus isn't sitting yet. And he cannot pick up a Cheerio, which I've read indicates delayed fine motor skills that could make it hard for him to learn to write. Sam doesn't as readily engage with people. Sometimes he doesn't respond to his name." Sam has climbed inside a toy box in the corner of the examining room, where he is handling germ-infested Legos. He looks up at me uncertainly. I have a sinking feeling I am betraying my sons. I decide not to mention anything else. "I should probably put a moratorium on my preemie reading list."

Gus is squirming, trying to get to the floor. I can tell I've lost our pediatrician's attention. He is thinking about the ham sandwich his wife packed him for lunch, hoping she slid a few Oreos into the bottom of the bag. I try to reel him back in. "Pediatricians must lose sleep worrying about their own kids because you know all the things that could possibly go wrong."

The pediatrician nods and reaches for his ear instrument. "You hope your children will be on the big yellow school bus just like everybody else. You're afraid the little bus that picks up the children with special needs will be pulling into your driveway each morning. We all are. No parent wants her child to have to take the little bus."

He throws this out nonchalantly, as if it's a line he uses often. Still, I want to embrace him. I'm surprised he has spoken so bluntly. Is there truth in what he says? Could it all boil down to my being afraid of the little bus?

"You've probably heard that preemies are at greater risk for learning disabilities." He is trying to examine Gus's ears, but Gus keeps yanking his head away from the instrument. "But your boys may not have other contributing factors such as intraventricular hemorrhages, a chaotic home environment, or a family history of learning disabilities."

"It's okay, Gus," I say, holding his head against my chest so the doctor can get a better look.

"Both ears are clear. I'm going to give him an antibiotic anyway to see if it helps clear up the cough."

"I just wish I could know right now that Sam's and Gus's aptitude for writing, or math, or memory, hasn't been compromised by their premature birth." As at every visit to the pediatrician, I can feel that my face is flushed, but now my eyes well up with tears. *Hold yourself together.* This pediatrician is talking to me as a peer. If I cry I'll just throw off the balance. I laugh. "I guess we'll have to wait and see."

"How about this?" he offers. "We'll give these guys until their next checkup at twelve months, and if you're still concerned we can have them evaluated by a psychiatrist and social worker for Early Intervention Services. Early intervention can help children overcome deficits before they can become an issue in school."

I have been seeking guarantees in vain, and I should know better. He has assured me that my apprehensions are no different from those of other parents. But he does not own a crystal ball. If I push him for more, he can only offer evaluations and referrals.

I leave the doctor's office and while driving to the park I call

Dan on my cell. "So you sold Sammy and Gus down the river," he says.

"I did not sell them down the river. I just don't think we should ignore problems if they arise."

"'If' being the critical word," he says.

"I didn't sell them down the river."

"Okay, okay. Just relax. There's nothing wrong with them."

Is my reluctance to have a psychologist evaluate the boys for early intervention while they are still at such a young, preverbal stage fueled by denial? Or do I realize that by inviting the psychiatrist to do her job I'm encouraging her to pin on each boy a diagnosis that is at best reductive? Why can't I bear to hear anything slightly critical about my boys? I vow to myself that I'll apply for help, if needed, down the road. But right now what seems most important to me is to be able to treat Sam and Gus just like babies. So, why then, given our feelings, did I have to needlessly alarm our pediatrician?

In the parking lot I strap the boys into the double stroller and push them to the playground where I set Sam down in the sandbox. I rest on a bench with Gus in my lap. A woman sitting beside me asks if the boys are from IVF.

"So was my daughter," she says, pointing to a little girl in the sandbox. "Four years and six tries."

"You must have been so happy."

"Not really," she says. "I spent most of my pregnancy worrying because the amniocentesis [a procedure that draws amniotic fluid out of the baby's sac to test for various birth defects and genetic diseases] showed that two of her genes were tangled, a piece of one had traded places with a piece of another. We decided to have her anyway although the balanced translocation put her at risk of retardation. But she's two years old now and as healthy as can be."

I look at the woman's daughter, a round-faced child with blond curls shoveling sand into a pail and pouring it out.

"She's beautiful," I say.

"It's pretty common, I think, for IVF babies to have a glitch or two. I guess there are some glitches in the process that still haven't been worked out. I've heard a number of stories about IVF kids who have something wrong with them."

I'm not sure how to respond. This is a horrible thought. Glitches are for computer programs and voting machines.

Sam has left the sandbox and is heading toward the swings. I excuse myself and catch up to him. I pick Sam up and carry the boys, one in each arm, to the swings.

Years ago in the town where I grew up, a grandmother backed her car out of her driveway and accidentally ran over her grandson. At the time my mom said, "If I ever did something like that, you couldn't hold it against me if I killed myself."

"Of course I could," I had replied. "You would make me grieve two deaths rather than one?"

But on a recent visit to my parents' house my mom said again, "Every day you're here that I back down the driveway and don't hit one of the boys I'm so grateful." She laughed nervously. "I may sound crazy, but it's true. If I were somehow responsible for Gus's or Sam's death, there is no way I could go on living. Do you understand?"

And this time I said yes.

It's not that I think Sam or Gus is going to die. I worry about accidents. But what I understand now that I didn't before my children were born is that if the danger I exposed them to through IVF and a multiple birth has damaged them, it may seem for the rest of my life as if I failed to see my boys in the rearview mirror. My reaction to this fear is to feel as if I've been hit by a car myself. My shoulders sag, my arms go numb like a limp raggedy doll. Am I overreacting?

I try to stop panicking by focusing on Sam and Gus.

I know their features by heart. Sam's expressions vary from

"come help me right this instant," to "leave me alone," to radiant pleasure, and somewhere deep in Gus's eyes he is always checking to make sure you love him enough. I carry Gus in my arms and his legs dangle heavily; sometimes he tries pushing off me to set himself free. Sam, on the other hand, usually hooks his legs around my body, evenly distributing his weight. Sam is quite a bit lighter than Gus now. So far not one aspect of their emerging selves has surprised me.

When, six months down the road, Gus is imitating everything we do, clapping his hands on car rides and singing "Wee wee wee" and Sam is pushing a fire truck, pressing on the siren again and again, it will all still make sense.

Although each day they wake up with a newly acquired talent, a way of laughing and diving down in their cribs to hide from me, I find that essentially they are who they were from the start. Which should assure me that I have not deprived them of anything vital. Napoleon Bonaparte, John Keats, Voltaire, Albert Einstein, Isaac Newton, Charles Darwin, Winston Churchill: *The Essential Guide for Parents of Premature Babies* is filled with illustrious figures throughout history who made their mark despite, or perhaps even because of, their shortened gestation.

A number of renowned scientists appear on the list. Einstein claimed that because he was developmentally delayed he did not stop to wonder about time and space until he was grown, at which point most adults were no longer giving it much thought. Regardless of the advantages or disadvantages former preemies have attributed to their unconventional starts, Sam and Gus have come through so far blissfully unaware of anything unusual in their mother's attentive nurturing and jittery joyousness.

Are our boys the exact same children they would be if I'd made it to full term? We will never know. Perhaps it's a worthless question. Even if Sam and Gus had avoided prematurity and its accompanying problems in their infancies, they would eventually have encountered difficulties during their toddler years and later in childhood. The boys would have faced and still will meet hardships ahead. And who they become will have as much to do with how they surmount these obstacles as with who they were at the start.

At home there's a message on our machine from Angela's mother saying that she had tried calling us and an automated voice had given her this number. Have we moved? "Well, anyway," she says, "I just wanted to tell you that Angela passed away. She died from complications due to her NEC. She had so little left of her intestines she could not digest properly and then developed an infection that killed her." Startled, I play the message again before saving her telephone number on the machine.

Gus wheezes, cough, cough, cough, as he crab-walks from the family room into the living room to check in with me again. Sam won't play patty-cake so we shake the rattles instead and I show him how to turn on the kitchen faucet.

I do not leave Gus's and Sam's side for several days. By the end of the week, with so much free time, Michelle has cleaned, washed clothes and windows, and the entire house is immaculate.

THE FIRST TIME SAM PULLS himself up he isn't crawling properly yet. He slithers up to the bathtub, reaches for the rim, and hauls himself into a vertical position. "How did he do that?" Dan asks. "I'm not ready for him to be standing. He's not big enough." He does look funny, absurd even, with his little body sprouting upright from the ground. He is nine months old.

On one of the last unbearably humid days of August, Gus sits up. He is crab-walking across the spare bedroom that serves as a storage room and stops at a toy that has caught his attention, a plastic pole with various colored rings on it. He plops his butt on the carpet and pushes himself into a sitting position. He sits per-

fectly erect, like a lady at a luncheon, as if there is absolutely nothing to it, and he begins to remove the rings one by one from the
post. He seems completely unaware that he is in a new posture, one
in which he can more easily see the world and operate his toys.
He does not eventually slump forward as Sam initially did. Gus
perches himself as if on the edge of a chair while he reassembles
the rings, then crab-walks to a book, and once again maneuvers
into a seated position.

Of course I am delighted. But I can't keep from thinking that it
is crazy to spend one minute more fretting over when the boys will
reach these ridiculous milestones.

My parents drive up to visit us over Labor Day weekend. My
mom and I take the boys to the kiddie pool at the town park.
There's not much else to do with infants who aren't yet walking
besides pushing them on swings or carrying them to the pool. We
bend over, dragging Sam and Gus around the pool, avoiding the
bugs and leaves floating on top. We smile at the other parents,
exchange our children's names and ages. I say, "They're nearly ten
months, but were born almost two months early, so they're really
only eight months." It's a question everybody asks and is not easy
to answer. *The Essential Guide for Parents of Premature Babies*
said to give their corrected age, but it sounds dishonest because
while the boys don't quite have the heft or agility of ten-monthers,
they cannot quite pass as eight months old, either. The boys can
now both pull themselves upright and it is obvious that Gus has
shot up in height. Sam is still shorter and built like a fire hydrant.
Although Sam does not look quite as skinny as Gus, neither boy has
the dimpled arms and legs, protruding bellies, or plump, round
faces that characterize babies. Their faces are narrow—Gus is
growing into his enormous eyes—and they resemble small boys
more than actual babies. Their hair is slowly growing; Gus's is

fine like mine, and Dan is already worrying that he will go bald early.

Perhaps the reason the guide on preemies suggests you lie and tell people your baby's corrected rather than gestational age is to spare strangers from having to come up with an awkward response. If someone tells you her baby was born prematurely, here are three responses you might think twice about: (1) With real sympathy, "That must have been so hard." The mother will think you mean hard for her child and will feel guilty. (2) Pragmatically, "You just need to be patient and give her time to grow up. My friend's preemies are now twelve years old and she still factors in their prematurity." This will tell the mother that her guilt will go on forever. (3) And finally, "Were you aware that the March of Dimes, founded by Franklin Roosevelt to defeat polio, now focuses on finding ways to prevent prematurity?" A mother will then think if only she had read the March of Dimes mission statement pledging to solve the silent crisis of premature birth in America she might have discovered a way to avoid her own pre-term labor.

I have found the best replies are optimistic if inane, like "I just love preemies. Aren't their tiny clothes so adorable?" or "It means they are going to be smart."

Sam has deep blue eyes, blond hair, and skin that tans. Gus is so pale he appears ghostlike, with dark hair and big hazel eyes. He has more of the characteristic traits of a preemie. People stop me on the street and claim Gus has the biggest eyes they have ever seen on a baby.

And I answer, "When he was first born those eyes took up half his face."

But I don't say, "You should have seen him at three and a half pounds without a chin, looking like ET, like a gasping goldfish." In fact, as time passes, I am veering in the other direction. I've shaved a week off their prematurity and added half a pound to their original weight. I imagine that by next year they will have been born at four and a half pounds, allowing for delays one might expect of a thirty-three-weeker, which are usually not marked and are rarely permanent.

After half an hour of wading through the water, our backs are killing us—my mother points out that she is years older than any-one else at the kiddie pool—and the boys are shivering and start-ing to fret. We lay them down on the grass, put on dry diapers and T-shirts and carry them back to the car where we pass back bottles of juice which they have finally learned how to hold. They now lit-erally grab their bottles away as though insulted you tried to help them.

At home I throw towels and suits into the dryer. My father and Dan are in the backyard trying to figure out the antiquated sprin-kler system. Sam has pulled himself up and is holding on to the tel-evision set, babbling at the heads on the screen. I ask my mom her opinion as to why Gus doesn't yet use consonants and Sam does. Sam says "dada" like it's a curse word. "A da! A da!"

"You promised that once he sat up, you would never fret again." With my mother's response I am reminded that my worries are just that, worries. Mothers of ten-month-old babies who were born extremely prematurely might very well be coping with debili-tating physical or neurological disabilities. As my mother finishes unloading the dishwasher she says, "Gus will get there. Right now he's just more interested in other things." She goes into the bath-room and pulls him out from where he has been playing with the pipes and trying to flush the toilet.

I glance at the three novels she brought for me, stacked neatly on the kitchen counter. I pick up the paperback on top, *The Secret Life of Bees*. "Isn't this corny? You really liked it?"

"I did," she says. "I thought it might be something for you to start with, to get you back into reading."

"Maybe it's just fiction that doesn't interest me right now. I should try a biography or a memoir. Did you know Phillip Lopate calls personal memoirs 'the voice of middle age'?"

My mother laughs. "You're hardly middle-aged." I have just turned thirty-two.

"Oh, but I am," I tell her, and then deflecting her look I repeat, "I am. I have a middle-aged soul."

"You'll feel better once you've found some new friends to laugh with."

"I get so tired of women asking for my children's names and not my own. It's like I've ceased to exist."

"It'll get easier, I promise," my mother says. She turns off the faucet, wipes down the counter with a sponge. "I forgot to tell you that my friend, Donovan Richards, has pancreatic cancer. Ronda sent an e-mail the other day saying that the tumor is malignant and inoperable due to its position."

"That's awful," I say. "Oh, I'm so sad for him."

"He's in his eighties. Don't be sad about it."

She is giving me this news so I will remember that now is not an especially painful time for me. And it works. I start thinking that I must write Donovan a note, send him a photograph of the boys.

The microwavable mini-pancakes are ready; I lift Sam and Gus into their high chairs and put on a *Baby Mozart* video, which is the only way I can get them to eat.

"You're turning off the Mets?" my mom asks. "With the score tied in the ninth?" She is horrified. "Sam and Gus are going to have to learn to eat without those videos at some point. I don't think they'll find DVD players at the cafeteria in college."

In the summertime my parents used to drive us to Shea Stadium for doubleheaders, where we were never allowed to buy the program or banners or even sodas, and my mom taught us to cheer in rapid baseball-speak, "Say hey Mookie, how 'bout swingin' one over the fence-y, that-a-way Mook, that-a-way Mookie!" I know the names of every player on the '86 championship Mets along with the rosters from the earlier years that they spent mostly in last place.

Once I moved away from home, I watched sports mostly out of nostalgia, or because Dan was interested. From April through October, whenever I call my parents, I hear sportscasters through the background blare of the television set. Does my mother ever miss the days when we piled onto the bed with her? Growing up, she listened to baseball games on the radio with her parents. In her midtwenties, newly in love with my father, she watched the Mets from a bar stool beside him in corner bars. She once drove me to three different shopping malls where we could not find a single Mets jacket amongst the racks of Yankees paraphernalia in the boys' departments. Now she looks on from her bed, a heavy wool blanket over her legs, while my father drifts in and out of the room because he can finally no longer stomach watching the Mets lose.

Have all of these familial memories deepened her love of baseball? Or perhaps being a Mets fan was always a private love for her, like reading novels and listening to Broadway musicals, personal passions that I latched on to tightly because her enthusiasm had infused them with meaning.

I am relieved to be reentering a reality in which children are encouraged to believe that life has meaning and they can accomplish anything they work toward. Even if, my mother used to tell us, people like you better if you fail. Katie, through her career in sports marketing, has expanded on her knowledge of baseball statistics, but I will have to reconnect more strongly with the Mets. Perhaps this is why I instinctively ached to have children of my own, to expand backward while going forward, to take up some additional space.

And now that I'm a mother, my life will be much happier if I have faith that Gus and Sam can realize their dreams, as big as they dare to dream them. Going as far back as I can remember, my parents have silently shouldered any awareness of my limitations, and even now I am uncomfortable with the thought of their someday inadvertently spilling the beans. I can quell any doubts the boys might voice as they begin to build their own lives. I will gladly sink their uncertainties inside me. Children are encouraged to suspend disbelief, but what if it's even more important to do so as parents?

Soon the *Baby Mozart* video is over and the boys are fussing to get out of their chairs. It's time to clean up, run a bath, read a storybook. I pull *Pat the Bunny* from the shelf and my father snaps photographs as I read to Sam and Gus. "Now you stick your finger through mummy's ring." There's a small round hole in the cardboard page for them to stick their fingers through. But they haven't quite mastered this part, and they both reach to turn the page.

Next I try *Goodnight Moon,* which used to be their favorite book, but as soon as I begin to read they crawl away.

After watching *Baby Mozart* a couple of times a day for weeks, reading the same book again and again, scraping food off the floor that never made it near Sam or Gus's mouth, all I want to do is head for bed. My letter to Donovan must be put on hold until tomorrow. I'm finding that whenever I schedule an activity in advance I end up wishing I hadn't, that the days on which I have nothing planned at all are better, more relaxed than if I am rushing around trying to dress the boys and get them into the car for a pre-arranged "playdate." The unfilled days feel liberating, like wide-open windows.

ON TUESDAY, their bag already packed and in the car, my parents stand watching Sam and Gus. The boys have planted themselves on top of one another while each plays with a different toy. "They treat each other like furniture," my dad observes.

For hours the boys will hardly seem aware of each other. Sam will fuss if I pick up Gus instead of him, but left alone they will play in their own space, not noticing that the other exists.

Then Sam will steal Gus's pacifier, and Gus will think it's the funniest thing in the world. He'll pursue Sam to try to get it back and Sam will crack up too. A few minutes later they are back in their separate universes, sometimes with Gus sitting on Sam's leg. Gus smiles every time he recognizes his own reflection in a mirror, but only occasionally does he delight in seeing Sam. Sam also takes his brother's presence for granted. At this point, the boys seem to serve as backdrops in each other's lives, moving fixtures in the scenery.

My mom reaches down to hug the boys good-bye. My dad says, "Grandma's crying again. She hates to leave her grandsons." It doesn't look to me as if she's crying, but I'm not sure. Probably he's just teasing her. I wish they would stay for weeks. Since when is everything more fun with my parents around? I carry Gus out to their car and watch as my mother, always the passenger, slides into her seat. She waves good-bye as my father backs down the driveway.

I CALL ANGELA'S MOTHER the day after she said they were having the funeral, fully expecting her not to be home. But she answers on the first ring.

"Hello?" I say. "It's Jenny. From the NICU. I'm so sorry Angela passed away. She put up such a strong fight."

"I know," says her mother. "That's the hardest part. She almost made it. She was recovering from her final surgery and she developed just a simple, common infection."

"It's terribly sad."

"But no one expects me to be sad. They keep saying you're so lucky her sister is fine, that at least I have a child. Someone actually said to me if Angela was going to die it was better that I never got to take her home. As if I didn't love her just as much in the hospital! As if a whole year went by and she still wasn't really my daughter because she hadn't been inside our house."

I think about how the publisher at my old company would not

rush to fill a silence. It suddenly seems like an act of respect for some gaps not to be closed.

"Did you take lots of pictures of Sam and Gus sharing an incubator?" ·

"A few," I answer.

"Angela and her sister never got to co-bed because Angela was always so sick. We have a couple of photos in which I'm holding her sister next to Angela's incubator on the day we took her home. I wish we had more of the girls together. I wonder if her sister will feel her whole life as if something is missing. You know the weirdest thing? The hospital just sent me a photograph of Angela. I think it was taken right after she died. She's wearing an unfamiliar gown and she looks really peaceful. I'm curious as to who dressed her and took this photo and mailed it to us. Do you think the hospital hired a photographer?"

"They might have," I say. The Polaroid-snapping Lamaze nurse comes to mind but I don't offer her up as a possibility.

"Anyway," she continues, "I only looked at it once before storing it away in a drawer, but somehow it's the image I'm starting to remember."

"Have you had the service yet?" I ask after a while.

"Yesterday. Several of the nurses showed up. Such sweethearts. They must have had to take time off work."

"I'm sorry I couldn't make it. We've moved up to Connecticut."

"Oh yeah. That's what I figured. How do you like it?"

"I'm still adjusting," I say. "But I think it's going to be okay. There's a lot more space for the boys to crawl."

"Her sister's finally started crawling too! She's all over the place. It's so exciting. I just wish I didn't feel the loss of Angela in everything her sister does. The first ultrasound we saw had two sacs. I've always thought of myself as a mother of two."

And now I can't resist responding encouragingly. It just comes out of me. "But her sister also brings you joy."

"It's true," she says. "She's a real fireplug. Already has command of a room. We're talking about having another." She confesses this as if it were something shameful. "Not to replace Angela."

"Of course not," I say.

I hear her doorbell ring. "Probably another casserole." She laughs. "I better get it. My husband's developed an addiction."

I don't say that we should get together sometime with the kids or for lunch, or suggest plans I doubt we'd keep.

I simply say, "I'll check in again soon."

And she says, "Thanks so much for calling. It was good to talk to you."

And I say, "I'll be thinking about you all the time."

And she says, "Take care."

THE BILLS FROM THE HOSPITAL continue to trickle in. They reach us in West Hartford, stamped with forwarding address stickers. I pile them on the desk and Dan goes through them once a month. Some of the invoices are for exorbitant amounts. Although our insurance is supposed to cover nearly all of the cost, just seeing the numbers unnerves Dan.

We are also billed quarterly for the two extra embryos from our IVF cycle that made it to day 5 blastocysts and are frozen together in a laboratory. One of them apparently looks especially good, and the last time I called, Dr. Morganstern said that given my history, if he were to help me get pregnant again he would suggest putting in just one of the thawed embryos. Dan asks how long we can leave Gus and Sam's brother in the refrigerator.

In the end Sam and Gus will have cost our insurance company a total of one million dollars. IVF comes at a high price, approximately $15,000, and insurance companies generally don't cover it. But couples contemplating the procedure can be reassured that insurance companies do pay the NICU hospital bills. A premature baby's stay in the hospital is typically seventeen days; this is longer than the average stay of any other type of patients. Because all of the equipment needs to be designed exclusively for small babies, the NICU is also the most expensive unit of the hospital to run. The electrical bill for a single bed in the unit equals the cost of electricity for a three-story house. Sam and Gus racked up sixty-four nights in those beds and just about every test that could be prescribed. Along the lines of the bionic Six Million Dollar Man, they have arrived with a sticker price: one million dollar twins.

WIN Fertility, Inc., is a company that for six years has been managing infertility benefits and offering infertility coverage to health insurance carriers and mid-to-large companies with healthcare plans on the principle that poorer outcomes and more financial harm is caused if employees do not have infertility coverage than if they do. The cost of pregnancy plans and neonatal care for uncovered infertility patients, whose treatment was determined by affordability, exceeds the cost of providing infertility insurance in the first place.

Lindsay tells me that the primary concern of Dr. Morganstern was not my boys. His interest is in trying to help the women who enter his office achieve their goal of pregnancy. Once his patient is pregnant, he has finished his job. Lindsay thinks there should be a pediatrician attached to infertility clinics to focus on what's best for the babies.

Infertility clinics in the U.S. have not been responsible for following the lives of the children conceived inside their offices. The statistics that are of primary concern to them end at the number of live births they produce. Although my clinic has conducted its own studies to look at the safety of IVF and ICSI, infertility clinics are not required to release their data to outside researchers. Only recently have many infertility clinics even begun to cooperate with outside researchers so that the children conceived through IVF can be tracked. The clinics allocate their own resources to bolstering their pregnancy rates, not to improving the long-term outcomes of any babies conceived there who might have been born prematurely. After all, a considerable investment of time and funds is required to follow huge numbers of ex-preemies. Preemies are at a greater risk of having heart attacks, strokes, high blood pressure, and diabetes later in life, and yet the results for Sam and Gus won't be in for decades. The present research on preemies focuses mostly on the big problems, on long-term issues of babies with severe handicaps. We may never know whether any subtle deficiencies Sam and Gus may suffer from stemmed from their prematurity. A staff writer for the *Washington Post Magazine* recently reported that the increase in premature twins, a result of fertility treatments, has forced an expansion of our country's special education facilities. Is this true? If Sam and Gus have problems at school, will they blame Dan and me for transferring them together instead of separately?

Reproductive medicine is largely unregulated in our country. In several other countries, including the United Kingdom, France, Australia, and Germany, there are laws to promote its safety. Our government has remained uninvolved in reproductive medicine, mostly to avoid the hot-button topics of stem-cell research and abortion. The debate in the U.S. has resolved around whether, just as a woman has a right to choose not to have a child, she should also be granted the right to medical treatment that could enable her to conceive a child. Although it is imperative to determine if a woman's right to health care should include the right to parent, shouldn't we also be asking ourselves what we can do to guarantee the safety of the children conceived with the aid of these treatments? In the United Kingdom there are various laws in place to protect IVF children. The U.K. has also implemented rigorous rules for stem-cell research and therapeutic cloning. While our government hesitates to map out guidelines on these scientific frontiers, American companies are sprouting up to clone dead pets for customers.

There have been, to date, virtually no studies published on the long-term health of IVF children. I didn't even notice this until Sam and Gus were born and I started thinking like a mother. How can we reconcile a mother's instinct to protect with the equally powerful biological, social, and economic forces that drives so many of us into the overcrowded waiting rooms of fertility clinics to take our chances? In the thesaurus a synonym for the verb "to mother" is "to protect."

Was Dr. Vanderbilt hesitant to worry me about the seriousness of a twin pregnancy because she considered me emotionally fragile from going through the stress of infertility? Or did my water breaking at thirty-one weeks truly surprise her? I've heard so many stories like mine lately, I can't help but wonder if she has delivered more than a few very premature babies since Sam and Gus.

For twins, the risk of dying by their first birthday is five to ten times higher than for a single baby. A singleton has twice the chance of being born healthy and free of birth defects that a twin has. The risk of cerebral palsy is eight times greater for twins than single babies. The increase in twin births by 65 percent over the past twenty-five years is due, largely, to the wildfire expansion of reproductive medicine. But is this a necessary correlation? In 2004 Belgian scientists conducted a study in which 367 women under thirty-eight years old did IVF. Half of the women had a single embryo implanted, the other half had two. Both groups had the exact same pregnancy rate, 37 percent. Based partly on this research, the Society of Assisted Reproduction Techniques is "applying the brakes" to reproductive procedures in order to reduce twin pregnancies. Having had success previously in reducing the number of triplet births, SART is now recommending that in cases with a favorable prognosis a single embryo be transferred. Advancing technology is allowing embryologists at a few leading clinics to differentiate even more between embryos that are likely to develop into babies and those that are not. The scientists pour sugar into the

petri dishes and the embryos that quickly absorb it have a 60 percent chance of becoming live babies. Only the Colorado Center for
Reproductive Medicine actually recommends single embryo transfers, and their patients rarely select this option despite the impres-
sive success rate.

For many older women, transferring multiple embryos is their
only reasonable hope to become pregnant. What is the right number of embryos for younger women embarking on their third and
fourth IVF attempts? Ovarian cancer has been linked to fertility
treatments in certain studies. Some of the psychiatrists in the
newly specialized field of infertility suggest that their patients
reduce the risk to their own health by undergoing as few procedures as possible, which means transferring more embryos per
cycle. It is a complicated matter. No two cases of infertility are the
same. But just because there isn't an easy solution, should we avoid
the discussion altogether?

If the technology had caught up with us, if we had conceived
just a few years later, there is the possibility that Sam and Gus
would not be twins. Had we transferred them a year or two apart,
would our boys still splay their arms and legs across each other as
though not even cognizant of where one body ends and the other
begins? Would they continually seek the other out to play, side by
side, in solitude? I acknowledge that my own IVF experience was
problematic. It's never far from my mind that our situation could
have been worse. And yet, although my feelings are conflicted,
whenever I look at Sam and Gus I am grateful that we cycled
through the infertility clinic exactly when we did.

On the first sunday night of daylight savings we feed the
boys dinner at what was their regular time, but with the time
change they become cranky and tired earlier, so we head for the
bathtub. By 7:00 they are in their pajamas, fussing, ready for bed.

But if we let them go down now we can't bear to think of the early hour at which they will wake us. So we bring them into our room and put on our clock radio. Dan lifts up Gus by his ankles and swings him upside down before dropping him on the bed. Gus's laugh is sweet like jelly beans. He flips over, comes straight back for more. Dan finds himself taking turns throwing Gus and Sam into the air. Then I dance with Sam to Dire Straits in front of the mirror while Dan helps Gus turn somersaults on the bed. All the while, Dan and I are trying to drink glasses of wine, which means that we have to take occasional gulps from our glasses perched on the dresser. There are babies in the NICU tonight being tended by the same nurses we had a year ago, the ones I liked and the few I didn't.

Sam is rubbing his eyes. "Let's put them to bed," I say. It's my job to end things before they go sour. As children, my siblings and I would horse around on my parents' bed and inevitably my dad would get tired and tell us to cut it out. But we would be way too wound up. "Damnit, I said enough!" he'd yell, and then my brother would jump on me and get sent to his room, and I would shout about the injustice and land in my room as well. The key is to cut things off in time.

We rest the boys in their cribs, each clutching his bottle, and head downstairs. Gus's cries follow us. The pediatrician in New York City told me early on that twins usually learn to tune out each other's cries, but I did not believe him. For the most part he's been right. However, once in a while, Gus's hollering does wake Sam up. On these occasions Sam screams bloody murder and Dan and I run in like a SWAT team. We sweep the boys out of their room and plop them on the couch downstairs in front of a *Baby Einstein* video. We let the tape run to the end and then put Sam and Gus back to bed with refilled bottles.

This evening, while making spaghetti with sauce from a jar, I stare at the clock and hope Gus stops crying before Sam wakes up. After fifteen minutes Gus is quiet. I eat an enormous bowl of spaghetti and fight off the urge to head straight to bed. I stay up with Dan to watch the second Lord of the Rings movie. When Dan was a boy, his father read the entire trilogy to him. I sat between Dan and my father-in-law at the Ziegfeld in midtown for part 2, *The Two Towers*. They both spoke the dialogue aloud along with the characters on-screen and I couldn't manage to tune them out enough to follow the story line.

"The obsession with J. R. R. Tolkien has got to be a guy thing," I say, reaching for *People* magazine during a particularly lengthy battle scene.

Before Sam and Gus were born I looked forward to the arrival of *People* in the mailbox on Friday nights. But now that I am drawn straight to the noncelebrity stories, which almost always involve children who are fatally ill, the magazine has lost some of its candylike appeal. Following the glossy not-quite-candids of Uma and Gwyneth frolicking on the beach in St. Barts come the "Coping" and "Crusader" sections in which a father tries to carry on after accidentally killing his baby and a mother works to raise money for the degenerative disease that took the lives of all four of her children.

This week's story is about a boy whose dream of playing major league ball was crushed by a brain tumor. Recently the boy got his wish to sit in the dugout alongside the members of his favorite team.

"It's not a big deal if Sam and Gus aren't into sports," I say. "Some guys aren't. We're just lucky that they're healthy. If it turns out they're not all that coordinated, you shouldn't be disappointed. Just because you were captain of the soccer team doesn't mean they'll be jocks."

"My dad's not an athlete," he replies. Dan's father, having just undergone his third embolization to remove malignant tumors from his liver, is on our minds. "I don't care if they play sports. All they have to be able to do is run around and have fun. Now shush.

Watch this part," Dan says. "It's all been leading to Gondor." Dan explains the significance of Gondor and Gollum, and Gandalf's transformation. I rest the magazine back on the coffee table and for the next hour I succumb to the magical world of immortal elves and dwarfs and wizards.

In late october i start reviewing books for the *Hartford Courant*. I am delighted that after my first piece runs, a paycheck arrives in the mail. The years I spent in publishing actually do mean something. Even way up here in Hartford, Connecticut, my new life is starting to connect back to my old one. The next time someone asks me what I do for a living I can answer in the present tense, not the past, not "I used to be," but "I am." And even though this is all hypothetical because the only questions I am ever asked are at the baby gym where I bring the boys on Wednesdays (What foods will your boys eat? and When do they nap?) and at the grocery store (Do you have a Shopper's Savings card? and Would you prefer paper or plastic bags?), still I am happy.

I also find the time to organize our first album with photos of Sam and Gus. Dan and I have taken photographs on any number of vacations over the years and the pictures are stacked in shoe boxes in the closet.

I've read that this pastime is becoming popular with mothers in America. Some are even getting together at scrapbooking parties. Assembling family photo albums has become a creative outlet. A desire to idealize the past led a grandmother into a photo shop to have a picture of one of her grandsons inserted into a family portrait taken at a reunion which he was unable to attend. A mother cropped her younger daughter's ex-boyfriend out of her older son's wedding pictures so as not to embarrass the daughter's new fiancé.

It seems that many mothers of all ages have a desire to create a cohesive family history. They seamlessly paste sun-washed prints of bonneted young brides and slick-haired grooms into puffy albums alongside their future children and grandchildren as if they all had been separated not by lifetimes but only crinkly, worn pages.

ALMOST A YEAR HAS PASSED since the boys' birth when, on Halloween, I start to feel sexy again. In college it was the one night of the year when I took off my Levi's and Patagonia and went forth in slinky black hot pants and fuzzy cat ears, thinking this outfit might land me a handsome cowboy or a Viking.

Sometime during the first year Dan and I were dating, Barbara Eden appeared on TV in an old rerun and the words "I love Jeannie" rolled effortlessly off Dan's tongue.

I threw a pillow at him. "How is it that you can say I love Jeannie but not Jenny? Jen-ny."

When Halloween rolled around I found Jeannie's trademark costume—a red velvet midriff-baring vest, the sheer pink balloon pants—at a magic store in the West Village.

I wasn't exactly transformed, and he didn't say anything, but as I stood at the top of the spiral staircase in my apartment and Dan looked up from the TV and smiled at me wobbling in furry high-heeled slippers, the bobby pins attaching my red velvet teacup hat and pink veil already coming loose, I knew he loved me. The expression on Dan's face was amused, but tender. He seemed aware that dressing up in an outfit I could not quite pull off had made me vulnerable. He jumped up from the couch and quickly kissed me with a purposefulness that spoke more of kindness than desire.

Perhaps it's the spirit of this night when the ghosts of the dead purportedly return to mingle with the living that dares me to flirt with truth. In the distant past on Halloween, conscious of winter's brisk approach, people would step out into darkness to "go a-souling." Young women believed that they could divine the name or appearance of their future husbands by doing tricks with mirrors.

Since I stopped pumping, my breasts have become smaller than they were before pregnancy. Dan asks, "Where do you think they went?" Katie says, "Do you think the same thing will happen to mine as soon as I have kids? Thank God Mom never let me get a breast reduction." But they now seem in better proportion to my small frame. I don't even mind my cesarean scar anymore despite its becoming keloid. No one ever sees it but Dan and me. During sex the scar serves to remind me that we succeeded at conceiving and bearing two children.

While putting together costumes for the boys on this warm Halloween afternoon, I think about what I will wear for mine. Not much, I decide. The leopard print bikini bottom that the saleslady made me buy after I told her Dan was wondering why I still wore maternity underwear months past my maternity. My Australian outback hat from my year in college studying abroad. My high-heeled, brown leather knee-high boots.

We take the boys out in the little red buggies they much prefer to their double stroller; push them down the road to a few houses, the cars' plastic wheels making a thundering ruckus that pulls people out onto their doorsteps as we approach; snap some photos of them as Winnie the Pooh and a pumpkin. Back in our driveway, Dan discovers a tick on his shirt collar.

"We should check the boys," he says.

I run my hands through Sam's hair, behind his ears, down his arms and legs. Then I rub my own arms and neck.

Dan pulls Gus out of his car and asks me, "What are you doing?"

"Checking myself for ticks."

"What about Gus?"

"You've got him, why can't you do it?" I ask before adding, "Or I can search him once we get inside."

"But you checked yourself? I'd rather have you check Gus. He's more important."

"Thanks."

"Isn't he supposed to be? If I had to prioritize whose lives were of consequence it would be the boys, you, me, then Michelle. Michelle would be fifth," he says pointedly.

A bright red Chevrolet truck has parked in the street in front of our house. Its owners must be out trick-or-treating. Painted on the rear window, sparkling under the street lamp, are the words, "In memory of Lisa 1958–2002."

Why is Dan fixated on our family's pecking order? Did he broker a deal with God while the boys were hospitalized? For what? His soul? Mine?

After Sam and Gus have gone to bed and we've taped a "Do not ring doorbell, babies asleep" sign over the bell, I reluctantly put on my Halloween costume for Dan.

He is not as surprised as I thought he would be. "Let's go to the basement," he says and smiles invitingly.

"I'm still annoyed. You pretty much ruined the mood."

"Listen, you're ahead of me. The boys should survive us. Wouldn't you want me to put them first?"

"It's just not a very nice thing to hear."

"I hope you would choose the boys over me."

"Okay. Enough." I am tempted to run back upstairs and throw on my sweats. I feel as sexy as Mrs. Potato Head.

"But I would rather see you in that costume than Sam and Gus, or Michelle. In that order," Dan says.

"Very funny." But I smile.

"Listen. You are my favorite wife."

I decide to let it go. In college I read an Irish proverb that a friend's mother had stuck on her refrigerator. It said, "The key to marriage is three things left unsaid each day." At the time the saying had seemed pathetic, but tonight it strikes me as kind. Have I changed so drastically? More likely our marriage, having been strengthened by surviving a difficult crisis, could still use some patching. With two babies in need of constant care, now is not the time to make major repairs. But leaving a few things unsaid makes it easier to shift gears and continue the climb.

Taking my hand, Dan leads us downstairs.

The basement of our house was decorated in the fifties. There are purple neon bulbs in the ceiling fixtures, and a string of blue lights is built into the bar. A row of swivel stools stands in front, and behind them is a wall of mirrors. We imagine the couple who lived in the house before us having wild naked parties down here. Recently, however, it has been taken over by a plastic slide from Dan's mother and a tent filled with plastic balls from mine. In a few weeks the room Dan declared was his when we bought the house, that he envisioned as his hideaway where he could watch Duke basketball and drink beer with his friends, has become Gus and Sam's official playroom.

My Fountains of Wayne CD just arrived in the mail today and I put it into the stereo and press shuffle so the song "Stacy's Mom" will get sandwiched between the Bruce Springsteen and Lucinda Williams CDs already resting in slots.

I know there are certain times in the month when women's bodies are more receptive to sex. It's biological. But it's too soon to let timing into my thoughts again. I push off the bar stool and Dan puts his arms around my waist.

ON THEIR FIRST BIRTHDAY, November 12, Gus rises to his knees and then stands unaided for a few seconds. He surfs in the air, using his arms for balance, before he drops down to the floor.

We invite a few acquaintances over for cake in the evening. The same neighbor who flew through our family room with her son because she didn't want him exposed to television tells Dan that she has started referring to me as "the snack lady." Apparently the neighbor can always tell that her one-year-old has been to our house because when she gets home from work he's covered in crumbs. So what if I'm guilty of fretting too much over whether my very thin boys have had enough to eat, to the extent that I will follow them around carrying boxes of Ritz peanut butter wafers. Her little boy is constantly reaching for my handbag, asking, "Crackers?" I don't allow myself to consider him a glutton, not even in my mind, just because at the same age all Sam says is "Dada" and Gus is monosyllabic.

I laugh along with the neighbor and Dan. A year ago at this time Sam and Gus were being rushed down to the NICU as I was sewn back together. Nothing can upset me today. I had anticipated that this birthday would be bittersweet. November 12, 2002, ranks as one of the best days of my life and also one of the worst. Over the past year I've hung on to January 14 as a safety net, professing it to be the boys' "real" birthday, and it may be a while before I am confident enough to let their due date go. A mid-November birth date puts Sam and Gus right before the cutoff of age eligibility for starting kindergarten, but I'll most likely take their adjusted age into account and enroll them in school the following year. My response to filling in "November 12" on medical slips and enrollment forms may always be complicated or the pain may fade with time. But now that the day has actually arrived again, I am cheerful.

Dan tells the neighbor about the new thing Sam does where he crawls over to you and says, "Dada," so you think he wants to sit in your lap, but really he wants you to lift him up so he can reach the light switch on the wall behind you. He loves flicking it off and on. "He's brilliant that way," Dan says. The neighbor volleys with a story about her son.

We sing "Happy Birthday" and cut a cake I've baked from a mix. Sam and Gus both clamp their mouths shut and throw back their heads, batting at the spoon with which I'm trying to feed them bites. Finally I just put the plate down in front of them, and Gus sticks his hand into it and shoves a piece in his mouth. Sam quickly escapes from the cake.

Later, after the guests have cleared out, Sam crawls into the bathroom and slams the door. He pulls himself up holding on to the toilet and bangs on the door. Gus knocks from the other side, and eventually Dan helps Gus to push it open. Surprise! They are smack in each other's faces. They both laugh and laugh in their Elmo party hats, and for some reason I can't quite pinpoint, most likely because they spend twenty-four hours a day together, it really is funny.

"I can't believe they're a year old," I say, dumping paper plates into a trash bag. "Sam and Gus aren't infants anymore. They have both come so far."

"You think we can get them on skis this winter?"

"Skiing is probably still a couple years off." I laugh, and hold out the bag to collect his empty beer bottle.

As Dan leans forward to drop in his bottle he says, "What if Sam and Gus want to go to Groton someday? Would we send them? Something worth considering. It's not that far off." I don't voice to Dan my fear that they will be in special education instead. Tonight that worry seems distant. Please let Sam and Gus have sound minds for remembering. Let them fire memories down those neural pathways that build love and meaning.

I am certain I won't be ready to let Gus and Sam fly away in just thirteen years. If their Synergis shots really work this winter and they don't wind up back in the hospital with breathing troubles from RSV, if they finally one day point across the street from inside their plastic red cars and exclaim, "Dog!"; if they learn how to read in first grade, how to subtract carrying over the digits in second, if they stand back up and wipe off their tears when the class bully swipes at them in third—and from their side of the fence it suddenly feels like much longer—won't I someday be ready to leave them?

I can almost picture Gus and Sam all geared up in their maroon-and-white uniforms, shoulder pads, Adidas cleats, metal lacrosse sticks. Sam's fine hair will be brown by then, but lighter than Gus's. And Sam will still be smaller. They have inherited Dan's narrow eyes and straight nose, so most likely somewhere not yet expressed lurk my clumsy genes. We won't need to blame any lack of athleticism on their being preemies when there are more amusing places to point. But we will not have forgotten. They will be running around the JV field smack in the middle of the campus circle, nowhere near the ball, and the chapel bells will be ringing in the center of time.

Over the thanksgiving weekend while we are visiting my parents in Florida, an older lady in a blue bathing cap wanders away from the aerobics class underway in the deep end of the pool to admire the boys. "Twins?" she says. "You are blessed." I nod. Although there are now twins everywhere, strangers still stop to admire Sam and Gus. If they are lucky, at the end of their lives, Sam and Gus will have known each other longer than anyone else. Since their earliest nights at home, I've heard soft syncopated snoring coming from their bedroom.

The lady in the bathing cap mentions her friend's twelve-year-old grandsons who recently came to blows over a girl who had dumped one of them for the other, and Dan says, "These two will never compete for love."

The lady brags that her son learned to swim at four, but then laments that once he joined the swim team he wouldn't let her come see his races. Eventually she wades back to her class and we carry Sam and Gus out of the pool and rub them dry in oversized beach towels.

We try taking the boys to the beach at sunset but the loud waves scare Gus and he starts to cry. Isn't the ocean supposed to mimic the sound of the womb? Could it be that Gus never particularly liked the womb?

At dinner that night my father says, "You're going to take Gus back to the beach tomorrow, right?"

The white bellies of small frogs are stuck against the glass doors behind him. We have to keep the doors closed or hundreds of them will hop into the house. "Maybe we'll give him a day off and try again," I say.

"Nah," my dad says, sipping his wine. "Take him back. He'll get used to it."

I'm sure it is partly the warmth of the sun following a cold New England fall, wearing light cotton blouses and my jean skirt all day, that makes me excited to see Dan when we close the door to our bedroom at night. Because the guest room has twin beds we snuggle under single sheets. But I am becoming increasingly convinced that my reignited desire for intimacy is cyclical. For a while now one week during every month finds me feeling more attractive and alert, aware of smoke rising up out of our neighbors' fireplaces, or the early birds chirping outside my window. Maybe going off the birth control pill, my stomach's expansion during pregnancy, the strange sensation of pumping breast milk, my anger that my body gave out have left me now feeling buoyant. Or perhaps what they say is true and women really do hit their prime in their thirties. Joking around in our high school dining hall after lunch, the boys used to say that by the time we girls hit our prime they would be old men. Back then the thought of a seductive mother made me cringe.

Sometime late in the night I hear rain falling. But when we wake early the next morning there is nothing but blue sky. Later Dan discovers that one of the local cartoon channels carries an animated *Stargate* modeled on his favorite program on the Sci-Fi Network. "This is perfect for Sam and Gus," he says, leaning back on the couch, his arms crossed.

Sam and Gus lose interest in the cartoon after a couple of minutes. Gus releases his hold on the couch and takes a single wobbly step toward me. He falls into my arms. I lift him in the air and shout, "Hip hip hooray! Hip hip hooray!"

My father who is trying to read the paper laughs and says, "You're so on top of them. Back off. Give them some space."

But just hours before our flight, it's my dad who, understandably, is craving space. He's used to quiet mornings with just my mother in the small house. I dress the boys in the only set of short sleeves I haven't packed. Sam, with his blond bed head and white-collared shirt, looks like he's just come in from a toddler tennis match. My mom, Dan, and I push the boys to the playground in their second pair of little red buggies, this set purchased by my mom. We pass a baby alligator lying on the bank of a pond. The golf course my parents live on was built on top of a swamp. Once the alligators get bigger the grounds crew calls a county hunter, who catches them and kills them. He is paid nothing but gets to keep the hides and meat to sell. But the little ones don't bother anybody. We pass black-and-white egrets drying their wings on the grass. At the playground Gus climbs up a ladder to the slide. My mother follows Sam over to the bucketed swings. Set in a canvas swing seat he flails his arms in excitement and bounces his legs. "He's got ants in his pants," Dan says.

As Sam flies through the air, he looks over and laughs at Gus coming headfirst down the slide. The mother of a toddler inquires about Sam and Gus's age and when I answer ten months she knows I'm lying. Gus is bigger than her son, who, it turns out, is fourteen months. At Gus's one-year checkup he ranked in the 50th to 60th percentile in height for his gestational age. And Sam has finally made it onto the chart.

What first year as a parent is not overwhelming? What life is not a risk?

While biologists are studying how to successfully freeze women's eggs, Sam and Gus are conducting their own experiments—with sliced bananas, which they throw off their trays and watch fall to the floor; with the chain from the lamp, which they pull to brighten the living room if the lamp doesn't topple over. They lean into the front door in the morning eager to be released to the outdoor open sky which seems to simultaneously excite them and put them at ease.

When Sam and Gus are older I will need to give them some room. But right now in exchange for pulling them around the pool, making their lunch, and generally loving them I am free to get as close to them as I want.

And there goes Sam crawling across the field away from the playground, my mother following close behind. He reaches for the wet wood fence to pull himself up and points through the bars as a shimmery car passes by on the road. A perfect breeze is loosening pinecones from the branches. I am sitting by myself in the sandbox amidst plastic shovels and pails.

"What are you doing?" Dan calls from the bottom of the slide as a pair of military helicopters from the nearby naval base fly overhead.

"I set up a play station."

"It's not a popular station."

"Just as well."

Gus comes flying down the slide, headfirst again, beaming. And I think, *There is nothing to stop you.*

I EMERGE FROM THE HOME OFFICE where I have spent the morning signing Christmas cards with the boys' photo on them and hear the fast pitter-patter of hands and feet on the hardwood floor: Sam and Gus heading to the stairs. The Christmas we were trying to get pregnant so many baby faces kept arriving in the mail, I couldn't keep straight whose baby was whose. I wondered where our friends had all gone and I swore that if I ever had babies I would not plaster them to cards. But then we developed the pictures of Gus and Sam smiling in their parent-propelled buggies as Winnie the Pooh and a pumpkin, and I thought, maybe just this one year. I addressed envelopes, listening to Sam push the heavy kitchen chairs around the floor below. The chair legs got stuck against the walls, and he cried out in frustration. How happy he will be as soon as he lets go and realizes he can walk without pushing so much weight. I stand on the landing, and am startled as the boys round the corner and come into view. Have they grown this much since this morning?

"Does Gus have his hair parted?" I ask Michelle.

Gus and Sam are singing yayas as they climb up the stairs. They edge each other out, laughing. The physical therapist in New York claimed that Gus was hypotonic. When I learned from our pediatrician that hypotonia was a neurological disorder causing low muscle tone, and that he believed that Gus's muscle tone was just like Sam's, I quit taking the boys to physical therapy. And look how strong they both are. Up they climb, like baby elephants. I filled out a questionnaire last week from Early Intervention Services. Then I threw it away. You are shaking your head. Maybe at thirteen months, Gus and Sam are not yet clapping their hands or waving good-bye. But you should see them coming up these stairs, the sheer, blissful determination on their faces. They are nearing the top, laughing even harder, egging each other on, I am laughing with them, and they know they have made it, just one more step.

DAY ONE—THE TALLY

Gus: 2

Sam: 8

Jenny: 6

Dan: 4

Total: 20 throw-ups

New Year's Day we catch a stomach bug. Gus is actually hit on New Year's Eve but he is so cheerful about it that we don't realize what he has until Sam joins him, throwing up his milk the following evening. Dan watches Sam curl up on the hardwood floor with his butt high in the air, quietly moaning and says he resembles me when I'm sick. Actually Sam does look like me at this moment. I am suddenly feeling queasy. Fifteen minutes later Sam is heaving up neon-yellow bile. "Can you clean him up?" I ask Dan. "I don't feel so good."

"This is not about you," Dan snaps. "Our kids are sick, you have to be a parent. None of this psychosomatic crap."

Sam falls asleep on the hallway floor. I make Gus a small bottle, and we carry them both to bed. Then I go into our bathroom and vomit six times. While I am leaning over the toilet I am thinking that I have to get downstairs to tell Dan. As soon as there's a lull I run down.

"I just threw up a million times," I say.

"You *are* sick." He smiles apologetically. "All of my little people are sick."

I sit on the couch. I smell frozen pizza. "Why don't you go up to bed," Dan says.

I lie in my bed, nauseated. I think, Please please make this go away. Please let me feel better. I promise I won't complain that I feel like a fifty-year-old though I'm really thirty-two. I will embrace my aging, tired life. I'll stop worrying about my boys; I'll be grateful for every day, blah blah blah, just let me feel better. I think I may die.

Dan finds it amusing that if I am sick, particularly with nausea, I think I am dying. But at my worst moments, I feel better imagining that there is an end in sight.

As a child, whenever I was sent to my room and was really pissed off, I would get into bed and envision my funeral. Everyone in town would be gathered in the little Lutheran church where we went once a year on Christmas Eve because my dad's ex-wife was a Lutheran. My friends and family would all be hysterical—a word I used all the time back then—and someone would play a tape I had recorded on my deathbed in which I talked about each member of my family, reeled off a list of wrongs he or she had done me, and then pardoned them one by one. I would start with the most recent obnoxious stunt my brother had pulled, like unplugging the electronic battleship game because I was winning, and then move on to forgive my dad for impatiently jumping to conclusions and sending the entirely wrong person, me, to my room. After I'd cried for a while I usually managed to fall asleep.

Since we've moved to West Hartford I have concocted an imaginary brain tumor on several occasions. How else to explain the fact that my neck always aches, that I am exhausted all the time and the only thing keeping me from napping instead of grocery shopping on the days Michelle is here is my fear she will tell people I'm lazy. Now, as my worries about the boys are abating a bit, it seems like the perfect time to get hit with a fatal tumor. And I know I will handle it well, affirming life for my family, acting brave in front of friends, and I hate that I already know this about myself.

Dan enters our bedroom and pulls down the covers on his side of the bed. I pretend I'm asleep so I won't have to talk. A few minutes later he gets up and I hear him vomit into the toilet four times. While he is in the bathroom, I turn off the alarm clock, which he has set for 6:30 in the morning, thinking he is going to go to work and leave me alone, sick, with two sick boys.

As he crawls back into bed I ask, "Did throwing up make you feel better?"

"I don't know, it hit me too fast to notice," he says. Then he asks, "Have you ever been smarter than I am?"

"Maybe."

"Did you really think you could turn off the alarm without me noticing?"

I manage to laugh, and he doesn't turn it back on. Soon he is snoring. But I feel too off-balance to sleep. My head and stomach hurt. Around five in the morning I hear a car pull up in our driveway and the thud of a newspaper landing on our front stoop. Some time after that, I fall asleep. By 6:30 both Sam and Gus are up. Sam is screaming: he still feels terrible. So do we. I give them both small bottles of grape Pedialyte. Sam throws up his immediately. We go downstairs and curl up on the couch and watch six *Baby Mozart* videos in a row. All I can do is get up, walk to the TV, and switch the tape every half hour. Then we put the boys back down for a nap, and doze off ourselves. We make it through the afternoon with more of the same. Gus has five bouts of diarrhea and Sam throws up three more times on the living room rug, our bedroom carpet, and his playroom carpet. At 7:30 we put them down for the night and fall into our bed.

The next morning I think will be better. But when the sun rises we are still weak and nauseous. Dan decides to give our home a name the way that some people call their houses "the Oaks" or "the Highlands." He christens it "the Vomitorium."

DAY 5 TALLY AT THE VOMITORIUM

Gus: 1

Sam: 3

Jenny: 0

Dan: 0

Total: 4

On the fifth day Dan finally goes to work. Sam eats a cereal bar and spits it up on me; I put the boys down for a nap, shower, then Gus throws up on me an hour later. I have done twenty-five loads of laundry; every set of the boys' pajamas has been washed at least half a dozen times. Whenever Sam or Gus vomit, I pour soda water on the rug, mush it around a bit, and remind myself that when this is all over I have to call in a professional carpet cleaner.

Each time Sam throws up he looks disgusted, and cries for twenty minutes even while I run a bath to try and distract him. All he wants to do is lie on the couch watching TV with his head on my lap like a ten-year-old. He grins and laughs at all the right moments, as when Al Roker gets pegged by a snowball.

Michelle arrives at noon and I expect to feel relieved. Instead her cheerfully booming voice grates on me. After everything she says she asks, "Do you understand what I'm saying?" and I have to hold my breath so I don't tell her to shut up. But then she takes over and I realize I can escape upstairs to return a friend's call.

The friend tells me she is about to become the first woman in her IVF clinic to transfer just one embryo. She's afraid of becoming pregnant with multiples because she has a friend whose preemie IVF twins have severe cerebral palsy. Her life has become one long trip to the offices of doctors and therapists. Her now-three-year-old girls cannot do anything by themselves, her marriage is falling apart, and she has admitted to my friend that she wishes she had never done IVF.

My situation is entirely opposite. I am thankful every moment of every single day that Gus and Sam are thriving. Not so long ago Dan and I would have been unable to produce biological children. I remember hearing of women a little older than myself who had trouble getting pregnant because their uteruses were malformed when *their* mothers took DES while pregnant with them. I would thank God we have come as far as we have in medicine. But recently I have read that some infertility treatments can have dangerous repercussions. Studies have been published in the Netherlands showing that IVF babies have twice the number of major birth defects like retinoblasma (a malignant tumor in the retina) as naturally conceived babies. Another study reported that ART babies in northern Finland have a four times greater risk of heart malformations. And in Australia a disproportionately large number of IVF babies have been diagnosed with Beckwith-Wiedeman, a syndrome in which certain organs, including the tongue, are enlarged. Can it be that in the petri dish recessive genes for enlarged tongues reappeared, along with predispositions to rare cancers not expressed for generations? Is it possible that undesirable mutations can occur in those dishes? Sporadic cases of genetic imprinting disorder have been diagnosed in IVF babies as well.

Dr. Morganstern claims that the findings at his clinic still show no increase in birth defects with their babies. Recently, in the most comprehensive study conducted in the United States to date, the American Society for Reproductive Medicine and the American Academy of Pediatrics concluded that the only increased risk factor in IVF pregnancies is prematurity. I'm able to convince myself that the research conducted in my own country is the most reliable. Although multiple pregnancies still present the greatest risks, it has now been proven that singleton pregnancies from IVF lead to very premature births three times as often as naturally conceived singletons, and women who have had fertility treatments tend to give birth two to three weeks earlier than women who did not have fertility problems when pregnant with the same number of babies. There may be a connection between prematurity and infertility treatments or infertility itself. Even low-tech infertility medications, like Clomid, are now suspected of increasing the incidence of preterm labor.

Perhaps someday risk-averse parents will sign up for genetic screening IVF procedures rather than gamble on a natural birth. But we are not there yet. When Sam and Gus head off to grammar school there will most likely be three sets of twins in each grade and an odd gaggle of triplets. And another ten years later twins may be back to being the rare exception, just one set in every grade, the way it was when I was young.

I would do it all over again tomorrow to have Sam and Gus. There is not a doubt in my mind that Sam and Gus are the two boys I was meant to have. In her toast at my wedding, Katie said that Dan and I had just made the greatest decision of our lives, for your spouse is the only family member you get to choose.

But I would choose Sam and Gus again and again and again. Gus, who turns around to seek our approval each time he slaps a spongy toy onto the side of the bathtub so it sticks, who overnight has started to babble "ma" and "bop," "bop" to indicate everything from a ball to a rubber duck and "ma" when he's reaching up his arms to be lifted from his crib after he tires of playing with his twelve pacifiers. Sam, who is so restless all day, and then sleeps so deeply at night. At three months Sam would cry when our car had to halt every few city blocks for a red light. Now we go to the mall to kill some time on weekend afternoons and he wails if we have to stop the plastic car he's riding in to wait for the elevator. Dan says, "It's cool, be cool, Sam." But he isn't until we're on the glass-walled elevator going up and he can watch the stores and people receding below. To have these exact two boys, I would stand once again by that crib in the NICU while their breathing momentarily stopped and the neonatologist on call, who I kept thinking I was going to like because he was so flamboyantly gay, breezed past prescribing more tests, X-rays, and echos without even stopping to look at the boys. I would hold Gus on my lap while a technician rubbed gel over his head for a follow-up brain scan to make sure that the bleed in his brain had resolved without forming cysts. Only this time I would know not to try to detect what was on the screen or ask the technician so many questions that drew the usual response: "If there was nothing here or if it was terrible I could tell you, but what I'm seeing needs to be interpreted by a radiologist." A friend of Dan's and mine who was specializing in radiology at the hospital had given birth to twin preemies the year before. She called the head of her department to look at Gus's ultrasound immediately after. The department head said, "You can tell your friend that her son's brain is beautiful." Do you hear that, Gus? She said you have a beautiful brain. I would try not to be frightened at the preemie clinic to see a set of twins no older than four or five with abnormally widespread eyes and flat noses waiting in wheelchairs. I wish I had talked to their mother. I would not snap at the physical therapist who shook her head, "Tsk tsk tsk," because you did not want to reach for her filthy toy. I would whisper encouragement in your ear, Sam, as you braved those first days. Now at last I don't even try to stop you from climbing out of the high chair the second we put you in; I appreciate that you came to us prepared for a fight. Those doctors helped to create you and they worked to save your lives, and there would be no selecting one of you over the other, even if it were just a matter of who got to come first.

Eight days later, we are finally healthy. The boys stop throwing up and start eating chicken nuggets again. It will be nearly a week before they are hit with their next bug, a common cold, which will get us kicked out of their toddler gym class. I drive through the snow to the grocery store to stock up on supplies, repeating to myself, They are well, I am well, we are well.

Epilogue

SHORTLY AFTER HIS SECOND BIRTHDAY Gus was diagnosed with mild intermittent asthma. It hasn't hindered him at all. Every morning we hold the inhaler over his nose and he counts to twenty. Then he says, "Sammy's turn," and we remove the Flovent medication canister from the face mask and hold the empty tunnel to Sammy's face so he can count to twenty. The pediatrician is optimistic Gus may outgrow his asthma.

When they were fifteen months old, Sam and Gus learned to walk, stumbling across the living room like very small King Kongs. They started walking at exactly the same time. At seventeen months, Gus said his first word, "apple," on Easter morning. Eight weeks later, standing in Dan's broken-down Ford Explorer, Sam shouted "go" like he meant it.

Once they said their first words, I lost track of any time line. At some point the boys learned their ABCs, colors, shapes, and how to count. Gus recited the words to his favorite books. Sam started to sing "Elmo's Song" in his crib every night before he fell asleep. Now they sing all day long. They throw their heads back and belt out the final words to the songs they know by heart, and every time we see them do it Dan and I say we must get out the video camera, but we still haven't.

As far as I can tell Sam and Gus have caught up to the children their age; I can no longer differentiate between their behavior and that of the other two-and-a-half-year-olds in their My Gym class. That I felt uneasy with physical therapists and pediatricians and speech pathologists seems silly now, but I suppose every parent, in her own time, finds the way that works best for her to treat her children as healthy and normal while also being open to services that could help them thrive. If our boys develop a few minor problems related to prematurity down the road, I know we will, with help, be able to handle them. I have so much confidence that Sam and Gus are curious, smart, charismatic, humorous, loving boys. Their quirks—that Sam still won't eat vegetables, that Gus insists on lining up spongy letters in alphabetical order along the bathtub wall each night—are just quirks into which I no longer read too much.

In addition to the lingering aftershock of spending nine weeks with the boys in the NICU my insecurities arose primarily out of guilt. By rushing us toward the most aggressive infertility treatment and then implanting two embryos at once on our first attempt at IVF I feared I had not taken every precaution to ensure the well-being of my children. In his book *How Safe Is Safe Enough* Philip Peters states, "The interests of future children are harmed when the birth of an injured child could have been avoided by changes in conduct resulting in a different, healthier child." During the first two years of the boys' lives it was not yet clear to me that they would grow up healthy and strong. If I had been pregnant with a singleton and delivered prematurely, I'd have found another reason to blame myself. I know a mother of a preemie who accused herself of not staying adequately hydrated. Dorrit initially believed herself to be at fault for having had a pedicure the same afternoon one of her twin boys broke his water—apparently an old wives' tale warns that foot massage can trigger labor. Mothers of preemies, and mothers generally, are often guilt-ridden. Holding ourselves responsible for what happens to our children may be less frightening than thinking that their fates are completely beyond our control.

But now that Sam and Gus are happy little boys, often laughing as they race each other around the house, I have relaxed. While kicking a soccer ball with them, Dan wonders aloud about their potential athleticism and I have to remind him that two-year-olds are generally clumsy and that a year ago all he wanted was for the boys to be able to run around and have fun, which they almost always do. I hope we will never take it for granted that this prayer was answered.

Sam wakes up in the morning and the first word out of his mouth is always, "Gussy?" It takes only a few minutes in Sam's absence before Gus asks where he has gone. Not a day goes by when I am not at some point overcome with gratitude that the boys are well. Leftover from their preemie days is my tendency to baby them slightly. I still let them carry bottles to bed. I can't bring myself to take away Gus's twelve pacifiers despite the emergence of an overbite (I have confined them to his crib). But maybe this will change now that the new baby has arrived.

When the boys were twenty-one months old, Dan and I decided we wanted to transfer one of our frozen embryos. Dan said, "It's time for number three to come off the bench." Although I was very nervous about becoming pregnant and possibly delivering prematurely again, the option of discarding our frozen embryos unsettled me more. Both Dan and I felt that we had started something by fertilizing and then freezing our additional embryos, and, if possible, we wanted them to have a chance at life. Although Dr. Morganstern and my new ob-gyn said that given my age, if I were to become pregnant with a single baby, I would not be considered high-risk, I did not fully believe them. If we were going to attempt another pregnancy, I wanted to do it before advanced maternal age became a risk factor as well. We had two remaining embryos, one viable and another not so viable, that unfortunately were frozen together and therefore had to be thawed at the same time.

Once I stopped breast-feeding my period began arriving every month for the first time in years. Dr. Morganstern was not surprised. He said that pregnancy and childbirth often helps regulate the cycles of his patients with PCOS. It meant that I was able to do a "natural" frozen embryo transfer. The clinic monitored my natural cycle and once ovulation occurred they scheduled me for a blastocyst transfer five days later. I did not have to take any medication at all.

Yet again I was fortunate that my transfer date coincided with the one day of the week that Dr. Morganstern performed procedures at the hospital. He walked into the operating room wearing his white coat and he looked both shorter and more humble than I remembered.

"The embryologist behind the glass wall told me to convince you to transfer both blastocysts even though, or maybe because, the likelihood of the second one taking is small." I looked up at the TV screen in the corner which had just lit up with two blastocysts. One was very fragmented. The other was a round cluster of hundreds of cells.

"I can't do it," I said. And then so as not to dampen the mood in the room and create bad vibes I added, "My twins are maniacs, I'd buckle under another set," though this was not what I'd meant.

Dr. Morganstern smiled. "That's what I told him." He stepped behind the glass wall and reemerged a minute later holding a catheter. "Just the one," he said.

When does life begin? I haven't a clue. But given my obstetric history, transferring more than one embryo was not a risk I could afford to take.

While I was pregnant, Connecticut became the fifteenth state to pass a bill requiring insurance companies to cover infertility treatments. It is estimated that this new requisite will cost each member with a health-care plan $2.50 per year.

A couple days short of thirty-six weeks into my second pregnancy, my water broke. The week before I'd had some spotting, which I'd reported to my new OB, a man whose resemblance to the Ralph Nader of twenty years ago alternately reassured and alarmed me. After running numerous tests which all showed the baby was healthy, the OB had concluded there was no cause for concern. The morning my membranes ruptured, I called my OB and a baby-sitter, then I showered, but I could not bring myself to pack a bag. Dan and I were quiet on the drive to the hospital.

The admitting nurse appeared to be in her midforties—tiny and tough. She hooked me up to an IV and said, "Another IVF pregnancy. It's rare that I see one of these go to term. It's like Mother Nature will only let you tamper with her for so long before she decides enough is enough." A couple of years ago it might have upset me to be matched up against the invincible Mother Nature as if I were a brash young Icarus. But from her tone of voice, I could tell she didn't intend for me to take her comment personally. She was merely reporting what she had observed. At this point in the game, with my family hours from completion, I thought it better to just wrap things up and not get into what was or wasn't natural.

The next nurse who arrived to take my temperature told me she was embarking on IVF next month at this hospital after a six-year battle with infertility. She said, "Successful stories like yours give me hope."

Leonard Thomas Quigley was born that night, calm and alert as an owl. Leo is named after Dan's father, who, sadly, passed away soon thereafter. Thomas, which means twin, seemed a fitting middle name since he was conceived together with Sam and Gus. He weighed six pounds. After staying overnight in the NICU for observation he was moved into my room in the morning.

I understand now, as I didn't before, that all childbirth experiences are shocking, painful, and extraordinary. At 7:15 p.m. Leo was not in the operating room with us and at 7:30 p.m. he was, bundled in my arms. Four days later we took Leo home from the hospital to meet his brothers.

Acknowledgments

RIGHT AROUND GUS AND SAM'S FIRST BIRTHDAY, I wrote a story in which a girl goes to boarding school and hears a joke about a guy in the woods during moose-hunting season, and I sent it to my friend, Heather Clay. She called and said, "I don't think it's a story about boarding school, or a story about a moose." She said it was about my boys in the NICU, and she helped me make connections I did not have the proper perspective to make on my own. So I recast it as an essay about the NICU and sent it to Jordan Pavlin, an editor and friend with whom I had worked. Jordan wrote back and said, "Don't you realize you're writing a book?"

But I would not have believed what I had written could become a book if Walter Minton, a brilliant publisher and an innately honest man who happens to be my father, hadn't said that he could see the subject matter lending itself to book form.

Without these three people and Dan Quigley—who finally came around after initially begging me to change his name to Frank—I would not have set out to write *The Early Birds*. And although life would certainly have gone on without this book, I am grateful to have had the experience of writing it.

Throughout the process my father kept saying that a manuscript only needs one editor. But I was fortunate to have two with different sensibilities. Jordan Pavlin continually pressed me to delve deeper into the experience I'd had becoming a parent of preemies. Jordan's enthusiasm was indefatigable; through several rounds of edits, with smart sensitivity and subtle powers of persuasion, she helped shape the book. My father asked for additional information—medical details about the usual course that preemies take and that Sam and Gus took specifically, who the neonatologists were and how they were trained, background material on the fields of reproductive endocrinology and neonatology. He suggested that I do my research, and because of him, I've written a more informative book.

Caroline Hall is one of the best friends from Groton whom I refer to in the book. Through the assurance her friendship has afforded me I have gained confidence as a mother and a writer. She always trusts that the story I'm telling is straight, and if I come off as a reliable narrator in these pages it's largely to her credit.

Were it not for Dr. Lindsay Thompson, I would not have made it through the NICU in one piece. Every night, over the telephone, Lindsay patiently put the day's medical setbacks into a language I could understand. She was also instrumental in hashing out many of the questions that arose while I was writing, and in proofreading the manuscript to make sure I'd described various procedures and issues pertaining to neonatal medicine correctly, improving upon the book's accuracy.

My agent, Eric Simonoff, wisely coaxed me into completing the manuscript on time. With two children and a third on the way I found a million ways to procrastinate, which I admitted to him, secretly hoping he'd offer to buy me additional time. Instead he counseled me to work toward making the deadline agreed upon in my contract. I also appreciate his prompting me to recall the difficulty I'd had deciding whether to return to work after the boys' birth.

Only because Michelle loves our boys so much and so well was I able to leave them in her care for hours at a time in order to write. Numerous mornings while typing at my computer, I listened to Sam and Gus downstairs laughing and playing with Michelle, and I have to think that their merriment seeped into the scenes I was writing. I am deeply grateful to Leo for providing the right ending.

Marion Minton read this book until her vision blurred and the various drafts bled into one another, and still was inserting commas, and correcting tenses, and sending e-mails with suggestions as to what "some reviewers might find annoying." While I tend to see Sam, Gus, and Leo for who they are, and not as extensions of myself, I hope that in mothering them I can be an extension of her.

Thank you . . . to everyone who offered thoughtful and perceptive editorial comments along the way: Will Minton, Katie Minton, Lane Minton, Cannon Campbell, Megan Quigley, Sarah McGrath, Liza Bainbridge, Dan Pope, Thisbe Nissen, Eleanor Furman, Dorrit Morley, Dawn Davis, Dr. Diana Edwards, and Sonny Mehta; to Marty Asher, Erinn Hartman, Abby Weintraub, Emily Molanphy, Kristen Bearse, Jenna Bagnini, Jennifer Marshall, Joy Dallanegra-Sanger, Kathy Hourigan, and the Knopf Publishing Group; to Lynn and Len Quigley for teaching us, through their example, how to build a wonderful life together; to all the Mintons and Dave Aisner, and all the Quigleys, Pfohls, and Kirbys, especially Matt Quigley, for unending support; to Lily Derwin and Leslie Congdon in West Hartford and Sue Joyse at Connecticut Children's Medical Center; to Dana Wechsler Linden, Emma Trenti Paroli, and Mia Wechsler Doron, M.D., the authors of *Preemies: An Essential Guide for the Parents of Premature Babies;* to The Center for Reproductive Medicine and Infertility and the Neonatal Intensive Care Unit at New York Presbyterian Hospital; and to Rebecca Smith at the March of Dimes.

I have pledged 50 percent of the royalties of the sale of this book, with a minimum donation of $10,000, to be provided to the March of Dimes.

March
of Dimes
Saving babies, together

March of Dimes:
Campaign to Prevent Prematurity

THE MARCH OF DIMES WISHES to thank the author for helping to increase awareness of the seriousness of premature birth and its consequences.

The March of Dimes's sole focus is the health of babies. Beginning with the Salk vaccine and the victory over polio six decades ago, we've continued to make advances—like neonatal intensive care units, newborn screening tests, and genetic therapies—that have saved the lives and health of millions of babies.

Today, our main focus is on the problem of premature birth. Prematurity affects half a million babies every year and the rate continues to rise. Through our national, multimillion-dollar Prematurity Campaign, we're funding top-notch researchers to find the causes of prematurity and ways to prevent it, educating families about risk factors and symptoms of preterm labor, and providing information and comfort to families with babies in neonatal intensive care through our NICU Family Support® program.

We want you to know about two of our online resources that pregnant women and new families will find particularly helpful.

- Share Your Story is our special online community for families of sick or premature babies. Here you can connect with others who've had similar experiences and who understand. Share your story, get information, and find emotional support at marchofdimes.com/share.
- The March of Dimes Pregnancy & Newborn Health Education Center® is the place where you can find answers to your questions anytime, day or night. For more information and to find out how you can help in the fight to save babies, visit marchofdimes.com.

About the Author

Jenny Minton graduated from Williams College. She worked in book publishing for ten years before moving out of New York City. She now lives in West Hartford, Connecticut, with her husband, Dan, and their three sons. Jenny is a freelance writer whose book reviews frequently appear in *The Hartford Courant*. This is her first book.